D0933935

CHABOT COLLEGE-HAYWARD

2 555 000 002352 T

Greatest

Fighter

Missions

BOOKS BY EDWARD H. SIMS

American Aces

Greatest Fighter Missions

Greatest

Fighter

of the Top Navy and Marine

Aces of World War II

HARPER & BROTHERS

Missions

ILLUSTRATED

by Edward H. Sims

Foreword by Admiral Arleigh Burke

Publishers New York

D
790
S542

*To Martha, my wife—
and
To the fighter pilots of World War II
who flew and fought alone, for life
and country, in so many skies*

GREATEST FIGHTER MISSIONS. *Copyright* © 1962.*by Edward H. Sims. Printed in
the United States of America. All rights reserved. No part of this book may be
used or reproduced in any manner whatsoever without written permission except
in the case of brief quotations embodied in critical articles and reviews. For
information address Harper & Brothers, 49 East 33rd Street, New York 16, N. Y.*

FIRST EDITION

Library of Congress catalog card number: 62–7921

Contents

vii

70452

Foreword

One of the most fascinating chapters of the war in the Pacific was the exploits of our Naval Aviators and the part they played in winning a conflict which was spread over hundreds of thousands of miles of water. Their performance was magnificent, and it is largely because of this effectiveness that the United States was able to win a decisive victory in the Pacific. In *Greatest Fighter Missions,* the author tells the dramatic story of some of the missions flown by the Navy's highest scoring fighter aces and their comrades in arms from the Marine Corps.

The young men who manned our Navy and Marine fighters came from all corners of the country. Most of these young, patriotic, hard-working, enthusiastic men came from our many colleges and were trained in flying schools throughout the nation. They were given rugged physical and mental tests to ensure they had the perfect co-ordination and quick reflexes necessary to win in air combat. They upheld the traditions of bravery, persistence and self-sacrifice which have made our Navy and Marine Corps outstanding.

In this book the author has painstakingly reconstructed the missions flown by men who had the highest dedication and devotion to their country. He has interviewed them, personally studied the battle reports, and has done everything humanly possible to authenticate the action in their individual missions.

In reading the book you will ride in the cockpit and go into battle with the top Navy and Marine aces of the war. You will be able to see the transition that came about after the early days, when some of our old fighters had to face the best the enemy had, until the latter stages of the war, when our fighter planes outclassed anything the enemy could put into the air.

This book is one of true adventure. It is a documented recording of the real, sometimes harrowing experiences. The missions were exciting, more exciting than any fictional account could be.

The performance of these men will create a sense of pride and inspiration in every member of every service, in every veteran, and in every American. I found the book rewarding reading.

Adm. Arleigh Burke, U.S.N. (Ret.)
Former Chief of Naval Operations

Washington, D.C.

Acknowledgments

In expressing my appreciation for encouragement and assistance in writing *Greatest Fighter Missions*, I should first mention Admiral Arleigh Burke, who, as Chairman of the Joint Chiefs of Staff in early 1958, was part of the motivation for this work.

During compilation, Admiral Burke completed his term as head of the Joint Chiefs and served two more as Chief of Naval Operations (he had previously served in this capacity, before being named chairman of the Joint Chiefs). This book finally emerges after his retirement from active service.

The Navy's foremost champion of the postwar era, and one of its all-time greatest commanders, Admiral Burke was a constant source of support and, more, a friend, to whom I cannot adequately express my gratitude.

I also want to thank the Navy's Mr. Herb Gimpel, who was generous with his aid from the beginning; Commander R. L. Bufkins, head of the Navy's Magazine and Book Branch, who withstood a storm of queries and requests without flinching.

When, finally, Commander Bufkins retreated to a higher post, Lieutenant Commander F. A. Prehn fulfilled many additional requests which helped make the accuracy of this volume possible. Captain Frederick ("Buzz") Lloyd and Admiral D. F. Smith, Jr., also were most helpful. Commander Will Hide handled several special and emergency requests with diplomacy and skill, for which I am grateful.

Mr. Cass Canfield of Harper & Brothers was a constant counselor and guide in the shaping of this work, as he had been earlier in the preparation of *American Aces*, contributing both encouragement and ideas for which I am sincerely appreciative. Mrs. Beulah Hagen, also at Harper's, is due my gratitude for her many suggestions and help.

Captain Jim Dowdell was of invaluable assistance; his support and his contribution were beyond measure.

President Robert Sumwalt and Dr. Edmund Yachjian, at the University of South Carolina, are due my thanks.

The outstanding art work displayed in the maps of the fighter missions was contributed by Warren Johnson, as was the jacket.

Mrs. George Zeigler, who typed the manuscript, contributed many suggestions and was of great help in meeting the many demands and deadlines.

Admiral W. A. Southerland's courtesy and co-operation aboard the *Franklin D. Roosevelt*, in the Mediterranean, is one of the most pleasant memories of the years of preparation of this book.

Captain Daniel J. Corcoran, Commander J. D. Pillsbury, in London, and Lieutenant Commander Bobby Lee Hatch gave valuable assistance. Captain Corcoran, in Naples, was especially helpful and gracious in expediting an assignment with the Sixth Fleet.

Lieutenant Charles R. Long, Admiral Southerland's aide, took particular trouble on my behalf, which was of considerable value. Admiral Robert Lee Dennison also is due my gratitude for his interest and courtesy in London.

To Admiral Jerauld Wright (Ret.) my special thanks are due. As Supreme Commander, North Atlantic Treaty Organization, Atlantic, Admiral Wright invariably extended his warm compliance with every request.

I am also much obliged to Admiral B. L. Austin, to Captain Richard L. Kibbe, skipper of the *Forrestal* at the time of my assignment aboard her, and to Admiral Muir Arnold, aboard *Forrestal*, for their courtesies.

Of course, I am unable, in this space, to list every Navy and Marine officer, and every member of the enlisted ranks, who extended a helping hand in the preparation of this book. Chief Shirley E. Ritter, at the Los Alamitos Naval Air Station, however, should not go unmentioned, and I hope the many others will accept my sincere thanks, in this form, for their generous help.

To each of the eleven aces themselves, who did their best to recall details of their most memorable missions in World War II—a war dropping further and further into the past—I also wish to extend my gratitude.

EDWARD H. SIMS

September, 1961
Washington, D.C.

Introduction

Greatest Fighter Missions is an attempt to re-create accurately, with the written word, the most thrilling, single mission flown by each of the highest scoring surviving fighter aces of the United States Navy and Marine Corps in World War II.

It is the natural sequel and companion to *American Aces* (1958), which described the most memorable fighter battle of each of the highest scoring surviving fighter aces of the U.S. Army Air Forces in World War II, and it follows the same procedure as its predecessor.

Each of the top-ranked Navy and Marine aces featured in these pages was sought out and interviewed at length, a process which required 25,000 miles of travel. In addition, the author, who was a fighter pilot with the U.S. Army Air Forces in World War II, served two hitches aboard operating carriers in connection with the preparation of this book. Records and memories were searched and the observations of others who were able to contribute information were sought. Every effort has been made—including the utilization of enemy sources—to verify time, altitude, location, and other details of each aerial engagement.

Care has been taken to avoid coloring of the facts, assumed dialogue, or anything that could not be verified. When you read that a certain Navy or Marine fighter ace turned left in a battle, this is what that pilot recalls, or believes to be the case. The author has attempted to achieve objectivity and accuracy without sacrificing the pace and adventure of these great exploits. Finally, after the missions included herein were reconstructed, they were submitted to the Navy Department for exacting review by Navy historians to ensure the greatest possible accuracy.

It is difficult to reconstruct a fighter mission, which covers so much territory in such a short time. Because of this, many persons lack a clear mental picture of what a fighter mission is like. Fighter aircraft carry only one person, the pilot; no reporters, historians or photographers go along to record the action and the details. The pilot, of course, is too busy to keep records.

Thus the greatest fighter battles, and the outstanding fighter missions of the war, have not been recorded in detail, accurately and chronologically, as have great land and sea battles.

It is my hope that *Greatest Fighter Missions* will fill some of the vacuum in the history and literature of Navy and Marine Corps fighter aces and their World War II exploits, as I believe *American Aces* did for their brothers in the U.S. Army Air Forces during the same period. It is also my hope that when the reader has finished this book he will know something of what it was like to take part in these great aerial encounters, step by step and minute by minute, and that he will have gained a new appreciation of what these brave but unassuming Americans endured and accomplished.

The great aces treated in this book include the six top surviving U.S. Navy fighter aces of World War II and five of the top six surviving Marine Corps fighter aces. A chapter is devoted to the most exciting mission of each, with accompanying map and pictures.

The number of aerial victories attributed to each pilot included in this book was determined from the list of accredited kills furnished by the Navy and Marine Corps. It should be remembered that lists of aces sometimes vary, are sometimes revised or brought up to date. (If these lists require correction, as happened in one case with *American Aces,* individuals concerned are advised to supply to the Navy whatever new or additional information they possess.) Victories described in this book were achieved by Navy and Marine Corps fighter pilots during official United States participation in World War II. The choice of which mission would be included was usually made by the ace himself. For reasons that will be obvious, the mission re-created was the most memorable to the ace involved.

The reader should keep in mind that conditions under which the aces flew varied widely, depending upon the period of the war. Thus, the early missions, such as that flown by Marine ace Marion Carl at Midway, in June, 1942, involved a relatively early model U.S. fighter, and enemy fighters superior to our own.

Later in the war, particularly in 1944 and 1945, the reader will sense the superiority of our fighters over the enemy's.

The Navy and Marines began the war with two fighters: the Brewster F2A (Buffalo) and the Grumman F4F (Wildcat). The former was suitable only as a trainer, though at Midway it was committed to action against the Zero with melancholy results. The first fighter seriously to challenge the Zero was the Chance-Vought F4U (Corsair). Eventually, Grumman's F6F (Hellcat) appeared and thereafter these two fighters dominated the skies.

The Japanese began the war with the best carrier fighter in the world, the Zero, which surprised U.S. fighter pilots with its speed, maneuverability and over-all performance. But the enemy failed to maintain his early lead as the war progressed and lost out in the production race. The impression prevails among many Americans that the Japanese enjoyed initial technical superiority in the first days of the war with the Zero, and that after the Zero had met its match Japanese technical development halted. The truth is that the Japanese developed fine fighters throughout the war, both new and improved models. Many of them, however, never got into mass production.

Probably the best Navy fighter developed by the enemy was the Shiden-Kai (Shiden 21). Some rate it as an equal of the P-51, but only 428 were produced. This fighter came into existence partly by accident, but it was superior in performance to U.S. carrier fighters in many respects. It entered operations in 1944, and was known to the allies as the "George."

The Type 5 fighter is generally considered to have been the best Japanese Army fighter. It was actually an improvisation, and became operational only in 1945. The airframe was originally designed for an inline engine, but due to an engine shortage, a radial engine was fitted to the frame and the results exceeded all expectations. The U.S. code name for the Type 5 was "Tony."

The Zero-Sen, of course, was the mainstay of the fighter forces of Japan, and with its fortunes Japan's fortunes seemed to rise and fall. At the beginning of the war the Zero was not only the finest carrier fighter in the world, but it could outperform the best land-based U.S. fighters.

The Japanese Navy furnished two companies its requirements for a new fighter in 1937. Only one accepted the challenge—Mitsubishi. That company completed the first prototype in 1939, and after six months of testing and modification the Navy accepted it later that year. When the Japanese struck Pearl Harbor, their Navy had over 400 Zeroes—model 21's. This was the model which so quickly established the myth of the aircraft's invincibility. More Zero-Sens were produced than any other Japanese warplane—over 10,000 in all. But by 1943 new U.S. fighters were superior to the 21's and the Japanese had improvements and modifications under way, a process which continued throughout the war. Many modifications of the Zero were given different code names by the allies. Thus "Hamps" and "Zekes" were not new fighters, but modified Zeroes.

Japanese Army fighters, in addition to the Type 5 and Kawasaki Hien Type 3 ("Tony"), included Nakajima's Type 97, Type 1 and Type 2 (known to the allies as Nates, Oscars and Tojo's), Type 4 ("Frank"), and Kawasaki's Type 2, known by the allied code name "Nick."

The Japanese Navy fighters of prominence, in addition to the Zero and its descendants, and the Shiden-Kai, included the Nakajimi Type 2 ("Rufe"), the Mitsubishi Raiden ("Jack"), the Mitsubishi Reppu ("Sam"), the Kawanishi Kyofu ("Rex"), and the Nakajimi Gekko ("Irving")—a night fighter.

Had the Japanese Navy been able to commit large numbers of Shiden-Kai fighters in the crucial years of the war, or had the Army been in a position to commit the Type 5 in any number, U.S. fighters would not have found the air war so much to their liking after 1943.

The Japanese pilot-training program also seems to have failed the mass-production test. When the war began, Japanese Navy pilots, particularly, were trained to a high degree of combat efficiency. But as they were eliminated—and the best carrier cadres decimated—there were insufficient replacements of similar quality available.

The Japanese produced a number of aces who scored more aerial victories than the most successful American aces—the late Richard Bong of the Army Air Force, with 40 victories, and David McCampbell of the U.S. Navy, with 34. The highest scoring Japanese ace, Hiroyoshi Nishizawa, was credited with 103 kills.

The highest scoring surviving Japanese fighter ace was Saburo Sakai, credited with 64 victories. His story has been chronicled in an interesting book, *Samurai*. Sakai shot down four American fighters in one day. Nishizawa shot down seven American planes in a single day over Rabaul—to set the record for enemy fighter pilots. (The record number of victories scored by an American fighter pilot on one mission was achieved during a mission described in this volume.)

The Japanese, like the Germans, kept their fighter pilots in action continuously throughout the war. There was no set system of rotation, such as that which U.S. Army, Navy and Marine pilots could look forward to. As a result, most of the top Japanese fighter aces had been killed by the war's end. Morale naturally suffered as a result of the extreme demands made on pilots.

Though the Japanese were notorious in exaggerating the results of their air and surface actions, the confirmed scores of their top fighter aces are probably not far off. (It is only proper to state, however, that U.S. records sometimes did not show losses claimed and credited to Japanese fighter pilots.)

The Japanese did not award medals to their outstanding fighter pilots, nor commend or promote them for courageous actions. This was contrary to Japanese military tradition. Only in the final months of the war, in 1945, was this tradition broken.

The Japanese (like the Germans) had nothing to compare with the heavy bombers of the U.S. Army Air Force. Japanese fighter pilots ordered to intercept and attack heavily armored B-17's and B-24's, and later B-29's, were deeply (and psychologically) impressed with the defensive firepower and armament of the U.S. heavies.

On the other hand, the Japanese Kamikazes (suicide planes) were something the United States could not duplicate. In the later stages of the war (organized Kamikaze attacks began in earnest in October of 1944) Kamikazes caused heavy destruction among U.S. ships. They were credited with 174 hits or near misses in the Philippines campaign and 279 hits in the Okinawa campaign! In these two campaigns alone the Japanese are estimated to have launched over 2,500 suicide planes!

Japanese fighter production was quite limited prior to mid-1943. According to a prominent Japanese aeronautical engineer, Jiro Horikoshi, monthly production of the famous Zero—the mainstay of Japanese fighter forces—averaged only 221 aircraft between April of 1942 and June of

1943. The peak in aircraft production was reached in 1944, when something over 2,000 Army and Navy aircraft were delivered monthly.

An American advantage of tremendous importance in the air war was the ability of U.S. engineers to construct airfields rapidly. Time after time the speed with which needed fighter strips were placed in operation aroused the envy and admiration of Japanese fighter pilots.

Tactics employed by American and Japanese fighters underwent a change after U.S. fighters became capable of matching the performance of the Zero. In the early stages of the war, U.S. fighters quickly learned to make a diving pass on the more maneuverable enemy fighters and escape with diving speed. Dogfights with the enemy were avoided.

United States fighters, working in pairs, soon developed the "Thatch Weave," named after Navy Commander Jimmy Thatch. This proved a highly effective defense in fighter combat. The weave featured a constant crisscross of two fighters, each capable of eliminating an enemy on the other's tail in the crossover.

Later Lieutenant Eugene Valencia developed the "Mowing Machine," a combat tactic involving four fighters, two making diving passes and crossing while the other two remained above. As the first two completed their firing passes they pulled back up and assumed the role of top cover for the other two, which now carried out diving passes.

The four-plane division Valencia trained and led shot down fifty Japanese planes using this tactic, a Navy record, and none of the four fighters was hit by an enemy bullet. Many other tactics were devised by U.S. pilots.

Japanese fighter tactics against the later American fighters, the F4U and the F6F, included the head-on pass, since enemy fighter pilots no longer possessed the speed to close these fighters from the rear—unless in a diving pass from superior height. The enemy fighters also often attacked U.S. bombers in head-on passes, at one time in the war dropping phosphorus bombs into the bombers.

Japanese fighter pilots, in the later years of the war especially, did not exhibit the teamwork displayed by U.S. fighter pilots. Often an enemy formation was decimated as trailing, or outside, fighters in a formation were picked off one by one, receiving no support from their comrades. Enemy pilots often flew in three-plane formations, which did not prove so effective as the American operational system of flying and fighting in one or more pairs.

There was no lack of bravery among Japanese pilots, and many did not wear parachutes, even though the chutes were available to them— and though commanding officers at some bases ordered their use. Relatively few of them were taken prisoner, as many believed in the Japanese military code or in the traditional Bushido (Samurai code)—which did not allow capture. A pilot who did not return from a mission was dead —there were no prisoners!

The fighter ace may well be a thing of the past. Today's interceptors, jets, fly so fast that dogfights as we have known them in two world wars are no longer possible. Even in the Korean War aerial encounters were, generally speaking, a matter of one pass at the enemy.

It was in World War I that the fighter pilot became known as an individual knight of the air, and there was a chivalry and romance to the aerial battles of that war which lives to this day in the literature describing the exploits of Richthofen, Bishop, Rickenbacker, and many others.

On the other hand, it was not until World War II that fighter pilots played such an important and sometimes decisive role in the outcome of land and sea battles. In that war it became obvious that the success of any major campaign, on land, sea or air, often depended upon the ability to establish control of the air.

The early and shocking victories of the Axis powers were made possible in large measure by the use of this new concept in warfare. Norway was won by Germany in 1940 through control of the air by the Luftwaffe, in spite of the presence of the British Navy. Hitler's generals would not undertake the invasion of England later that year until Germany had won control of the air. It was the RAF fighter pilot who held the fate of England in his hands in the summer of 1940.

The Japanese won their opening victories in World War II largely through superior air power, the air arm being the pride of the enemy fleet.

And so the fighter pilots of World War II hold a unique place in history. Quickly recognizing their importance, both the U.S. Army and Navy inaugurated large-scale pilot-training programs soon after the war began, setting high mental and physical standards for qualification as a cadet. Without overstating the case, it is accurate to say that the cream of the nation's college youth responded to the challenge of individual combat in the air.

HIGHEST-SCORING AMERICAN NAVY ACES OF WORLD WAR II AND CONFIRMED VICTORIES

David McCampbell	34	Alexander Vraciu	19
Cecil E. Harris	24	Ira C. Kepford	17
Eugene A. Valencia	23	Charles R. Stimpson	17

HIGHEST-SCORING AMERICAN MARINE ACES OF WORLD WAR II AND CONFIRMED VICTORIES*

Joseph J. Foss	26	Donald N. Aldrich **	20
Robert M. Hanson **	25	John L. Smith	19
Gregory Boyington †	22	Marion E. Carl	18.5
Kenneth A. Walsh	21	Wilbur J. Thomas **	18.5
	James E. Swett	16.5	

* To the nearest half aircraft.
** Deceased.
　† Boyington is also credited with six victories as a civilian flying with the Flying Tigers in China, prior to U.S. entrance into World War II.

Glossary

(The following words or initials are a few that appear in the chapters of Greatest Fighter Missions. The brief explanations given will acquaint the reader with their meaning.)

ABORT: To turn back before reaching the target.
ACE: Fighter pilot with five or more victories.
AIO: Air Intelligence Officer.
ANGELS: Altitude. "Angels thirteen" is 13,000 feet.
BANDITS: Enemy aircraft.
BARREL ROLL: Medium-speed roll, course remaining constant.
BB: Battleship.
BIG FRIENDS: Friendly bombers.
BLOWER: Supercharger.
BOGEYS: Unidentified aircraft.
CA: Heavy Cruiser.
C.A.P.: Combat Air Patrol.
CHANDELLE: Reversal of course by climbing turn.
CHARGE GUNS: Load guns.
C.I.C.: Combat Information Center.
CL: Light cruiser.
C.O.: Commanding Officer.
CONTRAILS: Visible trails of high-flying aircraft.
CV: Aircraft carrier.
DD: Destroyer.
DEFLECTION SHOT: Firing from side angle.
DIVISION: Formation of four fighters.
END SPEED: Take-off speed at end of carrier deck.
FLAK: Antiaircraft fire.
F2A: Buffalo (1), Brewster.
F4F: Wildcat (1), Grumman.
F4U: Corsair (1), Chance-Vought.
F6F: Hellcat (1), Grumman.
GAGGLE: Assemblage of loose-flying enemy fighters.
GROUP: Several squadrons.
HORN: Radio.
IFF: Identification, friend or foe (radar).
IMMELMANN: A reversal of course by half-loop and roll-out.
JINXING: To take evasive, erratic action to dodge flak.

KAMIKAZES: Japanese suicide aircraft.
LITTLE FRIENDS: Friendly fighters.
LSO: Landing Signals Officer (carrier).
LUFBERY: A circle of fighters in a tight turn.
MAGS: Magnetos.
MUSH: Sluggish flying performance (in thin air or at low speed).
OPS: Operations.
PRI-FLY: Control tower aboard carrier.
REVETMENT: Parking area for aircraft.
RISING SUN: Japanese flag.
SECTION: Formation of eight fighters.
SKIPPER: Commanding Officer.
S.O.P.: Standard Operating Procedure.
SPLIT-S: To half-roll and dive vertically.
SQUADRON: Formation of several divisions.
TRIM: To adjust control tabs for proper flying altitude.
TWELVE O'CLOCK: Straight ahead (hours of clock used to denote direction).
VAPOR TRAILS: Visible trails left by high-flying aircraft.
VF: Navy fighter squadron.
VMF: Marine fighter squadron.
WARDROOM: Dining room.

PART *1*

THE GRIM DAYS
OF DEFENSE

1 *Zeroes at Midway*

JUNE 4, 1942:

Captain MARION E. CARL, U.S.M.C.

IF one battle is to be selected as the most dramatic of the entire Pacific war, it must be the Battle of Midway. This battle was the turning point of the war against Japan, and includes all the elements of destiny and drama which make for stirring reading.

The first great Japanese offensive, completed toward the end of March, 1942, had won the Japanese success so completely that, according to Sir Winston Churchill, it surprised even the Japanese. Japan had established its authority over a vast stretch of new territory reaching south as far as the Dutch East Indies (Indonesia), west as far as Burma, and east as far as the Marshalls and Gilberts, both of which island groups lie considerably east (and north) of Guadalcanal.

The enemy high command debated its next move for some time and then ordered a second general advance, a bold expansion to the south and east. The principal effort in this second general offensive was to be an attack—by the largest fleet ever assembled up to that time—on Midway.

Admiral Isoroku Yamamoto, Commander in Chief, Combined Imperial Japanese Fleet, set as his first goal, in the Midway operation, the drawing out of the United States Pacific Fleet.

Yamamoto was fully aware of the need to crush the American fleet—in 1942—or risk the loss of the war. Because of this conviction, he favored the Midway operation. He believed Midway was important enough to U.S. Pacific defenses to force the American fleet to fight.

As a matter of history, Japanese and Americans had contested possession of the atoll, claimed by the United States in 1859, as early as 1903, when the U.S. Navy chased a party of Japanese away. That year the Navy began building a station on Sand Island (Midway Atoll comprises two islands—Sand, the larger, and Eastern, the smaller). It was in the 1930's that the Navy began to realize Midway's true value. Pan American Airways established an airport on Sand Island for its transpacific clippers and Midway's military significance was established beyond any doubt. The naval air station at Midway was commissioned in August, 1941, four months before the surprise attack on Pearl Harbor. By then a landing strip 5,000 feet long on Eastern Island had been completed and a major expansion of facilities was under way.

The atoll, 1,100 miles west of Hawaii, was the site of the westernmost military outpost in the Hawaiian Islands. The Japanese, if they possessed Midway, would be in a position to threaten Pearl Harbor, the foremost U.S. base in the Pacific, and Yamamoto was convinced an attack on Midway would force the United States Pacific Fleet to move in its defense, where his combined fleet would be ready to annihilate it.

The Japanese force engaged in the second general offensive was staggering in size and was divided into three mutually supporting fleets. There was a carrier striking force including four of the six carriers which struck Pearl Harbor. There was an occupation force consisting of battleships, heavy cruisers, transports, and seaplane carriers. There was the main body, commanded by Admiral Yamamoto, including the latest Japanese battleships, a light carrier and cruisers, and another carrier force, including two carriers and cruisers.

The three phases of this giant operation were to be the occupation of the western Aleutians by the second carrier force, the occupation of Midway by the occupation force, and a decisive fleet engagement to be achieved by the carrier striking force and the main body.

The Second Carrier Force was to open the offensive by bombarding

Dutch Harbor, in the Aleutians, June 3. The largest carrier striking force, including the carriers which attacked Pearl Harbor (two of which were the largest in the Japanese Navy), was to defeat the U.S. Pacific Fleet. The main body under Admiral Yamamoto, with the fast battleships, was to support the carrier force in operations against the U.S. fleet. On the night of June 5 Midway Island was to be assaulted by 5,000 troops of the occupation force.

The first hint of the enemy's interest in the westernmost of the Hawaiian Islands came on March 10. On that day a four-engined Japanese flying boat was detected off Midway and shot down after a fight with four Marine Corps fighters. Two other four-engined flying boats had attacked Oahu the night of March 3–4. They missed Pearl Harbor and dropped bombs, ineffectually, into Punch Bowl Crater, behind Honolulu.

Admiral Chester Nimitz, Pacific Fleet Commander, rightly evaluated the appearance of the four-engined aircraft as a likely omen of a future offensive toward Hawaii.

(Midway had not completely escaped Japanese attention in the December, 1941, attack, which caused such disastrous damage at Pearl Harbor. On the night of the Pearl Harbor attack [December 7], two Japanese destroyers bombarded the atoll briefly, inflicted fourteen casualties and some damage, and suffered hits from answering shore batteries.)

Thanks to outstanding work by intelligence officers, who had succeeded in breaking secret Japanese codes, Japanese plans and preparations were known in Washington as early as the second week in May. All available Navy, Marine Corps and Army Air Force reinforcement was scraped together for the impending battle and sent to Midway in the next three weeks. A PBY (Catalina) patrol squadron was rushed to the scene. An Army B-17 Flying Fortress squadron arrived. Four twin-engined B-26 bombers and six Navy TBF bombers reached the atoll.

A week before the battle, Marine Air Group 22 (on Eastern Island) received nineteen SBD-2's, the Navy's newest dive bomber, and nineteen pilots fresh from flight school. In addition, the Marines were reinforced with seven new F4F Wildcat fighters. Unfortunately, most of M.A.G.22's other fighters were obsolete F2A-3 Buffaloes.

Marine aircraft had been rushed to Midway shortly after Pearl

Harbor. Before reinforcements arrived for the Midway battle, M.A.G. 22 consisted of two squadrons—a dive bomber and a fighter squadron.

Nimitz was also scraping the bottom of the barrel for carrier strength to oppose the massive Japanese fleet.

In the end, the Navy managed to have three carriers in position north of Midway on the morning of June 4. Carrier *Yorktown* made it —after being damaged in the Battle of the Coral Sea—by reducing time in dry dock, at Pearl Harbor, from an estimated ninety days to less than two. She made port on the afternoon of May 27, was immediately put in dry dock, and over a thousand men, working day and night, completed essential and makeshift repairs in less than forty-eight hours.

On May 29 she was floated again, fueled and armed, and sailed on the last day of the month, in time to participate in the showdown battle. She joined *Enterprise* and *Hornet,* of Admiral William F. Halsey's Task Force 16, which had rushed southeast after the B-25 raid on Tokyo. These three carriers, under the command of Rear Admiral Raymond A. Spruance, plus the strength of the Marines, Navy and Army on Midway, were soon to be put to the supreme test. (At this stage of the war the U.S. Pacific Fleet did not include a single battleship with enough speed to operate with the carriers.)

Thus on the decisive day of battle, June 4, the main opposing forces were Spruance's carriers and the oncoming and formidable Japanese fleet. However, while these fleets rightly hold the center of the stage in any history of the engagement, it is with the dogged resistance of outnumbered Marine fliers of Marine Air Group 22, flying obsolete aircraft out of Midway and being slaughtered in the process, and especially with the efforts of Marine Captain Marion Carl, of Marine Fighter Squadron 221 (who was to become one of the great Marine air aces) with which we are concerned in this chapter.

Second Lieutenant Marion E. Carl, a native of Hubbard, Oregon, arrived on Midway on Christmas Day, 1941. He had departed San Diego on December 8, aboard the carrier *Saratoga,* which headed for Wake Island. Carl and fellow fighter pilots, and their F2A-3 Brewster Buffaloes, were to bolster U.S. defenses at Wake, but the island fell before *Saratoga* could land them. Therefore, *Saratoga* was diverted to Midway.

Carl and other Marine pilots at Midway had had almost six months to acquaint themselves with the area and practice combat techniques.

In March Carl was promoted to first lieutenant, in May to captain. By the end of that month, with a major invasion attempt expected any moment, Marine air strength numbered no less than sixty-four planes, including thirty-six dive bombers, twenty-one obsolete Brewster Buffalo fighters, and seven Wildcats.

Nimitz's orders, to the Marines on Midway, were that they adopt offensive rather than defensive tactics. That is, they were to strike the Japanese carriers, as well as defend the airstrip on Eastern Island! Carl, luckily, was one of the favored few who would fly one of the seven new F4Fs on that fateful June 4.

Shortly after nine o'clock on the warm, late spring Wednesday morning of June 3 a high-flying PBY (one of sixteen stationed at Midway) spotted a large convoy of ships steaming east toward Midway. Further reports that morning confirmed the size and direction of the armada. Longe-range Catalinas and B-17's based on Eastern Island launched a strike at the huge enemy transport force that day, 700 miles to the west. Hits were reported by returning pilots, but the claims proved optimistic. The Japanese fleet continued its approach, undamaged.

Marine pilots, certain that a decisive engagement would occur the next day, slept little on the night of the 3rd. The Pacific night was clear and warm and an air of tension gripped the island.

Carl is awakened in his tent by reveille at three o'clock in the morning of June 4, slips out of his bunk, dons khakis, and hastens to the mess hall. Thirty minutes later he is at the revetment where his F4F and crew chief await him.

The sun edges over the clear eastern horizon at approximately five o'clock. As yet there is no word from the operations center, located in a dugout near the main runway on Eastern Island. Radar has not picked up anything suspicious.

Forty-five minutes pass. The sky, now fully lighted, is almost cloudless. Carl and the maintenance crew pace back and forth in the sand, look up over the tropical, green palms into the western sky. All is quiet.

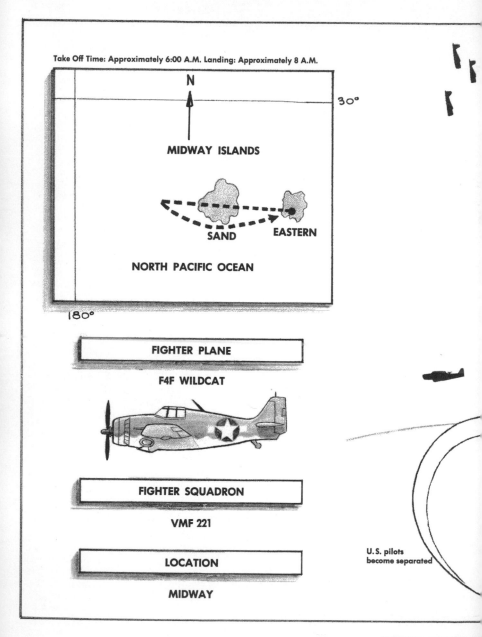

Take Off Time: Approximately 6:00 A.M. Landing: Approximately 8 A.M.

N

30°

MIDWAY ISLANDS

SAND   EASTERN

NORTH PACIFIC OCEAN

180°

FIGHTER PLANE

F4F WILDCAT

FIGHTER SQUADRON

VMF 221

LOCATION

MIDWAY

U.S. pilots
become separated

MISSION FLOWN BY

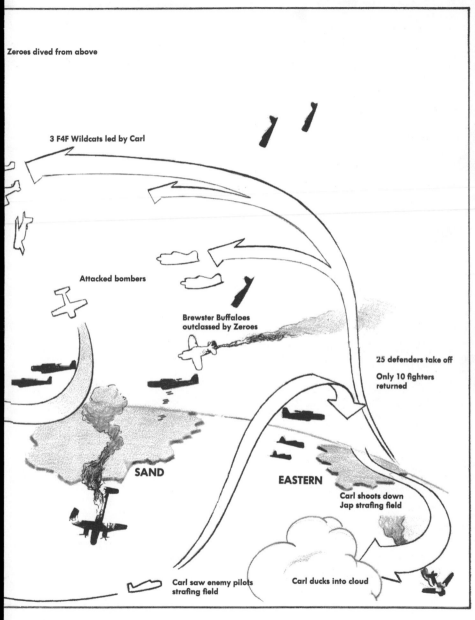

Zeroes dived from above

3 F4F Wildcats led by Carl

Attacked bombers

Brewster Buffaloes
outclassed by Zeroes

25 defenders take off

Only 10 fighters
returned

SAND

EASTERN

Carl shoots down
Jap strafing field

Carl saw enemy pilots
strafing field

Carl ducks into cloud

CAPTAIN MARION E. CARL, USMC, JUNE 4, 1942

Just before six o'clock a message from a PBY, to the west, comes in loud and clear on receivers: "Many planes heading Midway—three two zero—bearing distance—one five zero." Suddenly the air-raid siren wails, the scramble flag runs up at the "Ready Tent," and scramble orders are issued over the radio by Major Floyd B. Parks, commanding VMF 221's fighters. Similarly, Major Lofton R. Henderson, commanding the dive bombers on Midway, scrambles his pilots.

The enemy strike from Admiral Yamamoto's fast carrier force is now estimated at eighty to a hundred miles away. With the enemy so close, fighters and dive bombers take off on both runways. Carl, having hurriedly started his engine and strapped himself into the cockpit, taxies to the end of the runway, shoves the throttle to the fire wall. Creating a cloud of dust and sand, the roaring Grumman fighter gathers speed down the runway.

Soon the grayish, blunt-nosed, stubby F4F Wildcat lifts off the ground and is slicing up into the blue, heading west. Altogether, twenty-five defending fighters get off. Carl's group of twelve (five F4F's, the rest Brewsters), led by Major Parks, set off in the direction of the incoming Japanese. Captain Kirk Armistead's group of thirteen is directed to a location about ten miles out, to await a possible attack from another direction. The dive bombers already have set course for the enemy fleet.

Parks's twelve fighters, after a steady climb, reach 14,000 feet, and are now approximately thirty miles west of Midway. They are divided into two over-strength divisions (six fighters in a division). Carl, flying No. 6 in one of the divisions, trails behind the other five, constantly searching the sky. Nothing is in sight.

The steady roar of the 1,200-horsepower engine, excited orders which break radio silence, and the general air of tension combine to bring nerves to razor's edge. Carl checks gunsight and guns. He has never seen a Jap fighter but he knows he will see one today.

Once again he looks ahead. Suddenly, silhouetted against the water below, he sees specks. Aircraft! Seconds pass while eyes strain to make identification. Simultaneously, several pilots "Tally-ho" them over the mike! Bandits!

Flying low, at two or three thousand feet, the lead elements of the enemy's carrier striking force—single-engine bombers—are clearly visible ahead, below. Parks breaks radio silence, orders pilots to prepare to wing-over, right, in an overhead pass on the bombers. Other Japanese planes become identifiable below, but no enemy fighters have been located.

The U.S. fighters start down on the approaching enemy. Carl pushes throttle forward with left hand, hits right rudder, and follows Buffaloes and Wildcats down in a wing-over. The windstream screams as speed increases. The U.S. fighters open fire on the greenish-brown bombers,

Three SBDs (Dauntless dive bombers). They wrecked the Japanese fleet at Midway. (Navy Department Photo)

whose wings are painted with bright red rising suns. Having a position in the rear, Carl is able to observe the American attack. There are thirteen bombers in the formation; they take desperate evasive action, but several begin to trail smoke and turn out of formation.

Now, however, from behind, Carl gets an unexpected shock from a sudden glimpse—his first—of enemy fighters, Zeroes! They're diving on the American fighters! He yells a warning into the mike to other American fighter pilots that Zeroes are jumping them from above. No Zeroes had been sighted flying top cover—it was thought they were below with the bombers—but they had been there, somewhere. Carl must decide whether to complete his dive and pass on an enemy bomber, or defend himself against the diving Zeroes. Looking behind, and ahead, he decides he just has time to open fire, briefly, on a bomber.

The sight ring fills as the wingspan of the bomber appears to lengthen; his finger closes the stick trigger. Only seconds remain. Now! The six guns belch smoke and shells—a hundred a second! But there's no time to continue the attack. A Zero is quickly closing his tail. He jerks the stick into his belly, banks hard to the left, and streaks in the opposite direction from the enemy strike. Simultaneously, the bomber he attacked streams black smoke and falls out of formation.

Carl, the trailing American pilot and nearest target, and the first to sight the Zeroes, is alone in his maneuver. Taking advantage of the speed from his diving pass, he eases stick back and bites upward at a good clip. He will try to gain an altitude advantage, stays at full throttle. The other Buffaloes and Wildcats have passed through the enemy bombers, are pulling out of gunnery passes below in the direction of Eastern Island. Zeroes are fast closing on them, and soon a series of desperate, individual fighter actions commences. The Wildcat pilots are not as hopelessly outclassed, but Buffaloes begin to fall out of the sky at an appalling rate. As he climbs, Carl constantly glances behind. The Zeroes are turning around. They must continue toward Midway with the bombers! Carl reaches 15,000 feet, 17,000 feet, 18,000 feet.

Now alone, he must exercise caution. He banks right. The sky seems clear. No Zeroes in sight. He turns and heads back toward Midway, continuing to climb. He reaches 21,000 feet. In a few minutes he can see Sand Island, then Eastern. He rubbernecks constantly. No aircraft are visible. (Carl is unaware of it, but of the twelve fighters under Major Parks's command, nine have been shot down and two badly damaged.)

Sand Island draws nearer and nearer. Eastern is just ahead. Something is moving on Eastern. Carl takes a long look. Japanese fighters strafing the airstrip. He continues on course for several minutes, scanning the sky in every direction. No friendlies are to be found. There are so many fighters below that he hesitates to plunge into the fray, wondering where the American fighters can be. He circles slowly while the Japanese work over installations on Sand Island and the airstrip on Eastern. In ones and twos, enemy planes depart. Carl watches the number of enemy planes decrease, below, waiting for the best moment to go down and exact a measure of revenge.

When the enemy aircraft are reduced to less than a dozen—most of them having departed for their carriers to the west—Carl spots three enemy fighters in a ragged line, flying back and forth across the airstrip. Now directly over them, he pulls the stick right and pushes it forward, simultaneously pushing right rudder. The lone gray Wildcat roars down. Carl fixes his eyes on the yellow sight ring on the fixed gunsight, puts his right forefinger on the trigger button, and picks out the trailing Zero, just as all three start another strafing run on the airstrip. The F4F gains speed, the altimeter registering lower and lower altitude as Carl passes 5,000 feet, 4,000, 3,000. He eases back on the stick, banks left, overtaking the rear Zero. The enemy pilots, unaware of his approach, obviously think the air has been cleared of American fighters.

The wingspan of the last Zero widens in Carl's sight as the lone F4F walks up on the rear of the enemy plane. When the enemy is within range, Carl's finger presses the trigger and the Wildcat roars. A stream of armor-piercing tracer and ball ammunition pours into the enemy fighter. Pieces begin to fly backward; smoke streams from the wing root. At such close range the fire is devastating. A wing goes up. Carl continues to fire. The Zero staggers, noses down north of the field, a yellow stream of fire streaking backward from wing tanks. As Carl watches from 500 feet, the enemy pilot dives straight into the ground. Victory number two!

To his right, the second Zero is almost in range. Carl banks into a right-hand turn and closes for the attack. But now the third Zero flips into a sharp left turn, and almost faster than Carl can follow the action, the Zero is closing Carl's rear from the port quarter.

The Zero ahead is almost within range, but the Zero closing from the left, behind, is closer. Twinkling lights on the leading edge of the wings! The Wildcat staggers. Shells smash through the F4F before Carl can take evasive action. He banks right, then left, but the Zero stays on him. He's too low to dive away, nor can he outturn the more maneuverable enemy. Yet he must escape this fire, and soon, if he is to survive. At this desperate moment Carl notices a small cumulus cloud a few thousand feet ahead. He must get to it! Using maximum power, he points toward the cloud, at the same time jinxing for all he is worth.

The Zero continues to fire. Tracers streak by. Carl, having completely lost sight of his intended victim, somehow avoids further damage and plunges into the milky white! He will try a trick on the enemy pilot behind. With his left hand he grasps the throttle and yanks it all the way back. The Wildcat suddenly decelerates and appears to "brake" in the milky white. The pursuing enemy pilot, unaware that Carl has chopped his throttle, thunders into the cloud and races past. Agonizing seconds pass. Then, suddenly, clear blue sky and bright light again.

Now out of the cloud, Carl sees the enemy Zero just below to his left, not far ahead. The trick worked! Now he has him! He dumps stick forward, hits left rudder, and closes on the unsuspecting Zero. His trigger finger presses the firing button. Nothing! Carl is furious. Negative gravity has jammed the guns! He is only two hundred feet away, and could easily score another kill.

Meanwhile the Zero pilot, glancing behind, realizes his danger and begins to pull away, heading west to his carrier. Reluctantly, Carl banks left and heads back to Eastern Island, climbing as he approaches Midway again. The mystery to Carl is the absence of American fighters. None are in view. Down below he sees several fires burning on the field.

Meanwhile, the sixteen dive bombers which had taken off at about the same time as the fighters reach the Japanese carriers and go into the attack. Eight of the sixteen are shot down by defending enemy Zekes; another six are heavily riddled; two escape with only minor damage; no hits are scored on the carriers! Soon after Army B-17's attack from 20,000 feet, dropping 8,500 pounds of bombs each, but again there are no hits.

Eleven Marine Corps Vindicator bombers also arrive over the carrier force. Although overwhelmed by defending Zekes, they attempt to bomb battleship *Haruna*. Still no hits.

Carl continues to circle the field overhead, wondering where the surviving twenty-five fighter planes can be. He sees a few scattered fighters and bombers below, but the field is bare compared to the scene at five that morning. He calls the tower, and as radar shows no enemy planes in the vicinity, he gets permission to land. Easing back on the throttle, he starts down, lowers his landing gear, and approaches the runway cautiously, scanning the landing area for fires and bomb craters. The runway is clear (the Japanese had intentionally spared it).

It is only 8:00 A.M. when he touches down at seventy knots and taxies to his revetment. Crewmen and other pilots hasten to the plane and excitedly inform him that only ten pilots, of the twenty-five who had taken off, have come back—including himself.

Even more discouraging is the report that only two fighters, including Carl's, are capable of taking off again. Nevertheless, armorers and crewmen gas and arm these two fighters with all speed, and Carl gets ready to take off immediately. He hardly has time to collect his wits when orders come to scramble again. He and fellow Marine Captain Bill Humberd gun their fighters off into the west at approximately 8:30. These two are Midway's remaining fighter defense!

TBF torpedo bomber (Avenger). Their sacrifice insured victory at Midway. (**Navy Department Photo**)

Carl's Wildcat is marked by shell holes from the previous battle, but the engine performs normally. As the two planes circle the field and climb, the battered dive bombers and torpedo bombers begin to return from their carrier strike—many of them badly shot up. (Of twenty-seven dive bombers, fifteen return, most of them badly damaged. Of six torpedo bombers, one returns! And all that the bombers can report are either unconfirmed claims or no hits on the Japanese fleet.)

At this moment, approximately 9 A.M., the returning Japanese striking force was preparing to land on the four enemy carriers to the west.

Unknown to Carl, thoroughly discouraged and depressed despite his first aerial victories, the desperate fighting of Midway pilots in their obsolete aircraft had laid the groundwork for a great American naval victory.

If a military evaluation of the situation had been taken at that moment, it would have seemed that the Battle of Midway was moving inevitably toward a Japanese victory. Though the enemy had lost a small number of carrier planes, he had destroyed over half the aircraft on Midway and inflicted considerable damage on the installations on both Sand and Eastern islands.

Yet the gallant defense by Midway's fighters had accomplished enough to prove decisive in the events which were now to follow. Even before the Japanese pilots had landed on their carriers, the strike commander radioed an opinion that there was "need for a second strike wave."

Basing his decision partly upon the recommendation of the air strike commander, Vice Admiral Chuichi Nagumo, commanding the carriers, ordered his bombers to arm and fuel for another attack on Midway. The need for a second attack, to completely neutralize the island's defenses, was to make the Japanese carriers especially vulnerable in the next few hours. It meant the bombers were to remain on the flight decks being refueled, leaving the carriers "sitting ducks" for an American attack. Fortunately for the Americans, Nagumo was not aware of the American carrier force now approaching from the north.

Now arrived, perhaps, the greatest hour of the war in the Pacific for the Americans.

Early that morning American carriers *Yorktown, Enterprise* and *Hornet,* which had been stationed in an appropriate position by Admiral Chester W. Nimitz, had been informed by spotter planes of the presence of the four enemy carriers to the south. *Enterprise* and *Hornet* launched a strike with all available planes shortly after seven o'clock. *Yorktown* launched her striking force soon after 9 A.M., just as the striking force from the former two carriers was approaching its prey.

At first even this carefully planned attack, which was to prove so devastating, appeared doomed to failure. The torpedo planes reached the enemy carriers first. Defending Zeke fighters, spotting them approaching, swarmed to the attack. A slaughter ensued. Of forty-one torpedo bombers which attempted to attack the carriers thirty-five failed to return! Nor did they score any hits on the carriers.

This was similar to the failure of the Marine and Army attack, from Midway, earlier that morning. However, the low-level attack of the torpedo bombers drew Japanese defending fighters down to low altitude, and this now paid an immense dividend. Thirty-seven dive bombers from *Enterprise* and *Yorktown* arrived on the scene. The Japanese carriers, fueling and arming bombers for another strike on Midway—made necessary by the gallant Marine defense—were now to be paid off for Pearl Harbor.

The American dive bombers winged over into the attack. The four carriers were in a boxlike formation, protected on the sides by battleships, cruisers and destroyers. *Akagi*, the flagship of the fleet, as she had been at Pearl Harbor, was on the starboard flank. About a mile behind was sister ship *Kaga*. Several miles to the left steamed the other carrier division, consisting of *Hiryu* and *Soryu*. Until now these four carriers had survived repeated strikes by land-based bombers without suffering a single hit, but their time had come. Lieutenant Commander M. F. Leslie, leading seventeen SBD dive bombers from *Yorktown*, dived on *Soryu*. Lieutenant Commander Clarence McClusky, from *Enterprise*, leading thirty-seven SBD dive bombers, divided his force. He ordered one squadron to follow him, in an attack on *Kaga*, and another to dive bomb *Akagi*.

Commencing his attack from 14,500 feet, Leslie led his seventeen dive bombers down on *Soryu* as she was turning into the wind to launch her second strike on Midway. Three hits with 1,000-pound bombs were scored at approximately 10:30 A.M. One penetrated the flight deck forward, exploding in the hangar below, another struck amidships in the midst of fueled and armed planes, and a third hit near the after elevator. The entire ship became a sheet of flames. *Soryu* was abandoned in twenty minutes.

McClusky's dive bombers scored three hits on flagship *Akagi*. One hit the elevator amidships, another the flight deck on the port side, and a third exploded in the middle of aircraft on the flight deck. The carrier was enveloped in flames and the crew ordered to abandon ship.

Four hits were scored on *Kaga*. One bomb landed near the bridge, killing everyone there. Other bombs landed amid aircraft on the flight deck and penetrated gasoline and bomb storage areas below decks. In minutes *Kaga* was a mass of flames.

Three of the enemy's four fast carriers were now doomed. Rear Admiral F. J. Fletcher and Rear Admiral R. A. Spruance, commanding the U.S. carriers, had done their job well. But, stung by this savage

U.S.S. Yorktown being hit by bomb during battle of Midway. (Official U.S. Navy Photo)

attack, the lone Japanese carrier, *Hiryu*, mounted an immediate strike against the American carriers, and managed to exact a measure of revenge.

Three hits were scored on *Yorktown*, which had—through such heroic repair efforts at Pearl Harbor—barely managed to make the scene in time to participate in the battle. Unlike the Japanese carriers, *Yorktown* did not sink immediately. In fact, she managed to carry on after the first attack from *Hiryu*. But two hours later another attack from the remaining enemy carrier doomed gallant *Yorktown*. Two torpedoes from the second Japanese attack wave struck *Yorktown*, rupturing fuel tanks on her port side and jamming her rudder.

Though *Yorktown* remained afloat for two days, due to valiant efforts of her skipper and his salvage crew, she was a derelict, and was finally sunk by a Japanese submarine. However, her conqueror was avenged within hours. Fletcher, rightly guessing one enemy carrier was still in operation, had dispatched ten scout bombers to search for her. After a search lasting over three hours they finally located *Hiryu*, two battleships, three cruisers, and four destroyers steaming north.

At 3:30 P.M. *Enterprise* launched twenty-four dive bombers (ten of them *Yorktown* aircraft).

These dive bombers were led by Lieutenant Commander McClusky. They located the enemy carrier at about five o'clock. Though *Hiryu* was making thirty knots and was better prepared to defend herself than her three sister carriers, McClusky's dive bombers scored four direct hits. They started uncontrollable fires and doomed *Hiryu*. The last of the four carriers successfully bombed did not sink until next morning. Yamamoto, shocked by this immense disaster, called off the invasion of Midway.

Carl touched down, in his shell-marked Wildcat, before noon, after his second flight of the day. The extent of the Marine achievement was as yet unknown and unappreciated. Nor did Carl realize how narrowly he missed engaging a second enemy carrier strike with two planes. Understandably, Marine pilots who had flown the Buffaloes were bitter. All were depressed. None was more disgusted than Carl, even though he had scored his first kills, on his first combat mission—on the way to becoming the Marine Corps' seventh ranking ace in World War II. (Carl was soon to go to Guadalcanal, where he would shoot down another fifteen enemy aircraft, and be shot down himself in September.)

Carl's achievement, and that of those flying with him on June 4, 1942, at Midway, was in providing sufficient opposition—with obsolete equipment—to compel the Japanese to prepare a second strike against the island. Had the initial enemy carrier strike knocked out Midway,

Japanese cruiser afire after attack by Navy and Marine planes at battle of Midway. (Official U.S. Navy Photo)

Admiral Nagumo's carriers would not have been so highly vulnerable to the attack of American dive bombers.

Indeed, they would have had more fighters ready to launch, and the outcome of the battle in that hard-pressed spring of 1942 might have been entirely different. Such was the contribution of VMF 221 and all those who defended Midway on June 4.

For "extraordinary heroism" in the Battle of Midway, Carl was awarded the Navy Cross. Before the war ended he had received two Navy Crosses, five Distinguished Flying Crosses, fourteen Air Medals, and a number of other medals and decorations.

Today, still in the Marine Corps, a colonel rather than a captain,

Carl has over 10,000 hours in fighter planes. He was among the first Marine pilots to fly jets. He is the only Navy-Marine rocket pilot, having held the world's speed record in 1947 and the world's altitude record in 1953. He is serving on the Joint Staff of the Joint Chiefs of Staff, as this book goes to press.

2 A Scramble at Guadalcanal

AUGUST 30, 1942:

Captain JOHN L. SMITH, U.S.M.C.

THE United States checked the Japanese tide at sea in June of 1942. It was in August that U.S. Marines landed on Guadalcanal and began the struggle which gave American forces their first victory over Japan's combined land, sea and air forces.

Guadalcanal is an island in the Solomons that few Americans had heard of before the war, and one no American commander would have selected as the best place for a decisive struggle between Japan and America. Yet, because of its strategic importance, for more than six months it was the site of a desperate struggle between the air forces, fleets and soldiers of the United States and Japan.

The Solomon Islands include two parallel rows of islands—Choiseul, Santa Isabel and Malaita, and below them, on a parallel northwest-southwest course, New Georgia, Guadalcanal and San Cristobal. At the northwestern end of the chain, above the big island of Bougainville, lie New Britain and New Ireland. Guadalcanal itself lies northeast of Australia, well to the east of Australia's eastern coast.

Following up their sensational opening victories, the Japanese had advanced steadily southward and eastward. They established a major base at Rabaul, on New Britain, and New Ireland, and then reached out to the hot jungles of Guadalcanal in June, 1942, where they landed a small contingent of troops and began construction of an airfield, also disembarking troops at Tulagi, on nearby Florida Island.

Rightly concerned about the Japanese envelopment of Australia, the United States' reaction was the country's first major move toward checking the enemy's overland advance. The initial plan called for the landing of a Marine division in the Solomons on August 1. When it was discovered that the Japanese were building an airstrip on Guadalcanal, it became even more important to capture the island. As it turned out, however, delays postponed the American landing until August 7, which was just in time, since the enemy airstrip would have become operational that month.

On August 12 the first U.S. aircraft, a PBY, landed on what was to become Henderson Field (named after Major Lofton R. Henderson, commander of Marine dive bombers at Midway). It carried Lieutenant William S. Sampson, U.S.N., who pronounced the field in operational condition.

The Marines were to furnish Henderson's fighters. Pilots would be carried to within flying distance of the field by the carrier *Long Island*, from which they would take off. The need for air power at Guadalcanal had become critical following the naval disaster at Savo Island. The day after the Marines went ashore a Japanese task force slipped through the navigable water known as "the Slot" and launched a surprise night attack on the U.S. force screening landing operations. Sunk were cruisers *Astoria, Quincy, Vincennes* and *Canberra. Chicago* was heavily damaged.

The Savo Island disaster completely changed the naval complexion of the Guadalcanal operation. American naval forces pulled out, including the American carrier force and its fighter pilots. On the night of the disaster the Japanese admiral in command missed a golden opportunity when he turned away, after his stunning victory, six miles from U.S. transports feeding the American landing.

When American naval forces withdrew, the transports dumped their supplies on the beach—as far as was possible—and departed also. Thus those ashore, left to their fate, desperately needed air support.

It was relatively slow in arriving. The first Marine squadrons assigned to Guadalcanal were VMF 223, commanded by Captain John L. Smith (a fighter squadron), and VMSB 232, commanded by Major Richard C. Mangrum (a dive-bomber squadron). Smith's pilots were inexperienced and he wisely exchanged some of his green fliers for more

An F4F Wildcat, the U.S. Navy's early fighter, taking off from a carrier. (Official U.S. Navy Photo)

experienced veterans in a nearby squadron. Because of this and other delays it was not until the afternoon of August 20 that *Long Island,* escorted by cruiser *Helena* and destroyer *Dale,* launched the two Marine squadrons into the wind 200 miles southeast of Guadalcanal. Nineteen Grumman F4F Wildcats and twelve Douglas SBD Dauntless dive bombers set course for Henderson Field, and at five o'clock that afternoon Captain Smith landed the first American fighter on Guadalcanal.

That very night there occurred the heaviest fighting of the campaign up to then; continuous firing was heard by the aviators only 3,000 yards east of Henderson Field. This was the Battle of the Tenaru River, sometimes called the Ilu River, or Alligator Creek. The Marines won it handily, for the Japanese attacked with only 900 men—having underestimated the strength of the invading American force.

This proved to be the first of a long series of enemy attacks on Henderson Field, and for Smith's fighter pilots a foretaste of operational conditions and dangers unsurpassed in severity by those experienced by any other group of pilots in World War II. As the situation of the Marines on Guadalcanal deteriorated steadily from August until October, when it reached crisis proportions; the pilots and crewmen of these planes carried on daily attacks against superior enemy forces, with only tents on the edge of the field for shelter, the most meager rations, often reduced to Japanese rice, subjected to enemy strafing attacks, naval bombardments, and shelling from Japanese Army howitzers, constantly suffering from malaria-carrying mosquitoes and dysentery.

Enduring this ordeal, they rendered invaluable service, shattering the myth of the Zeroes' invincibility. For the first time in the war, U.S. fighters rising from Henderson Field exacted a heavier toll of attacking Zeroes than they suffered themselves.

Flying the Grumman Wildcat, the best American-built fighter available, which could not in all circumstances stand up to the Zero, Marine pilots began to tackle large invading flights of Zeroes from August 21 onward, and did not hesitate to dive into enemy formations which outnumbered them substantially. From a psychological standpoint this was of great value to the morale of U.S. aviators in all services.

In October, when speculation about a possible American withdrawal began to creep into official conversation, it was Marine air strength based on Guadalcanal that eased the crisis and spelled the difference between victory and defeat.

The constant and devastating attacks of Marine fighters and dive bombers, supplemented by a very small U.S. Army fighter force and by somewhat larger reinforcements of carrier fighters, which flew in from time to time as the battle progressed, caused most of the Japanese air and sea losses in this critical period.

Had it not been for this air striking force, the Japanese could have landed unlimited troop reinforcements on the western end of Guadalcanal. As it was, the enemy suffered heavy losses at the hands of Marine aircraft in his attempts to do so. The fact that the Japanese could not properly reinforce Guadalcanal, even though they maintained naval

70452

Take Off Time: Shortly after 10:00 A.M. Landing: Approximately noon.

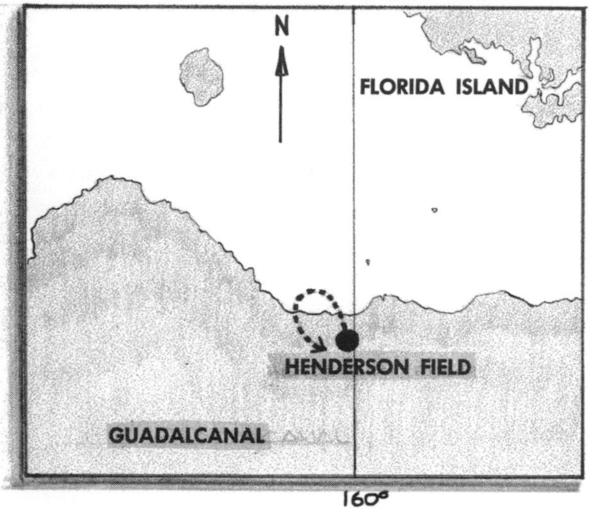

N

FLORIDA ISLAND

HENDERSON FIELD

GUADALCANAL

160°

FIGHTER PLANE

F4F WILDCAT

Large enemy raid

FIGHTER SQUADRON

VMF 223

LOCATION

GUADALCANAL

MISSION FLOWN BY:

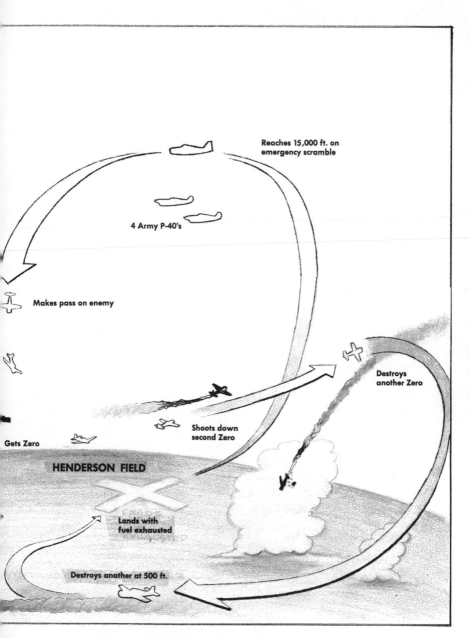

Reaches 15,000 ft. on
emergency scramble

4 Army P-40's

Makes pass on enemy

Destroys
another Zero

Gets Zero

Shoots down
second Zero

HENDERSON FIELD

Lands with
fuel exhausted

Destroys another at 500 ft.

PTAIN JOHN L. SMITH, USMC, AUGUST 30, 1942

superiority during most of the campaign, proved to be the key to the U.S. victory. Although often outnumbered two to one by the enemy's air forces at Rabaul and Buin, the Marine pilots achieved and maintained control of the air throughout the bitter months that saw Major General Alexander A. Vandegrift's gallant 1st Marine Division prove its superiority over the Japanese Army.

Captain John Lucien Smith was born in Lexington, Oklahoma, and attended the University of Oklahoma. In 1936, after graduation, he joined the Marines and served for two years as an artillery officer, after which he was ordered to Pensacola, Florida, to become a Marine pilot. He served in dive bombers for a time, then was transferred to a fighter squadron which was being sent to Wake Island.

However, Wake fell before the squadron arrived, and it was put ashore at Midway. It was there that Smith learned his trade as a fighter pilot. He was called to Pearl Harbor immediately before the Battle of Midway, and given the task of organizing Marine Fighter Squadron 223, which he did.

After landing at Guadalcanal, he became the first American to shoot down an enemy Zero. Cruising with a flight of four Wildcats at 8,000 feet over Savo Island, Smith sighted six Zeroes 2,000 feet above him— a distinct advantage for the enemy. He attacked, and his was the only victory of the day. It provided an ominous note for the Japanese command, since it revealed the presence of American fighters at Henderson Field.

The grim nature of the aerial campaign that followed is reflected in the statistics in this comparatively short period all but six of Smith's twenty-one pilots (nineteen planes) became fatalities or casualties. Of the six who were ordered out of Guadalcanal on October 13, including Smith, many, again including Smith, had been shot down, had survived, and had returned to combat operations. Others had suffered injuries or illness and returned to duty.

It is with Smith's experience on August 30, nine days after his first victory, that this chapter is concerned.

It is 4:30 in the morning when Smith awakes in his tent, and pulls on his field shoes and khaki-issue shirt and trousers. Outside, the first traces of light are beginning to separate still green palms. It is a muggy day. (VMF 223 has been in action only nine days and already six of its original nineteen fighters have been lost. And the air battle is obviously increasing in intensity, the Japanese reacting strongly to the arrival of U.S. fighters on Guadalcanal.) After dressing, he swallows a breakfast of coffee and captured Japanese cookies (somewhat similar to vanilla wafers). He walks out to a blue-and-white F4F Grumman fighter, on the edge of the field, and carefully warms up the engine, causing a roar that can be heard for miles in the morning stillness. Leaving the F4F, and his crew chief, at the revetment, Smith makes his way to the Ready Room tent, located in the middle of a coconut grove, between the beach and the runway. It is just after five when he enters.

Squadron 223's orders are to maintain a close standby until dawn plus thirty minutes. In the Ready Room pilots await a signal from a warning system comprised of coast watchers (Australian and native) located on the islands to the northwest. In recent days the Japanese have been raiding Henderson Field every morning. The 30th should be no exception.

After a short while Smith and other VMF 223 fighter pilots return to their fighters and continue their wait. It is now thirty minutes past dawn. There is still no message from the warning system, so pilots gather in a small wooden building that serves as Operations, near their planes and on the edge of the field, and settle down to a game of cards. The sun rises higher in the eastern sky, revealing a mass of cumulus clouds over the blue-green waters of the Slot and Sealark Channel, but still no warning comes. It is eight o'clock.

Eight Marine pilots, flying Wildcats, are ready to scramble. A number of Army pilots, some flying slower P-40's, are also available. (Later that same day, the remainder of Marine Air Group 23's flight echelon would arrive, additional fighters and dive bombers, but as of the morning of the 30th, U.S. fighter strength at Henderson Field, above which the aerial battle of Guadalcanal was rapidly increasing in intensity, was at a low ebb.)

Smith glances intermittently at the clock in Operations as he plays cards. Since scoring the first Marine air kill in the Solomons on August 21 he has shot down four additional enemy planes, to become an ace with five victories. He is the first American fighter pilot to achieve such a score at Guadalcanal. Another hour has passed. It is after nine o'clock.

The telephone in the shack rings and Smith answers. An excited voice on the other end reports a large flight of Zeroes, "on the way," and a "large flight of Betties" following—all flying at medium height. The pilots, including the Army pilots, bolt from their chairs and run out of the shack and head for their aircraft.

At briefing Smith had told his men to rendezvous about eight or ten miles east of Henderson Field. Then, in combat formation, they would return to the area of the field. As he runs to his fighter he notices high banks of cumulus clouds to the north and west. It is clearer to the east. This will allow an orderly rendezvous to the east, by which time perhaps radar will have picked up the direction from which the Japs are arriving. (Henderson Field boasted one of the early radar sets; on it the direction of an enemy air strike could not be determined until the attackers were at the northwest end of the island—about ten minutes away.)

A shotgun shell fires and the Pratt and Whitney engine roars into life. Smith had signaled Corporal Erving Yach, his crew chief, as he sprinted up to the big fighter. Now Yach is busy helping him with his harness and gives him tense words of encouragement. Smith waves good-by, guns the fighter, and heads for the end of the runway. It is almost ten o'clock in the morning.

Moments later the roaring Pratt and Whitney pulls the fully loaded blue-white F4F off the runway, and the stubby Marine fighter skims over the palms into the east. Smith watches behind him, as Lieutenant Charles Kendrick, his wingman, and the other pilots lift safely off the field. They follow on an eastern heading at maximum climb. Down below, Cactus Control (Base Operations) has no further information. Smith decides to try a bit of bluffing, in an effort to confuse the enemy concerning his true strength. He reports in over the radio as the commanding officer of one squadron and then another. If the Japanese are monitoring radio transmissions, this will indicate that several squadrons of U.S. fighters are forming up over Henderson Field.

Only a handful of U.S. fighters, however, are climbing into the blue sky of the east. As the Wildcats reach 10,000 feet, superchargers of the two-stage engines cut in. Pilots check guns. The Wildcats are armed with six 50-caliber guns and a complement of 1,850 rounds of ammunition, divided between armor-piercing, ball and tracer. The P-40's are armed with 20-millimeter cannon but are limited in performance by their low ceiling.

As the Marine fighters continue their climb above 10,000 feet, the P-40's break off, but continue to keep the F4F's in view above. The Army pilots have no oxygen and can't operate higher than 10,000 or 12,000 feet, where supplemental oxygen is a necessity.

Down below, Cactus Control reports coast watchers have lost the enemy in heavy cumulus clouds to the west. Several times they have been sighted again, only to be lost once more. Now they have been found again, very close to Henderson Field! Smith looks at his altimeter; he has reached 15,000 feet. He calls to his fighters to begin a turn to the west, hoping to intercept the enemy over the field. The F4F's wing into a left turn, and the P-40's below follow suit.

Cactus Control radios: "We're pretty sure they're in the area now!" Smith levels off, points his nose straight for Henderson Field, almost due west. But the enemy is not yet in sight. He is cruising at 165 knots. Scattered clouds have moved in from the west, below, and begin to obstruct vision, at times obscuring Smith's view of the Army pilots at 12,000 feet. The Wildcats approach Henderson Field, every pilot rubbernecking in an effort to spot the Zeroes. (While bombers also were expected, the fighters would be at a higher altitude, and the U.S. pilots wanted to locate the enemy fighters first, since the Zeroes would be positioned to dive on the Americans attacking the slower Japanese bombers below.)

The eight Wildcats cross directly over the field. Still no sight of the enemy! Momentarily, Smith loses sight of the Army fighters below, and scans the sky for them.

Suddenly a voice comes in over the radio receiver: "Zeroes over us! Jumping us! We're right north of the field!" Frantically Smith scans the sky north of the field. He sees them! Twenty-two newly painted black-brown Zeroes! They're making it hot for the P-40's. Already two parachutes are billowing in the sky below. Instinctively Smith slams into a diving right-hand turn, ordering the others to follow, and the Marines rush to the aid of their badly outnumbered Army comrades.

The battle is 3,000 feet below, and the two surviving Army fighters are carrying on a twisting, turning fight with the more numerous Zeroes. Smith orders each Marine pilot to pick out an enemy fighter. He picks up speed as he roars downward, and squints into the light circle of his fixed sight. The first four Wildcats are now well ahead of the second four; Smith sets course to close the top four Zeroes with his leading four Wildcats. He begins to ease back on the stick, making better than 300 knots, drops left wing, and slices into a left turn behind one of the four dark Zeroes. Now he can see the rising sun red ball on the wings of the Zero straight ahead; his finger grips the trigger button.

Henderson Field on Guadalcanal, showing damaged aircraft in fore-ground. (Navy Department Photo)

Behind, at full throttle, the other three blunt-nosed Wildcats of the lead flight swoop down on other Zeroes in precision fashion. The enemy fighters are making only about 230 knots, banking slowly to the left, oblivious to the danger as the F4F's close in rapidly from behind. The range is down to nine hundred feet.

Smith eats up the distance between the planes . . . eight hundred feet . . . seven hundred! The enemy's wingspan fills the sight. He is on him. Now he presses the trigger button! Six 50-caliber guns shake the F4F. White smoke streaks back from his guns. Tracers show the gunnery pattern is converging dead on the Zero ahead. Strikes are numerous. The enemy aircraft sheds pieces, smoke and fragments. Smith holds the trigger button down. His prop nears the Zero's rudder. Flash! A yellow ball of fire fills the sky; the stricken fighter wings over slowly, trailing black smoke, begins to plunge to the earth below. Smith streaks close by, pulling up to avoid the debris. Victory No. 6!

So co-ordinated has been the attack, the other three Wildcat pilots also achieve complete surprise. In sixty seconds, as if by the turn of a switch, three other Zeroes burst into flame, disintegrate, plunge earthward. Four victories in a minute for Smith's lead flight!

But other Zeroes have overwhelmed the slower Army fighters, and all four have been shot down. The second flight of Wildcats is now about to gain a measure of revenge. They dive into the gaggle of Zeroes farther below. Several trails of dark smoke soon mark the path of burning Zeroes. The enemy, too, like the P-40's, has received a rude shock from above, and the Zeroes scatter widely.

Smith pulls back on the stick and clears his rear. The three pilots in his flight are in place; all report victories. The four F4F's begin a slow climb—seeking the Zeroes which have scattered. None are in view at the moment. The enemy bombers have not yet been sighted, either from the ground or by any of the American fighters. All eyes scan the sky to the northwest.

From ten o'clock, ahead, a lone speck emerges from a cloud. Smith follows the enlarging object closely. Zero! No doubt the enemy pilot has climbed to this altitude to help his comrades, but now he becomes the hunted instead of the hunter. With his left hand Smith pushes throttle full forward, dips right wing, and with right rudder knifes into a turn behind the Zero. His wingman, and the other two Wildcats, follow. Because the Zero had been forced to climb, the enemy's speed is reduced; the Wildcats close the gap immediately.

Smith keeps both eyes on the sight ring, his hand on the trigger. He watches the wingspan of the Zero grow wider and wider as he rushes up from behind. In seconds he's in range, presses the firing button! The streaks of shells begin to register; in a few seconds pieces of the Zero fly backward. Now they become a veritable shower. Smith keeps firing. He sees the cowling of the Zero fly back, and part of it strikes his canopy, but causes no serious damage. The Zero trails a fatal streak of red and yellow flame. A half-burst of about a second, and it blows up in an orange flash. The enemy pilot has no chance to bail out. Victory No. 7!

Smith has two victories in less than five minutes. But the battle is not over. And he still hasn't located the bombers. The division being intact, he radios: "Charge your guns." Smith points the blunt nose of the F4F northward, over the water, to get a good general view, and scans the sky for the unsighted bombers. He still can't find them. After a few minutes, not having seen anything, the four fighters execute a left turn, then another, which puts them on a southward heading— toward Henderson once again. All eyes search out the sky ahead, above the field. And Smith spots a suspicious object dead ahead.

At twelve o'clock, on a collision course, a low-wing silhouette grows larger. Smith, in the lead F4F, points his nose at the oncoming bogey and studies the silhouette. At this instant someone yells: "Bandit ahead!" Instinctively Smith tenses as he keeps his eyes on the rapidly approaching enemy fighter. His finger slips up on the trigger button. He hardly has to change course. He is automatically in a firing pass! The enemy fighter now gets bigger and bigger. In range!

Suddenly light flickers come from the Jap's wings—an intended death message from the enemy pilot! Smith presses the trigger in reply; his six 50-caliber guns roar, and the Wildcat shakes. The two fighters are closing at 500 knots. The F4F's behind Smith follow, pilots watching: it is the division leader's fight.

The Zero comes on, wing guns still flashing. His finger on the trigger, keeping his fighter on collision course, Smith maintains a murderous fire on the oncoming enemy. If neither is fatally hit, one pilot will have to change course. Neither loses nerve. The two fighters streak together. Now, at last, the Zero begins to trail smoke. Pieces fly backward. It is beginning to break up under the impact of hits! And then—a burst of flame! The enemy fighter explodes.

Dangerously close, Smith rams the stick forward, diving beneath the debris of the burning enemy fighter. Some of the pieces from the stricken Zero strike the F4F of his wingman, Lieutenant Kendrick, but cause only superficial damage. The enemy pilot did not get out. Smith's third victim leaves a vertical smoke trail in the sky as it plunges toward Henderson Field below. Victory No. 8!

The sky is clear of Zeroes. Smith takes a moment to look around him.

His four-plane division is no longer intact. Both his and Lieutenant Kendrick's F4F were hit by many pieces of his last victim's aircraft. The clouds are beginning to close in from every direction, and visibility is steadily decreasing, which will make joining up again difficult. The cloud ceiling is likewise lowering. (The cloud build-up Smith observed to the west earlier in the day is now over Guadalcanal.)

Smith dips his left wing and banks into a spiraling left turn, descending to 9,000, 8,000, 7,000, now 6,000 feet. He glances around, looking for Kendrick.

"Kendrick, where are you?" he transmits. "I'm short of fuel, circling the north shore, west of the field," comes the reply. "Wait there. I'll join up and we'll go in to the field together," Smith orders. The lower he descends the heavier the clouds. Scud is everywhere. Smith searches for Kendrick. He is now down to 3,000 feet, 2,000, 1,000! His fuel gauges show an adequate supply of fuel; he therefore wonders if Kendrick's tanks are leaking. He is flying east along the north shoreline, now down to 800 feet. Still he can't spot Kendrick. He continues east, only a few hundred feet above the shore.

Over to the left, ahead, he spots two aircraft. One could possibly be Kendrick. But why two? He banks into a slow left turn, applying full power, and begins to close the gap. Visibility is limited, and he can't identify the aircraft, though he's within 700 feet. He eases up closer . . . 600 feet, 500 feet. A shock! Zeroes! The two fighters, in close formation, have almost certainly been strafing the field while the air battle raged above it.

Smith grabs the silver-colored handles of his gun chargers, charges them, and maneuvers the nearest Zero into his sight. He is already within 300 feet! The Zero is only a few hundred feet above ground, and Smith, alone, is risking the chance that the other enemy pilot ahead will circle behind him, get on his tail, once he opens fire. His attack is highly dangerous because the Zero is far more maneuverable than the F4F. Nevertheless, pointing his nose at the Zero to the right, lining him up in the gunsight glass, Smith once again presses the trigger.

The guns roar. Tracers mark a steady path toward the enemy victim. The Zero literally staggers under the weight of the fire of six guns at such close range. The stricken enemy pilot pulls straight up. Smith is not dislodged by the maneuver; he yanks back on the stick and maintains fire on the Zero, which now begins to trail flame and smoke. The

F4F's fire is too much. The Jap fighter's left wing suddenly lifts, the right wing drops. The Zero noses over, right, into a dive.

The canopy flies off. Streaming flame and smoke, the plane disintegrates as it plunges earthward. It goes straight into the ground, only a few hundred feet below.

For an instant Smith watches the Zero burn. There was no parachute, nor was there time to use one. He begins to rubberneck rapidly, remem-

Guadalcanal's northern coast. (Navy Department Photo)

bering the other enemy fighter, in an effort to locate him. He S-turns and searches the sky behind; the other Zero has apparently had enough. Victory No. 9!

He flies east, following the coast. In the excitement of the last two kills he has not kept landmarks in view. He is not sure of his position. He resumes the search for Kendrick, also checking all quarters of the sky for the possible appearance of the other Zero. But no plane, friend or foe, is in view. Then, ahead, he recognizes the Lunga River.

He circles the river to identify it positively, then sets a homeward course which should lead him to the field. The clouds on all sides have lowered considerably. Navigation becomes a major problem. Kendrick's whereabouts is a mystery; Smith figures he must have already returned to the field. In a few minutes, his navigation proving true, familiar landmarks begin to appear. He roars on, low over the palms. Then, ahead . . . Henderson Field! He crosses the runway and prepares to land. The tension eases.

He calls Cactus Control, reporting in. The reply is comforting. Everyone else is down; he is the last to return. He swings the big fighter into a left turn, cuts his speed to 75 knots on the approach, gradually hauling back on the throttle. He settles steadily and touches down, safely. Canopy back, he turns off the runway and slowly taxies to his revetment.

He can see a group waiting for him; some jump up and down. Kendrick has landed, and told ground crewmen and pilots the big news—the Oklahoman has scored three or four kills, increasing his victory total from five to eight or nine! As he taxies into the crowd, someone yells the inevitable. How many victories had he scored? With a grin, Smith replies, "Four," and holds up four fingers. Everyone smiles or exclaims; there is an extra appreciative smile from Corporal Yach.

Among those waiting is Lieutenant Colonel Ray Scollins. Scollins reports excitedly that, according to the latest count, fourteen of the twenty-two Zeroes were shot down in the day's battle. Smith is elated. The bombers had never appeared. (They had turned back, because of the clouds and foul weather, and only the Zeroes reached Henderson Field.) Four Army P-40's were lost and six other Army fighters were badly damaged.

Scollins and Smith discuss the mission, and the pilots who achieved victories. Armorers and crewmen immediately begin to load the guns and fill the tanks with gasoline. Congratulations pour in from all sides. Smith is able to relax.

The Japanese had suffered a bloody repulse only nine days after they had lost their first Zero to a defending U.S. fighter. It was an important aerial victory, though much hard fighting lay ahead. Smith was to shoot down nineteen enemy planes before he had finished—and was recalled from Guadalcanal as the leading American air ace.

As leader of the first Marine fighter squadron at Guadalcanal, and the first squadron to explode the myth of invincibility of the Zero, Smith's performance in the summer of 1942 stands as one of the great efforts of World War II, and one of the inspirational examples in U.S. military history. He was awarded the Congressional Medal of Honor, by a grateful Congress, in recognition of his contribution to victory in the struggle for Guadalcanal.

His lightninglike destruction of four Japanese Zeroes on August 30, in a Wildcat and outnumbered, is more impressive when one remembers that in each case he was up against a thoroughly trained, veteran Japanese fighter pilot. These were the same pilots who were responsible for the stunning Japanese victories in the opening phases of the war and were greatly superior to most of Japan's later-day pilots. And Smith was not flying an F6F or an F4U, which enjoyed a wide performance margin over the Zero.

The citation accompanying Smith's Medal of Honor reveals official recognition of this all-important accomplishment. It reads:

For conspicuous gallantry and heroic achievement in aerial combat above and beyond the call of duty as Commanding Officer of Marine Fighting Squadron Two Twenty-Three, during operations against enemy Japanese forces in the Solomon Islands Area, August–September, 1942. Repeatedly risking his life in aggressive and daring attacks, Smith led his squadron against a determined force, greatly superior in numbers, personally shooting down sixteen Japanese planes between August 21 and September 15, 1942.

In spite of the limited combat experience of many of the pilots of this squadron, they achieved the notable record of a total of eighty-three enemy aircraft destroyed in this period, mainly attributable to the thorough training under Major Smith and to his intrepid and inspiring leadership.

His bold tactics and indomitable fighting spirit and the valiant and zealous fortitude of the men of his command not only rendered the enemy's attacks ineffective and costly to them but contributed to the security of our advance base. His loyal and courageous devotion to duty sustain and enhance the finest traditions of the United States Naval Service.

Ironically, Smith had been ordered from Midway, just prior to the climactic Battle of Midway, to form VMF 223. At that time he felt deprived of an opportunity to participate in the war's aerial fighting. In less than three months, however, he wrote his name in immortal letters in the sky over the sand and coconut palms of the little-heard-of island of Guadalcanal.

It was there that the Japanese land advance southeastward, in the Pacific, was checked in World War II. John Lucien Smith, the leader of VMF 223, probably did as much as any man to halt the tide of that advance.

3 *A Dip in the Sea Off Malaita*

NOVEMBER 7, 1942:

Captain JOSEPH J. FOSS, U.S.M.C.

THE most famous Marine fighter ace to emerge from World War II was probably Joseph Jacob Foss, of Sioux Falls, South Dakota.

Foss shot down more enemy planes in the Pacific than any other Marine, and, moreover, was the first American fighter pilot to equal the record of Captain Eddie Rickenbacker, of World War I, who was credited with destroying twenty-two enemy aircraft and four balloons. Foss was to go on to fame and success after the war, also, being elected governor of South Dakota, and more recently, commissioner of the American Football League.

His combat duty was performed during the most rugged period of air fighting in the Pacific war. He arrived at Guadalcanal on October 9, 1942, just four days before then-ranking Marine ace, Captain John Smith, was withdrawn from combat, and achieved the almost unbelievable record of shooting down twenty-three enemy aircraft in little more than two months' time!

As executive officer of famed Marine Fighter Squadron 121 (with which we will again be concerned later in this book), Foss played a leading role in the crises of October and November, 1942, when things were blackest at Guadalcanal. The contribution of VMF 121 in the defense of Guadalcanal is apparent from a quick look at the records. The squadron set the record for the most enemy planes shot down in a single tour. It was not a cheap conquest. Of some forty pilots who arrived with the squadron in October (flying 400 miles from carrier *Long Island* to Henderson Field) practically half were lost in a hundred days.

Six days after Captain Foss had landed at Guadalcanal the naval picture had become so grim that Admiral Chester Nimitz admitted: "We are unable to control the sea in the Guadalcanal area." Nimitz added: "Thus our supply of the positions will only be done at great expense to us. The situation is not hopeless, but it is certainly critical."

Nimitz spoke one day after Foss and other Marine pilots had the realities of their situation brought home by shells from two Japanese battleships. They boldly stood offshore and wrought devastation to Henderson Field and other United States installations on Guadalcanal. That bombardment killed a number of pilots, including Foss's old instructor at Pensacola Naval Air Station, Ed Miller. United States stock sank even lower when, on the morning of October 15 (after Henderson Field had been shelled for the second successive night, this time by enemy cruisers), Foss and other pilots could see enemy transports lying off Tassafaronga, unloading Japanese troops and supplies, unhindered, ten miles away.

And, as Samuel Eliot Morison notes in *The Struggle for Guadalcanal*, even Secretary of the Navy Frank Knox, usually an optimist, sounded bleak on the 16th when he refused to make a prediction about Guadalcanal, adding, "But every man will give a good account of himself . . . everybody hopes that we can hold on."

The situation was again desperate in November. After having failed to push the Americans off Guadalcanal in October, the Japanese determined upon a more massive effort.

The last great Japanese effort to bring in large-scale reinforcements to Guadalcanal was turned back in November, in a series of fierce air and naval battles, culminating in the naval Battle of Guadalcanal—perhaps the fiercest single warship engagement of the entire war.

Interestingly, after this Japanese bid to retake Guadalcanal had been turned back the fortunes of war seemed to shift to the Allies, not only in the Pacific but in other theaters of the war as well. It was at this time that Field Marshal Erwin Rommel's Afrika Korps was beaten at El Alamein, and it was at this time that the German armies failed in their bid to capture Stalingrad, and were cut off, from behind.

Thus a critical point of the war in the Pacific, on land, was reached in November of 1942, and it is with that period that we are concerned in this chapter.

In their effort to retake Guadalcanal in November the Japanese decided to commit the entire 38th Division—a much larger troop effort than had been attempted thus far. Because the cost of transporting troops to the western tip of Guadalcanal had been made excessive by Marine, Army and Navy airmen, the Japanese resorted to the use of cruisers and destroyers to bring in the men and supplies. According to Captain Tameichi Hara, of the Imperial Japanese Navy, in *Japanese Destroyer Captain,* twenty Japanese destroyers were used in the period of November 2–10 to land the Japanese Army's 38th Division on Guadalcanal. The Japanese also apparently used at least one cruiser in this reinforcement effort. It was the task of the airmen on Guadalcanal to hinder this reinforcement as much as possible, since the Navy—as related above—had lost control of the waters around Guadalcanal.

Marine pilots on Guadalcanal were not unaware of the Japanese ascendency in the area. They knew the American carrier *Hornet* had been sunk October 26, in the Battle of the Santa Cruz Islands, that carrier *Enterprise* had been damaged, as had the new battleship *South Dakota.* As a result, Admiral William Halsey, commanding American naval forces in the area, had fewer capital ships to oppose the enemy at this time than he had had several weeks earlier. And Halsey was soon to lose two cruisers and four destroyers, and other cruisers and destroyers damaged, in the aforementioned murderous Battle of Guadalcanal on the night of November 12–13.

The Marines were aware of the fact that the enemy was increasing his landings of troops on the western end of Guadalcanal. General Louis Woods, who had just relieved Major General Roy F. Geiger, commanding the First Marine Air Wing at Henderson Field, knew the Japanese had landed troops successfully from destroyers on November 2.

Therefore, when a dive-bomber scout plane reported, November 7, that eleven Japanese warships had been sighted, north of Florida Island, steaming toward Guadalcanal, Generals Geiger and Woods and every Marine air officer in a command job knew what was to be done.

The enemy's intention was to land troops after dark, and the American air strike had to be launched immediately, so the enemy warships could be bombed while there was still daylight.

Colonel William Wallace, commanding Marine Air Group 23, of which VMF 121 was a part, and Major Leonard ("Duke") Davis, commanding officer of VMF 121, hurriedly brought word of the sighting of the enemy ships to the operations area of Fighter 1 (a fighter strip southeast of Henderson Field). A strike composed of F4F fighters and SBD dive bombers was to be launched immediately. Foss was to lead eight of the Wildcats (F4F's), each of which would carry 200-pound bombs. The SBD's would carry 500-pounders or 1,000-pounders.

That afternoon, Saturday, November 7, the sky at Guadalcanal was overcast. There were scattered thunderstorms and no blue sky was to be seen. As Foss and his fellow Marine pilots scrambled "on the double" to take off as soon as possible, hurrying from tents between the tall palm trees (once cultivated groves), back in the United States attention turned to football, where on this Saturday the 1942 season was coming to a close. Would Illinois, Iowa, or some other team win the conference championship in the Big Ten? Would Georgia or Georgia Tech (both undefeated at this date in 1942) win top honors in the Southeastern Conference? On Guadalcanal boys just out of college were fighting and dying in a completely different world.

Foss had only minutes to prepare to take off. The ex-farm boy (his father of Norwegian ancestry, his mother Scotch-Irish), twenty-seven years old, had graduated two years earlier from the University of South Dakota. He had been on the college boxing team and had been a member of the track team, and his father—before he was killed in an automobile accident in a storm in 1933—had taught him to shoot.

The young captain had no idea, then, that he was destined to receive the Medal of Honor from President Franklin D. Roosevelt. The grim realization which faced him at the moment was that he, and the others in his group of eight fighters, were to act as decoys—to draw fire—while the SBD's attempted to drop their heavier bombs on the enemy warships.

And back home, while people that Saturday were preparing for parties and dances and complaining of the shortage of gasoline and tires, and sugar, Foss was putting on his life preserver and other flying gear and

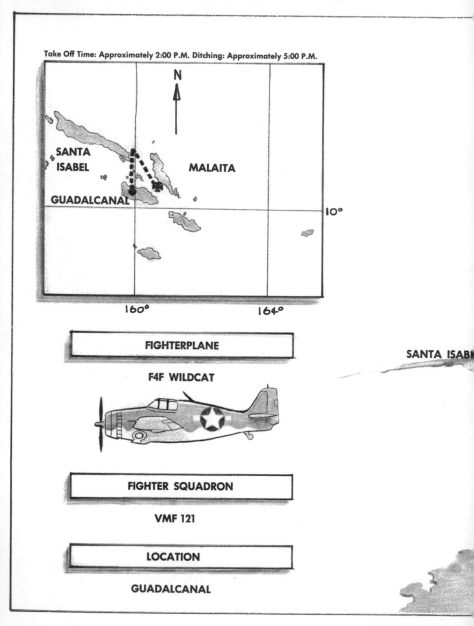

Take Off Time: Approximately 2:00 P.M. Ditching: Approximately 5:00 P.M.

N

SANTA
ISABEL

MALAITA

GUADALCANAL

10°

160°   164°

FIGHTERPLANE

F4F WILDCAT

FIGHTER SQUADRON

VMF 121

LOCATION

GUADALCANAL

SANTA ISAB

MISSION FLOWN BY

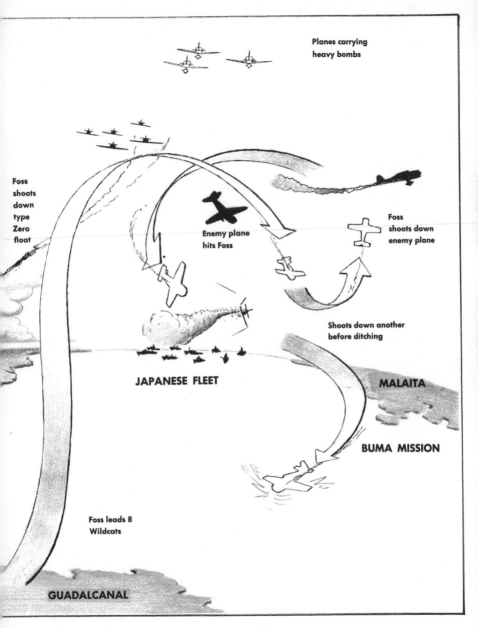

Planes carrying heavy bombs

Foss shoots down type Zero float

Enemy plane hits Foss

Foss shoots down enemy plane

Shoots down another before ditching

JAPANESE FLEET

MALAITA

BUMA MISSION

Foss leads 8 Wildcats

GUADALCANAL

CAPTAIN JOSEPH J. FOSS, USMC, NOVEMBER 7, 1942

running to his F4F Wildcat, which stood off the end of the runway of Fighter 1, camouflaged, under swaying palms. He didn't have time to think back to the occasion when he first became interested in flying, when a squadron of Marine fliers staged an air show at Sioux Falls in 1932. Three years later, in 1935, Foss paid $5 for his first airplane ride. Then, in 1937, he paid $65 (on the installment plan) for his first pilot-training course, beginning in a Taylorcraft.

At the University of South Dakota, in 1939, he took a Civil Aeronautics Authority flying course, and when he graduated he had a hundred hours of flying time. In 1940, soon after World War II began, but before the United States was involved, Foss hitchhiked to Minneapolis to enlist in the Marine Corps Reserve. Of twenty-eight men applying that day only two were accepted, and luckily for the United States, one of them was handsome, dead-serious Joseph Jacob Foss.

Foss was seated in his blue-gray Wildcat. The number 13 which had been painted on the side of his plane had been changed to 53 by superstitious crewmen. He yelled "Clear!" The prop began to spin, smoke belching from blue stacks. Other props were beginning to turn on the edge of the field, and soon the Wildcats were taxiing to the end of the runway. That afternoon seven SBD's, led by Major Joseph Sailer, Jr., and three TBF's, led by Lieutenant Harold H. Larsen, were carrying the Marine's big bombs. Altogether, twenty-three Marine fighters were taking part in the operation, as well as eight P-39 fighters.

The enemy warships could not be allowed to reinforce Guadalcanal without an all-out effort to stop them. Already, earlier in the week, the Japanese had succeeded in landing reinforcements to the east of the Americans. Since the enemy's major strength was on the western tip of the island, it was evident he was preparing a squeeze movement, in which the American foothold would be assailed from both sides. Back in the United States, on this very day, November 7, an Associated Press dispatch reported:

"The Japanese landed troops and reinforcements earlier this week to undertake a squeeze maneuver. . . . So far, American positions to the east of the airfield (where the Japs landed) are unchanged. . . . The threat has only been checked, rather than eliminated."

The newspapers also told of Japanese attacks, in strength, which had been repulsed by American forces the day before. Therefore, the pilots flying north to intercept the enemy fleet that day were fighting the battle of the Marines on the ground, just as surely as they were fighting their own.

Foss roars down the runway and lifts into the gray; soon he and the other Marine fighters are climbing into an overcast sky, leaving the white coral sands of the Guadalcanal coast behind. According to sighting reports, the Japanese warships are due north of Florida Island, Florida Island being in view ahead. Foss checks his instruments, charges his guns, by pulling up the three levers on each side of his seat, and then letting them snap back. His six 50-caliber guns are loaded with armor-piercing, incendiary and tracer ammunition—the tracers being spotted in every fifth space in the belt.

Now the Wildcats are approaching 10,000 feet, and Foss begins to scan the sky ahead more carefully. He also takes time to look behind him and mulls over tactics he will use in the strike at the enemy fleet. The SBD's are nearby, all eyes are fixed on the blue waters now visible north of Florida Island, for the first sighting of the enemy ships.

It is now more than thirty minutes since take-off. The U.S. fighters are still climbing. They reach 12,000, 13,000, 14,000, 15,000 feet, still below the overcast. As the altitude increases vision increases. Now Foss can see ahead, under the overcast, fifteen or twenty miles. But there's no sight of ships. He checks his gunsight and engine instruments. The Wildcat's engine is running smoothly, and everything has proceeded orderly so far. Florida Island has passed far behind; the U.S. dive bombers and fighters continue onward and upward.

Foss keeps scanning the ocean ahead, right to left. And then . . . he is the first man to see them. Not ships. With his left hand on the throttle, his right on the stick, still climbing, Foss focuses his eyes on suspicious specks off to the right. He takes a long look. Enemy planes! He pushes the radio transmitter button: "Bandits! There they are! Two o'clock!"

Other Marine pilots, quickly turning their attention to the right, and ahead, detect the silhouettes of six float-type Zeroes. They are descending, moving from right to left. Foss, dropping his bombs preparatory to combat, instinctively banks slightly to the right, to take up a position for an attack. He takes seven of the twenty-three fighters with him, the others staying with the SBD's—who continue on toward the Japanese fleet, dead ahead. Foss eases the throttle all the way forward, keeping his eyes glued on the six enemy fighters. They continue to descend, apparently not having noticed the eight F4F fighters now approaching rapidly from the south.

Foss can recognize the dusty, gray-green color of the Zeroes, and can make out the rising sun on each wing. Now he is closing rapidly, and the enemy planes, perhaps descending to take position ahead of their warships to the north, are oblivious to the approach of death from behind. Foss shoves the stick forward. The enemy fighters are rapidly descending, and the Wildcats continue the pursuit in a diving left turn—still undiscovered.

Foss checks his sight and fixes his eyes on a Zero ahead, the farthest left. The distance is rapidly closing. Other American pilots concentrate on other enemy victims. The Zeroes fly on and continue to cross to the left. Foss now banks hard left, realizes he will make a deflection shot, since he'll be turning inside the enemy. The Wildcat rapidly walks up on its victim. Foss has his finger on the trigger. He takes a quick glance behind him. Other Wildcats are closing other Zeroes from behind.

The enemy's wingspan grows wider and wider. He must restrain himself and wait until the Zero is in range. Still the enemy makes no move. The gray-green wingspan is now filling the sight ring. At that instant Foss presses the trigger. The Wildcat staggers from the recoil of the six guns. The tracers mark a deadly, converging course into the Zero to the left. For an instant nothing happens, as the 50-caliber shells slam into the stricken enemy aircraft. Foss holds his firing lead, from about a 60- or 70-degree angle. Shells rake the enemy. Suddenly the Zero disintegrates! The enemy's tanks have exploded, and pieces fly backwards. Foss maneuvers to miss them and levels off as he watches the remains of the enemy plane fall through the air. Victory!

Surprised, he notes a parachute opening below. The enemy pilot has survived the fatal explosion. He quickly glances around him. Some of the other Wildcats are following Zeroes down in power dives. Several other Zeroes fall, burning. Foss recognizes his friend, "Danny" Doyle, chasing one Zero to the deck. He glances at his altimeter . . . 7,000 feet.

Up ahead, now in view for the first time, looms the enemy fleet! The quarry is found. The warships leave white wakes in their paths. Three parallel lines of warships, and a warship on each flank, are steaming due south. Three ships form each of the columns, the center column being slightly ahead of the columns on each wing. A cruiser and ten destroyers! The cloud ceiling above is solid, but visibility is excellent below, and Foss can see the bombers flying up from the south to attack it. Now he gathers his pilots together by radio. They are climbing once again—to regain precious altitude.

A Suisei (Judy), Japanese Navy dive bomber, sinking after being shot down during an unsuccessful attack. (Navy Department Photo)

Only six of his men, however, respond to the call. The enemy fleet is not far away, and Foss must assemble the Wildcats and lead them in an organized attack. Even though his F4F's are decoys, their attack will be a vital part of the over-all air strike, since the antiaircraft guns on the warships below will divide their fire between the Wildcats and the SBD's and TBF's, carrying heavy bombs and torpedoes.

Foss checks his pilots. Danny Doyle, who dived to the deck after a Zero, is missing. Now the ships ahead are beginning to turn, as they spot the American planes coming in for an attack. Foss presses the mike button: "Reverse order—attack!" Since Foss is the leader of the seven Wildcats, the reverse order of attack means the seventh plane in formation will attack first, etc. The enemy fleet is now ahead, to the right, and the Wildcats prepare to peel off in their dive.

The warships below are spreading out, and the Marine pilots prepare to begin simulated bomb runs. The peel-off will be made from 10,000 feet. The first of Foss's seven F4F's peels off to the right. Foss will be the last of the seven to attack.

As the lead Wildcats go into their dives, Foss notices a suspicious speck ahead. A bogey—approaching rapidly! The unidentified plane is on a converging course. Friend or enemy? Foss keeps his eyes fixed on the approaching aircraft, which is now quite close and still on a converging course. The other F4F's dive on the fleet. He continues watching the unidentified aircraft. Now the silhouette becomes clear. Another enemy float plane! This one is a two-seater!

The enemy aircraft is almost on him. Foss banks sharply to the right. The Jap passes so close he barely misses the Wildcat with his wing. The enemy pilot cuts his throttle and his lighter plane almost seems to "brake" to a stop. Foss, still turning right, notices a gunner in the rear cockpit—aiming straight for 53. It's a shrewd maneuver. The enemy pilot apparently attempted to ram, then chopped his throttle, to slow down enough so his rear gunner could hit the Wildcat.

Thump! Thump! Thump! Hits! The Wildcat shudders, is taking heavy punishment. Holes rip through the cowling and wings. One smashes through the canopy, leaving a hole in the glass the size of a walnut. Momentarily paralyzed by the sight of the enemy gunner squarely facing him, firing away, Foss has absorbed many hits. Now he rams the stick full forward with his right hand; the Wildcat drops, nose down. The engine still runs smoothly. Foss, aroused, his fighting instinct taking over, pulls back on the stick, keeping his eye on the enemy plane above, and begins a fast-climbing approach to avenge the first round.

He will approach from underneath, for a belly attack. He pulls the Wildcat into a steeper and steeper climb. Foss uses full throttle and speed gained in the dive to climb at a steep angle. The enemy plane begins to fill the sight ring. He pulls back on the stick. He must fire quickly, for the Wildcat won't hold this steep angle forever. The slower enemy cannot run away. His wingspan fills the sight. Fire! This time, again, tracers prove the six 50-calibers perfectly aimed. Shells rip into the exposed belly of the enemy two-seater, and pieces fly back.

A stream of smoke begins to trail from the enemy two-seater. A yellow flash—gasoline ignites! The second victim explodes also; the two-seater wings over and begins a plunge toward the ocean below. Foss watches two chutes billow. Victory number two, after a close call! His aircraft is damaged—how badly he doesn't know.

Foss looks below. He's directly over the enemy fleet. Ships are turning in every direction and the F4F's and other American planes dive on them. One enemy destroyer sends up a pall of smoke. Another of the ships—the cruiser—has apparently been hit.

Foss's thoughts are interrupted. Out there to his left, below, something is moving. He observes carefully. Another enemy two-seater! A glance at his engine gauges. The engine seems to be running smoothly enough, but Foss wonders about the extent of the damage he has sustained. Will the F4F stand up under maximum stress and strain? He'll gamble. He'll go after the enemy plane to his left.

He hits left stick and left rudder, and starts a diving left turn. He eases forward on the throttle and watches as the enemy silhouette grows larger in his sight ring. The wind rustles through the hole in the canopy and creates noise and vibration. Still Foss concentrates on the grayish-green enemy two-seater ahead and below, to the left. He is closing rapidly, his speed builds up in the dive. His finger is in place on the trigger button once again.

He's approaching the enemy at a slight angle from behind, and this time the enemy gunner in the rear doesn't see him. The wingspan widens. Foss keeps his eyes intently on the victim ahead. Closer and closer. The wingspan fills the sight ring. He presses the button! For the third time the six 50-caliber guns roar, the Wildcat shudders, and a stream of lead converges on the victim ahead.

Immediately the enemy plane begins to stagger under the impact of the shells. Foss keeps boring in, firing, now at almost point-blank range. The enemy's wing goes up and the plane seems to quiver. The two-seater blows up in front of Foss's eyes. He pulls up and looks back. The remains of the enemy two-seater, burning and trailing smoke, are plunging straight down toward the enemy fleet below. Victory number three!

Foss looks around the sky. The ceiling is lowering. Down below he can see Wildcats circling, having delivered their attacks on the enemy ships. Foss points his nose southward and calls for his fighters to join him. He will head home. He can see the ceiling is lower; the weather ahead will be thick. An F4F is approaching. Foss notices that it's shot up worse than his own. He signals him to come in closer. He will accompany the cripple home. Two cripples join up!

But once again his eye warns him in time. Behind, converging fast, he notices silhouettes of fighters! At this instant his engine begins to miss. The shells which struck him have taken their toll after all. He has a sinking feeling in his stomach. He rams the throttle all the way forward. He'll run for it! The engine responds, but unevenly. He looks back again. Zeroes! Many of them. And, as is the custom of enemy pilots, they're fast converging on the two cripples.

Foss, now desperate, looks at the clouds ahead. The worsening weather may be their only chance. Just then his engine cuts out altogether! Silence. Now it roars back into action! Every few moments it cuts out, and then cuts in again. Foss pushes the stick farther forward, diving down and heading for the nearest cloud cover. The Zeroes come on, more than a dozen of them. Foss feels for his comrade, also trying to make it back with a damaged Wildcat. Zeroes are after him too! The gauges on the instrument panel react strangely as the engine roars on and off.

The cloud ahead draws nearer, and the Zeroes behind draw closer. Foss can do little to protect the other crippled Wildcat; he will be lucky to survive himself. Now the Zeroes are fast closing his rear. He must get out of the line of fire . . . now! He pushes the stick forward, almost dives into the nearest cloud bank. The milky gray rushes forward and envelops him, just as the Japs, behind, are almost in range. Foss is flying in thick stuff, with a missing engine, hoping the enemy will not be able to follow. He watches the altimeter . . . 7,000 feet, 6,500, 6,000 feet. As long as he is in the cloud he is safe, but it's quite an ordeal, flying without full power, with an engine liable to cut out at any minute.

The altimeter registers 4,500, 4,000, 3,500 feet. Whump! The engine cuts out completely. Now it resumes, and the instruments on the panel jump back and forth. Rain begins to spatter the canopy. Now, suddenly, he plunges out of the bottom of the cloud, at about 3,500 feet, over the water below. He glances behind. No Zeroes in sight. (Unknown to him at the moment, the Zeroes have caught the other crippled F4F and are shooting him down.)

The rain, below the cloud, is coming down hard. It spatters against the front of the canopy with such impact and splash that Foss finds visibility almost nil. However, he can dimly make out, to the left ahead, the shoreline of an island. Malaita!

It has to be Malaita—a long island in the southern Solomons, since Foss knows he is northeast of Florida Island, and Malaita is the only large island in this direction. Foss glances behind him, to be sure the Zeroes are not slipping up on him. He is down to 2,500 feet. The engine gauges are in the red. He's now five or six miles from the coastline, to his left. The rain is still heavy; he will try to make it to the island, and then decide what to do.

The right wing of the stricken F4F rises a little as Foss banks slightly left and the blue-gray F4F, running rough, with holes in wing and fuselage, battered by the heavy rain, inclines downward toward the coast and the rain-swept palms of Malaita Island. Through the rain, to the left, Foss catches a glimpse of a small village. He aims the blunt nose of his air-cooled engine toward it. If worst comes to worst, and he can't make it farther than that, at least he will find human beings there.

But Foss can't remember if this part of Malaita Island is in Japanese or American hands. Will he be falling into a trap? Are enemy soldiers stationed on this coast? Searching his memory hard, Foss descends. Now he approaches the shore, banks right, to fly along the coastline. Whump! The engine cuts out again. Foss looks at the altimeter. He's at 1,500 feet.

He pushes the canopy all the way back. The engine is knocking heavily, the whole airframe vibrating. He prepares to ditch. Will the same heavy weather that saved him from the enemy prevent his rescue, or sighting, by the people of the village to the left? The engine is failing! Foss knows at this instant that he will ditch. The altimeter reads 1,000 feet. He banks slightly to the right and decides to go into the water about a mile away from the village shore. Now he throttles back; the engine is fully silent.

He can clearly see the swell of the ocean, maneuvers to skid along the swell in a smooth ditching—as all Marine and Navy pilots are trained to do. But the battered Wildcat reacts sluggishly. Foss is suddenly just over the waves. He eases back on the stick. A big swell rises up in front of him. The ocean is coming up fast! He eases farther back, but the Wildcat slams into it with a crunching sound. The canopy slams forward, closes, and Foss wonders for a split second whether he will bounce, skid along on the water, or sink. To his dismay, the Wildcat is rapidly settling in the water. Suddenly water is over the wings, sloshing up to the level of the canopy. The Wildcat is sinking fast! The canopy is still closed, and Foss is strapped into his seat.

Frantically he reaches up to pull the canopy back. Stuck! By now the waves are closing over the top of the canopy; the Wildcat is sinking! His parachute chest-strap is unbuckled, but he has forgotten to unbuckle the two leg straps. As he struggles to get the canopy open, the parachute remains strapped to his legs, and begins to soak up water, now pouring into the cockpit. Everything around becomes dark green. He is under the surface . . . sinking farther and farther! Foss can't open the canopy. Fear races through his mind, that the aircraft will hit bottom and turn over on its back, trapping him forever.

Water is now high in the cockpit, and the F4F is continuing to sink. He lunges at the canopy handle and yanks at it with all his strength. The desperate heave finally breaks it open. Foss jerks himself clear. The parachute, however, to which he is still attached, rises first, pushes his head down. Foss is belching water and desperately gasping for breath. In these seconds he realizes that he has only a few more to live unless he reaches the surface. The chute continues to pull him up, and finally breaks the surface. Foss fights desperately to get his head above water, to the side of the chute. Instinctively, as the act of a trapped man, he pulls the cord of his Mae West. The life preserver suddenly inflates. It shoves his upper body around the chute, to the surface. He gasps in free air.

It is a few minutes before he regains normal consciousness and is able to breathe, after belching up much water. He is a couple of miles off Malaita, in the expanse of water between Florida and Malaita islands. He rests, trying to get his strength back, still shaken from the close call of almost being entombed beneath the Pacific in his shattered fighter.

He remembers the briefings on the tides in this area—and the warning that the tide between Florida and Malaita runs at 14 knots. If the tide is against him, he will never be able to swim to shore. He can glimpse the shoreline above the waves, every so often, and so he rests, momentarily, trying to determine which way the water is running and what he will do.

Foss can't be sure which way the tide is running. He decides he will start swimming, now, while it is still daylight and while he still can see the shore ahead. He swims slowly, in an effort to conserve his strength, but keeps at it. His strokes get heavier and heavier; he swims on and on. Foss worries about sharks, prevalent in these waters, and remembers to break one of his emergency capsules, which is supposed to keep sharks away.

As he continues to swim he notices the dye in the water remains around him. Discouraged, he realizes he's making very little progress. Doubts about his chances of being picked up race through his mind. If he had been on a morning mission he would have all day to be spotted in the water. However, the scramble at Guadalcanal came at two o'clock. Foss estimates it's now about five o'clock, or later. He doesn't have much daylight left. The weather above is poor and minimizes chances that search aircraft will spot him in the water. He continues to swim, even though progress is slow.

For a long time he swims toward shore. It's quite obvious he's making little progress. But he refuses to accept the agonizing conclusion. He swims on and on. Finally light is failing. It's getting dark. He must have been in the water for some time. He looks at the shore, still about two miles away, and realizes he'll never make it before darkness sets in, if ever.

And so he relaxes, again, in the water, and breaks another capsule to keep the sharks away. This could be the end, and he has the satisfaction of knowing he shot down three enemy planes on the mission, if it is to be his last. He wonders if the enemy fleet was stopped, and how much damage was done. He thinks about the tents back at Guadalcanal, the primitive conditions—now they seem luxurious as he floats in the choppy water and darkness descends over the Pacific.

His thoughts drift back to the United States, 8,000 miles away. Still farther away, on this November 7, 1942, thousands of American troops are invading North Africa—unknown to Foss—and a hundred miles west of El Alamein the beaten remnants of Field Marshal Erwin Rommel's army are now in headlong retreat. The high tide of the Afrika Korps has been passed in Africa. At Stalingrad, on this very day, Nazi attacks are beaten back and the tide is turning there.

A wire service reporter, writing thousands of miles on the other side of the world, repeats a Russian communiqué: "On the battlefield northwest of Stalingrad, where the Russians are pressing the Germans hard to relieve Stalingrad, Nazi and Russian artillery maintain a fast duel." (This was the prelude to the Russian attack which cut off the German army besieging Stalingrad, the worst disaster yet encountered by the Wehrmacht.)

And in the newspapers in the United States, on this very day, advertisements are urging Americans to: "Sell your idle tires to Uncle Sam now." And the newspapers on November 7 report the stock market is registering gains, a belated reaction to the victory of Field Marshal Bernard Montgomery at El Alamein! So investors and the fortunate citizens back home are making money. Foss is fighting for his life under a darkening sky, in the running, chilly waters between two of the Solomon Islands, far, far away in the Pacific.

Now it is dark. Foss has stopped swimming. He is conserving his strength. The rain has stopped, but all is silent around him, except the splashing of the waves. No lights are to be seen, even though he looks in the direction of the village every time the water lifts him high enough to see the shore. Time passes, and Foss is sure he is playing a losing game. It is totally dark. He wonders how long his Mae West will remain inflated and how long he can float before he attracts sharks. He breaks another capsule of shark preventive. There have been so many jokes about these capsules. He wonders if they work. So far, he has escaped the attention of dreaded sharks.

He is not sure he saw it! He keeps looking in the direction of the shore. Again! A small light. The waves hide it, and it goes on and off. He is alert, completely tense. He is sure he saw a light. And now, for the first time, he knows something is moving in the water close to him. Every so often it cuts through the water on one side or the other. It comes to him suddenly! Sharks! He breaks another capsule, but, unmistakably, the sharks are all around him. Perhaps they have been there for some time and he has been unaware of it. Now that he notices carefully, the sharks are on all sides, and only the darkness prevents him from seeing their fins quite clearly. His thoughts jump back to the light. It keeps appearing, in the direction of the village. The sharks make him frantic. He has almost forgotten to wonder whether Japanese or Americans are in control of the village. With fins knifing through the water around him, he's ready to see either.

The light is closer. It's moving! It must be a boat. Yet Foss hesitates to utter a sound. He treads water, keeps his eyes fixed in the direction of the light. It steadily comes closer. Now a black object is visible ahead, moving toward him. Still Foss remains silent. It is some kind of boat—it looks like a native canoe. It is coming straight for him.

He watches as the bow approaches within ten feet, five feet. Have they seen him? How could the boat approach so close? Now the bow is on him. The boat is passing almost directly over him. He ducks his head under the water momentarily, desperately trying to decide what to do. Now he raises his head and listens. The talk he hears is a mystery. It sounds like broken English. It is utterly dark, and the light is now shining in the other direction. He realizes, at this moment, he is between the outrigger and the canoe itself. Heart throbbing, Foss still remains silent, watching the canoe, just a few feet away. He sees figures moving in the boat, but still he cannot understand the language being spoken. Suddenly, one of the men in the boat speaks, loudly and clearly: "Let's look over here."

A wave of relief sweeps over him. Foss yells back: "Yeah—right over here!" The light flicks off. Foss sees a couple of natives pick up clubs and lift them menacingly. He yells: "Friend! Birdman! Aviator! American!"

Foss can't understand the jabbering. But the natives, now directly over him, do not attempt to club him. One of the men in the boat leans over in his direction and holds out his arms. He paddles a foot and reaches out to grip the outstretched arms. Tommy Robinson, an Australian sawmill operator, pulls the South Dakota pilot into the canoe.

A native gives him a tug, in the way of a helping hand, to get him into the bottom of the boat. Then Foss looks up and realizes a priest is in the boat. "I'm Father De Steinberg," the priest says. Just at that time a flying fish smashes into the light and knocks it out. Had that happened earlier, Foss might never have seen the light. But he has seen it, and has been rescued, and relief and thankfulness swell up inside him. He asks:

"Where are you from?"

"We're from Buma Mission." (Buma Mission is the small coastal settlement he saw from the air.)

Slowly they make their way to shore, Foss explaining what had happened, and asking how they had known he was out in the water, two miles off shore. A native had seen him crash. The native had excitedly exclaimed: "There's a birdman out there in the sea!" As a result of the native's sighting, several canoes started out from shore, in search of the pilot, who just might have survived.

The boat finally reaches shore, and once ashore, Foss relaxes and talks to Robinson and Father De Steinberg. The priest offers Foss his bed, and, emotionally and physically worn out, Foss accepts. Soon he is sound asleep.

Morning revealed a beautiful village, and island, and Foss decided, if he survived the war and had the time, to go back and spend several weeks on the island. The feel of land, the smell of foliage, and the security of earth below his feet joined with the beautiful scenery to make him feel thankful he was alive. But Foss knew he should get back to Guadalcanal, and so he spread out his parachute, which had floated near him throughout the afternoon and evening in the water and had been picked up with him, in a clearing on the island.

It was Sunday, and Foss wondered if his comrades would be looking for him. He didn't have long to wait for an answer. A sleek American fighter flew down the coastline several hours later and spotted the chute. The pilot radioed Guadalcanal. Back at Operations, on Guadalcanal, Jack Cramm, an old friend, prepared to take off in a PBY-5A— to investigate the parachute sighting. And, later in the day, the PBY-5A landed off the coast opposite the little village. Cramm, taxiing in to shore, soon learned it was, indeed, Joe Foss who had survived and was awaiting rescue.

Foss thanked his rescuers profusely, bade them good-by, and boarded the PBY-5A for the return trip to Guadalcanal. Now he learned that one of the American plane's heavy bombs had hit the Japanese cruiser the day before, and that two pilots had put torpedoes into her. The P-39's which had also taken part in the strike had shot down five enemy planes. Marine fighters had destroyed nine, including the three Foss shot down. Two others had been accounted for by the other planes. A fellow Marine pilot in his flight, William P. Marontate, had also scored three kills. Three American fighters had been lost.

Foss was soon back at Guadalcanal, once again enjoying the "luxury" of the primitive fighter base. He was asked about possible injuries and his physical condition, and he declared himself ready to fly again.

As a result, on the very next day, Monday, the 9th of November, he was ordered into action.

Unknown to Foss at the time he treaded water in the dark off the shore of Malaita Island was a danger he never encountered—because he was unable to swim to shore. Off the coast of the village the water was infested with crocodiles. At this particular spot along the coast they were numerous and deadly, and had Foss been able to swim in to shore he would have encountered them.

And so, Foss had been lucky to survive the ditching of his crippled plane on the afternoon of November 7, considering all the dangers involved.

He remained on operations at Guadalcanal until just prior to Christmas, when he received a short leave. He returned to combat on New Year's Eve, and remained until February, when he was ordered out of action. By that time he had shot down more enemy aircraft in the Pacific—twenty-six—than any other Marine would destroy in World War II! (Foss returned to combat later in the war, but added no more victories to his record.)

And, unknown to him at the time, his effort of November 7 was to count heavily in earning him the nation's highest honor, the Congressional Medal of Honor. Six months later, at the White House, on May 18, 1943, the following citation, in tribute to his gallantry, was read aloud to a distinguished assemblage of Americans:

For outstanding heroism and courage above and beyond the call of duty as Executive Officer of a Marine Fighting Squadron at Guadalcanal, Solomon Islands. Engaging in almost daily combat with the enemy from October 9 to November 19, 1942, Captain Foss personally shot down twenty-three Japanese planes and damaged others so severely that their destruction was extremely probable.

In addition, during this period, he successfully led a large number of escort missions, skillfully covered reconnaissance, bombing and photographic planes as well as surface craft. On January 15, 1943, he added three more enemy planes to his already brilliant successes for a record of aerial combat achievement unsurpassed in this war.

Boldly searching out an approaching enemy force on January 25, Captain Foss led his eight Marine planes and four Army planes into action, and undaunted by tremendously superior numbers, intercepted and struck with such force that four Japanese fighters were shot down and the bombers were turned back without releasing a single bomb. His remarkable flying skill, inspiring leadership and indomitable fighting spirit were distinctive factors in the defense of strategic American positions on Guadalcanal.

After this citation had been read, the Medal of Honor was presented to Foss by President Roosevelt. In his tour of duty at Guadalcanal, Foss had made three dead-stick landings on Henderson Field in planes crippled by enemy bullets. Thus, counting his close call in the waters off Malaita Island, Foss had managed to survive landings in four badly damaged fighter planes.

In addition to the Congressional Medal of Honor, Foss was awarded the Distinguished Flying Cross from Admiral William F. Halsey, personally, for heroism and extraordinary achievement in shooting down six Zeroes and one bomber during the crisis period at Guadalcanal of October 13 through October 20, 1942.

In 1943, after being ordered out of Guadalcanal, he was returned to Marine Headquarters in Washington, thereafter to be sent on a tour of Navy preflight schools and naval air stations, where Marine pilots were in training. He then helped sell bonds in a nationwide tour of the United States. His second tour of duty in the Pacific began in February, 1944, when he resumed combat flights around Emirau, in the St. Matthias group, but enemy planes were scarce and he failed to add to his illustrious record.

He was discharged from the Marine Corps in December, 1945, after the war had ended, and tendered his resignation from the Inactive Reserve in September, 1946, to accept a commission in the South Dakota Air National Guard. In 1950 he was promoted to the rank of colonel, and in 1953 he was advanced to the rank of brigadier general in the South Dakota Air National Guard.

In 1954, after having served in the South Dakota House of Representatives, he won an overwhelming victory in the race for governor, and after having served in that capacity he was later named commissioner of the new American Football League, with headquarters in Dallas, Texas, a job he holds as this book is written.

The importance of the effort of Marine pilots on November 7, and their efforts in this period of the war in general, cannot be overestimated. In the period during which Foss served the Japanese made three major attempts to retake Guadalcanal from our forces—which had seized it in August, 1942, in the first American counteradvance of the war.

And though the attacks of pilots on the afternoon of November 7 did not stop Japanese reinforcement efforts nor even the warships which were the targets of Foss's Wildcats that afternoon, the losses inflicted on warships and transports by pilots flying from Guadalcanal were so exorbitant that the Japanese finally decided to abandon their reinforcement efforts.

The enemy later admitted that American air strength was so formidable in the area it had become impossible for the Japanese Navy to deliver sufficient troops and supplies to Guadalcanal. Shortly after the battle between Japanese warships and American fliers on November 7, the Japanese committed heavier warships to the effort to reinforce their battle for the island. The result was that they lost two battleships and a number of other warships.

The climax in this long struggle to control the waters around Guadalcanal came November 14, just one week after the action described in this chapter, when the Japanese attempted to send large-scale troop reinforcements, in a major convoy, to Guadalcanal. All afternoon, on the 14th, every plane on Guadalcanal that could fly was loaded with bombs and attacked the transports of this convoy. The day produced the greatest slaughter of Japanese troops by American airmen in the entire campaign. By evening seven transports, ranging in tonnage between 5,000 and 9,000 tons, had been sunk. Another four were crippled, and managed to make Guadalcanal only to be beached there, where they were gutted next day by the same pilots who had hit them the day before and by the destroyer *Meade.*

It is estimated that only 4,000 Japanese troops out of the 10,000 in that convoy managed to reach Guadalcanal. Many were drowned, though many were later rescued from the water by destroyers. Out of the entire convoy only five tons of supplies—260 cases of ammunition and 1,500 bags of rice—were put ashore.

This, according to Bob Sherrod, in *History of Marine Corps Aviation in World War II,* was as great as any victory Marine aviators participated in throughout the war.

When Marine airmen finally won the battle to control the waters around Guadalcanal, those in command of American forces on the island, and at higher headquarters, realized the tide had finally turned and that the Americans were on Guadalcanal to stay. It was the first great combined land, sea and air victory by American forces in the Pacific in World War II.

4 Gun Duel Over Tulagi

APRIL 7, 1943:

First Lieutenant JAMES E. SWETT, U.S.M.C.

By April, 1943, Guadalcanal had been without Japanese troops for two months. The great Marine fighter aces of the bitter days, such as Smith and Foss, had established their immortal records and departed.

Henderson Field and Fighter 1 and Fighter 2, the auxiliary fields, were no longer frequently disturbed by enemy bombing attacks. The Japanese had lost their long struggle for Guadalcanal and had no plans to recapture it.

The war had just passed its turning point, and some Americans back home now talked victory "next year"—1944. There was hope of an invasion of occupied Europe "this year"—1943. On the Russian front the Germans had met disaster at Stalingrad, and in the Pacific the Americans now had begun the long island-march to Japan with a landing on New Guinea.

With Guadalcanal no longer the "front line," some of the pilots sent there in the spring of 1943 wondered whether they would see much of the enemy. Japanese air power had not been finally decimated, of course, but it was not much in evidence that far south. Certainly the new arrivals would not experience the grim competition for aerial supremacy over the island that earlier pilots had encountered.

One of the pilots sent to Guadalcanal at this time was destined to be one of the great Marine aces of the war. James Elms Swett, of San Mateo, California, touched down on Guadalcanal's famed Henderson Field only weeks after Japanese troops had evacuated the island. He was then twenty-two years old, only recently a student at San Mateo Junior College, where he had enlisted in the U.S. Naval Reserve as a seaman second class on August 26, 1941. The war was to engulf America a hundred days later.

In October, Swett had been appointed an aviation cadet. He won his wings, as Marine second lieutenant and single-engine pilot, in the Marine Corps Reserve, on April 1, 1942. At that time—early 1942 —United States forces in the Pacific had not won a battle, and the war was in its darkest stage. Though Swett earned his wings at Corpus Christi at this critical period of the war, it was more than a year before he saw an enemy plane on a combat mission.

From Corpus Christi, Swett was sent to Quantico, Virginia, to receive additional training, and then to San Diego, California, to begin carrier training.

While the turning points of the war were occurring in the Pacific (the Coral Sea and Midway battles), Swett was assigned to training chores in the United States. He finally checked out on a carrier, which was actually the converted excursion ship *Wolverine* on Lake Michigan, and was declared proficient in carrier landings and take-offs.

Late in 1942 he was shipped back to San Diego, where, after another period of training, he was ordered aboard United States seaplane tender *Pocomoke* (AV-9), headed for Pearl Harbor.

By the time *Pocomoke* reached the Hawaiian Islands, however, the enemy's most serious threats to recapture Guadalcanal had been turned back.

Another period of training was Swett's lot, as he edged closer and closer to a combat zone, moving from Pearl Harbor to the New Hebrides on a jeep carrier. There he established living quarters in a tent city on Espiritu Santo, one of the New Hebrides islands. Espiritu Santo is the northwesternmost major island in the New Hebrides, and lies 555 miles southeast of Guadalcanal, across the Coral Sea. So

Swett was now only a little over five hundred miles from a combat zone.

When he quit his tent quarters at Espiritu Santo to board a DC-3 transport, headed for Henderson Field on Guadalcanal, it seemed to Swett and other Marine pilots that they were to see a legendary land. For six months newspaper headlines in the United States had described the exploits of U.S. pilots at Guadalcanal, attacking enemy bombers, battling enemy fighters, and leading attacks on enemy bases to the northwest.

At Henderson Field Swett was assigned to Fighter Strip 2, to the east of Henderson. By this time Guadalcanal was home for a number of Army P-38 Lightning fighters, P-40 Warhawks, and P-39 Aircobras, as well as Navy and Marine fighters and Army and Navy bombers.

It didn't take Swett long to learn that most of the activity on Guadalcanal was offensive. The Americans had switched over to the attack and were raiding Japanese bases farther up the Solomons. Frequent raids were made on Santa Isabel Island and on the Japanese base of Munda, in the New Georgia group, and on Kolombangara.

The F4F Wildcats, which Swett would fly, did not have the range to fly all the way to Bougainville—the principal enemy base in the Solomons. (Marine pilots flying the F4U Corsair had greater range and enjoyed a sufficient radius of action to make the round trip to Bougainville, and one such flight will be treated in a later chapter of this book.)

At Fighter 2 Swett was assigned to VMF 221, a fighter squadron which would end the war second in the corps in the number of planes shot down. However, the beginning of his tour of duty with VMF 221 was not auspicious. The days passed and things were strangely quiet. American planes raided Japanese bases up the Slot, but this was the extent of combat experienced.

Unobtrusively, though, events were building to a climax and would soon produce action aplenty. But there was little warning of the sudden turn of events which was now to take place. Swett had been on Guadalcanal for several relatively quiet weeks when April 7, 1943, dawned over the Solomon Islands.

Unknown to American pilots on Guadalcanal, on that April 7, 1943, Imperial Japanese Headquarters had decided on a major air offensive to extract a measure of revenge for the loss of Guadalcanal. Admiral Isoroku Yamamoto, chief of the Combined Fleet, had personally planned the assault. To be certain it was successful, and delivered in overwhelming strength, he ordered carrier pilots from four Japanese carriers—*Zuikaku, Zuiho, Junyo* and *Hiyo*—transferred temporarily to land bases in the Solomons.

Ninety-six Navy fighters, sixty-five dive bombers, and a number of torpedo planes joined forces with the land-based 11th Japanese Air Fleet, which consisted of eighty-six fighters, twenty-seven dive bombers, seventy-two twin-engined bombers, and a number of torpedo planes.

Altogether Yamamoto (who later was to be shot down and killed by an American fighter pilot over Bougainville) had at his command between three and four hundred planes for the air offensive designed to avenge the loss of Guadalcanal.

This was a formidable force. Admiral Yamamoto had good reason to expect impressive results from this massive concentration of aerial striking power. Since he was employing twin-engined bombers, his air fleet would carry a greater weight of bombs than that which struck Pearl Harbor on December 7, 1941.

As admitted by Masatake Okumiya, one of the authors of *Zero,* the assemblage of warplanes put together by Admiral Yamamoto at this time constituted the main strength of Japan's first-line air power.

Quietly, and without launching major air strikes, Yamamoto built up his air strength at Rabaul and adjoining bases, preparatory to the opening of the offensive, set for April 7.

The only clue to impending developments was a raid by a very large force of Zeroes on April 1. But no bombers accompanied these fighters and the attack was not followed up. On April 6, however, a U.S. photographic reconnaissance plane reported a heavy increase in the number of aircraft on various enemy fields in the northern Solomons. The P-38 pilot who spotted the concentration estimated enemy aircraft at Kahili airdrome alone, on southern Bougainville, at 114—against 40 spotted on that field a day earlier. At another field, near Ballale, the presence of 95 enemy aircraft was reported, whereas the day before none had been visible on this field.

As these sightings and estimates were weighed by intelligence, it became obvious that something big was in the making.

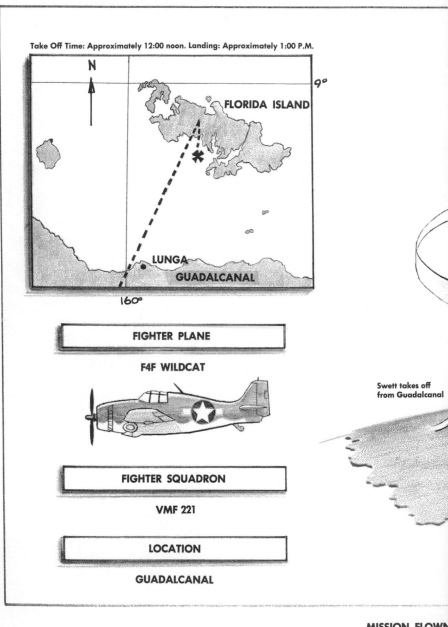

Take Off Time: Approximately 12:00 noon. Landing: Approximately 1:00 P.M.

N

9°

FLORIDA ISLAND

LUNGA

GUADALCANAL

160°

FIGHTER PLANE

F4F WILDCAT

FIGHTER SQUADRON

VMF 221

LOCATION

GUADALCANAL

Swett takes off
from Guadalcanal

MISSION FLOWN

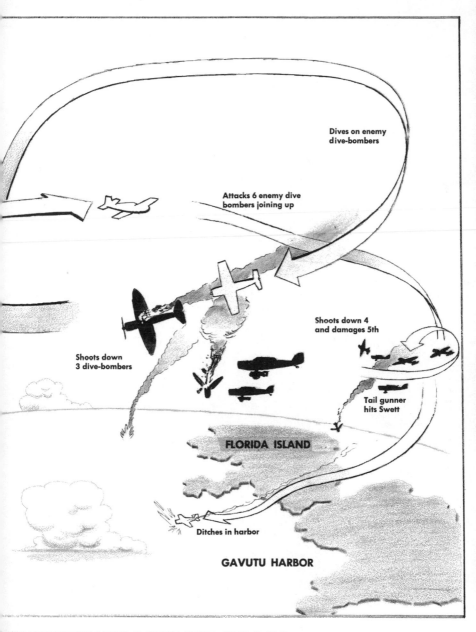

Dives on enemy
dive-bombers

Attacks 6 enemy dive
bombers joining up

Shoots down 4
and damages 5th

Shoots down
3 dive-bombers

Tail gunner
hits Swett

FLORIDA ISLAND

Ditches in harbor

GAVUTU HARBOR

FIRST LIEUTENANT JAMES E. SWETT, USMC, APRIL 7, 1943

On Wednesday, April 7, at 3:30 A.M., Jim Swett was awakened in his tent on "Strafer's Heights." He was to fly the dawn patrol. He dressed hurriedly and breakfasted at the mess hall, where there were "more flies inside than outside," downing his usual breakfast of Spam and peanut butter.

The dawn patrol was a precautionary and standard defensive tactic, and this morning four F4F Wildcats would perform that duty. When Swett reached his fighter he was not overly excited or enthusiastic. Nothing usually happened on the dawn patrol, and thus only four fighters were taking off.

He climbed into the cockpit and soon the big radial engine thundered into life, belching ripples of smoke. In seconds Swett was taxiing toward the runway, the other three Wildcats in line. In a few minutes the four Wildcats had lifted into the brightening sky, and now turned on a northwest heading, climbing at approximately 150 knots.

Looking down, Swett could see the tall palms almost parallel to his course, along the northern shore of Guadalcanal. He was soon flying over the western end of the island, where the Japanese had held out for six months after the Marines landed. The four Wildcats passed very close to Savo Island, just north of the western tip of Guadalcanal, and the scene of several fierce naval battles in recent months.

Now the shore of Guadalcanal was passing behind, and Swett and his three comrades were rapidly gaining altitude. On the radio Swett called "Recon," code name of the fighter director located on the Russell Islands, thirty miles off the tip of Guadalcanal, in the direction of the enemy's bases farther up the Solomons. The dawn patrol circled the Russells, acting as a lookout, in position to flash a warning if enemy planes attempted to surprise American installations on Guadalcanal. The lieutenant (j.g.) who was on duty at the Fighter Director Center (Recon) that morning was gay, as usual. Swett, "Knucklehead" to the lieutenant, exchanged flippant comments on various subjects as he watched the Russell Islands drawing nearer and nearer ahead.

When over the island group, the Wildcats began circling slowly to the left, leveling off, on station. Eyes searched the sky, especially to the northwestward, for any sign of enemy aerial activity. Two hundred miles to the northwest, enemy pilots were now busy with preparations for the opening strike of Yamamoto's air offensive. Crewmen were warming up more than a hundred Zero fighters, and in addition, armorers were loading bombs on many Japanese dive bombers and twin-engined land-based bombers, which would soon be in the air.

Swett, a couple of hours of monotonous patrolling around the Russells ahead of him, relaxed and enjoyed the view of the deep-blue water of the Solomon Sea below. Despite reports of the day before, of greatly increased enemy air strength, the general suspicion among American pilots was that Japanese reinforcements were defensive—since hardly anyone expected them to launch a major attack on Guadalcanal, which the enemy high command now accepted as irretrievably lost.

Engines roared monotonously as Swett and the three other pilots continued to circle the Russells. Half an hour passed, and then an hour. Swett eyed his gasoline gauges and kept his eyes on the sky to the northwest. Nothing in sight. Now the division had been patrolling for an hour and a half, and still the minutes ticked on. The weather remained good, with the sun rising steadily in the east. It was now mid-morning. The division had been on station over the Russell Islands for more than two hours. Recon below reported nothing going on. It was a dull morning.

Finally, with fuel considerations entering the picture, the dawn patrol broke off its conversations with Recon, below, set course at approximately 120 degrees, and headed home toward Guadalcanal. It had been an uneventful patrol, and soon the shores of Guadalcanal were visible. Minutes later Fighter 1, Henderson Field, and Fighter 2 all came into view. The four Wildcats, spread out in landing pattern, descended with gear and flaps down, and touched down on Fighter 2 without incident.

This was the end of flying for the day, pilots thought, and they taxied toward their revetments on the edge of the field in the coconut palms.

Just as the four pilots were pulling themselves up out of their cockpits, jumping down off the wings of their planes, the routine part of the day ended. The word was flashed—from coast watchers—that a major enemy air attack was on the way. Island watchers, up the Solomons chain, reported very large formations of aircraft heading southeast—apparently toward Guadalcanal. Crewmen and pilots were hurriedly making preparations for take-off of every available fighter. And the four Wildcats which had just flown the dawn patrol were now hurriedly refueled and prepared for another take-off.

Across the waters of Ironbottom Bay, U.S. ships, both warships and merchantmen, hastened to get up steam and pull out of Tulagi and Gavutu harbors, on Florida Island.

It was well they did, for on their way down the Slot, now very near, were 177 enemy aircraft—110 Zero fighters and 67 Val dive bombers. Coast watchers had already begun to estimate the enemy's number, and while they reported the armada as a tremendous one, most of them nevertheless underestimated its true strength.

Swett had been ordered into the air again, as fast as possible, and as soon as the big blue Wildcat was refueled, he was seated in the cockpit, and shouting a few parting words to crewmen waving good-by. Already a four-fighter patrol had taken up station off the Russell Islands (the second shift of the day) and, altogether, some seventy-six fighters were in various stages of the defensive scramble. Warnings went out all over the island, to troops and installations everywhere, to the ships in Indispensable Strait to the east, and south of it, that a major enemy air strike was expected almost momentarily. "Condition very red," the radio warned.

Now Swett, again leading a division of four Wildcats, was ready for take-off. Fighters were scrambling from four fields and radio chatter was heavy. He signaled his division by hand, rammed his left hand forward, for full throttle, and the Wildcat lunged forward, pushing him back in his seat, and began picking up speed as it rumbled down the strip.

In his brief stay on the ground Squadron Commander Captain Robert Burns had assigned Swett the job of leading a division. He was to call commander, Marine Air, once airborne, for specific orders. Swett contacted the commander at Fighter 1. His orders: head immediately for Tulagi Harbor, protect targets from Japanese dive bombers, certain to be included in a strike of such size as that now coming in. Swett banked toward Tulagi, climbing at 140 knots.

Tulagi Harbor is almost due north; Swett sets a course of 10 degrees. The coastline of Guadalcanal passes below into the background, and Swett scans the skies to his left, the northwest, the direction from which the enemy planes will come. All pilots tingle with anticipation. The enemy is certain to visit Tulagi.

Swett recognizes a familiar voice over the radio. It's Captain Smiley Burnett, on patrol over the Russells, where Swett was earlier:

"Holy Christ! There's millions of 'em!" Burnett screams.

Swett's four Wildcats are up to 10,000 feet. He knows the enemy will be over Ironbottom Bay, between Guadalcanal and Florida islands, in minutes. He pushes his hand against the throttle, increases climb angle. All pilots in the division, and every other one, have eyes glued to the northwest. Swett's division reaches 12,000, 14,000, 15,000 feet! The first stage of the supercharger cuts in.

Swett again checks his electric gunsight, the two electric orange rings with pip in the middle. He checks gun switches. Now the altimeter reads 16,000, 17,000 feet. Fighters are rising in separate groups all along the coast of Guadalcanal. Swett is now almost over Tulagi Harbor. Below, he can see U.S. destroyers. Most of the ships have escaped, but a few are in the area, and Swett wonders what will happen to them— if many Japanese dive bombers appear over Tulagi.

Seconds are agonizing minutes. For Swett, and some of the other pilots of VMF 221, this will be the first time they have seen the enemy in combat. And Swett thought he had missed out on the big days! Suddenly, to the left ahead, at ten o'clock . . . His heart jumps. Swett sees fifteen or twenty aircraft, headed straight for Tulagi Harbor. He shouts into the mike: "Tally-ho! Ten o'clock!"

Tension and excitement grip all. Seeing the enemy for the first time, Swett realizes the American pilots are outnumbered twenty to four. He glances hurriedly around him. His Wildcats are strung out loosely. He moves stick left and kicks left rudder. The left wing dips, and the stubby, low-wing Wildcat, roaring at full throttle, aims her oval nose on an interception course with the enemy. Swett carefully eyes the silhouettes now closing. Below them is a second gaggle of dots. Dive bombers, on course for Tulagi Harbor! The question, in Swett's strategy, is whether he can intercept the Vals in time. Now excited cries fill the air as many Americans sight groups of enemy aircraft.

Swett has not yet fired his guns at an enemy aircraft, and fortunately, now that he is soon to need them, he remembers that the ordnance crewman at the field crammed fifteen or twenty extra rounds into each gun. Swett estimates he has 450 to 420 rounds per gun, divided between tracer, armor-piercing and incendiary ammunition. That gives him a total of 2,500 50-caliber shells.

The distance between the dive bombers and Swett's Wildcats steadily lessens. The silhouettes ahead grow larger and larger. Suddenly the dive bombers bank left, preparing to wing over into dives. Swett kicks right rudder, his left wing comes up in a right turn, and he sets course to follow. The Vals begin a shallow decline, enemy pilots obviously picking out targets in the harbor below. From above, a yell comes in over the earphones. Zeroes sighted directly above!

Now the Zeroes turn the tables on the four Wildcats. The Wildcats are in position to surprise the Vals, but it is the unexpected Zeroes who

A Zeke, or modified version of the famous Mitsubishi Type O fighter, the best carrier-based fighter in the world at the outbreak of the war. (Official U.S. Navy Photo)

are diving on the Wildcats. Swett, now in a tight spot, glances back. Does he still have time to hit the Vals? The Zeroes are close to the three F4F's behind, which have become strung out, and the Vals are not too far ahead—now going into steep dives.

He slams the stick forward, and the engine roars as the air-speed indicator needle turns rapidly to the right. He'll go for the Vals! It's a calculated risk; he'll gamble the Zeroes can't catch him before he catches the Vals.

The Zeroes are diving into the attack. He is plunging after the Vals (the other three Wildcats are not yet in position to dive after the Vals) and his speed will enable him to stay far enough ahead of the Zeroes to escape their fire.

The Vals ahead, slowed by their bombs, are doing about 200 knots.

Swett closes the distance steadily, making 300 knots, his speed increasing.

The enemy dive bombers are more clearly in view, and Swett—in his first sighting of the enemy—carefully looks them over. They're a light brownish-gray color. Swett believes they must be new. He notices bright red "meatballs" on their wings.

The Wildcat continues to gain. Swett glances behind him; the Zeroes are not gaining. Wild battles now break out all over the sky, in every direction, and noise and shouts fill his earphones. Forcing himself to concentrate, Swett keeps his eyes fastened on the nearest dive bomber ahead, almost within range.

The enemy's wingspan already fills the inner 50-mill sighting circle. Swett waits for the wing to fill the 100-mill circle. His guns are boresighted to converge at 300 yards; soon the enemy will be in perfect range. The Val ahead continues its dive on a ship below, the rear gunner apparently unaware of Swett's presence. Almost within range, Swett notices a bomb exploding in the harbor below.

Now, however, only one thought dominates his actions. The gray-brown dive bomber is in range, dead ahead. Instantly, eyes fixed on the sight, Swett pulls the trigger! The six fifties vibrate; a streak of shells roars out into the surprised enemy aircraft. Black smoke begins to trail back; the Val is already burning fiercely. Swett is so close he stops firing.

He rams the stick slightly forward, to dive underneath the burning bomber. The Val now begins to spin, out of control, toward the water below. Swett is by him in a flash, with his great speed, and now, sliding to the right, has the next Val in sight.

A bomb explodes between a big tanker and a corvette nearby. The Vals are beginning to score. Swett's altimeter registers lower and lower altitudes, 8,000, 7,000, 6,000 feet. With greater diving speed, the Wildcat rapidly approaches the second Val, as the dive continues. Swett hardly has time to realize that on his first combat mission, the first time he fired at an enemy, he has scored a kill! He is already after victory No. 2. A quick glance behind; his tail is clear. A tremendous aerial battle, in every direction, is developing—though at the moment Swett is the lone American fighter attacking the dive bombers.

Now the second Val draws closer, and closer. The Val is slightly to the right, and quickly the enemy's wingspan approaches the 100-

mill light circle. In range! Fire! Swett holds the trigger button down a couple of seconds. Aim perfect again. A sudden explosion ahead, a white-yellow flash in the center. The Val has disintegrated. The diving Wildcat plunges through falling debris of victim No. 2 and shoots out toward the water below. The altimeter registers 3,000, 2,000 feet!

Ahead, to the left, Swett sees another Val, about ready to drop his bomb. He kicks left rudder, left stick, and maneuvers to line up the third Val in his sight. He has scored two kills, but now time is running out. He must pull out of his dive soon, and he will be on the deck with the enemy aircraft. And on the deck, Swett knows, Zeroes can easily outmaneuver Wildcats. He will be in a dangerous, lonely position, what with over a hundred highly maneuverable Zeroes in the sky above.

He is closing the third Val fast. Seconds drag, as he waits for the enemy wing silhouette to lengthen, showing he is in range. Swett is a thousand feet above the water. Finally, in range! Swett's right forefinger presses the trigger. The guns roar again. Tracers shoot out ahead. The Val, ahead left, is being hit. Swett keeps firing. The Val won't burn! Now the enemy dive bomber ahead is pulling out of his dive.

Swett pulls back on the stick and blood drains from his head. The Wildcat responds and begins to come out of the dive—following the Val ahead. Gravity pulls hard, but Swett avoids a blackout. He keeps his eyes fixed on the enemy silhouette ahead, now skimming over the water toward Florida Island. Swett nervously looks behind him. No Zeroes yet! Suddenly he feels a heavy vibration, which seems to come from his port wing. He glances to the left. A gaping hole is visible in his wing! Also, his outboard gun has been hit, and knocked partly out of the wing. The flaps on his left wing are badly damaged. Still, the engine is running smoothly. Swett looks for Zeroes. None on his tail. What hit him?

The Val ahead is in range. Disregarding the damage to his left wing, Swett maneuvers to get the enemy back in his gunsight. He has already poured as many shells into him as he used to knock down his first two victims. But the Val won't go down. Now the enemy aircraft is streaking over the treetops of Florida Island. He is less than 500 feet. Swett maneuvers rudder to box him in his sights.

Now! A short burst! The Val is hit again. Swett keeps firing. He is

almost on top of him, firing at point-blank range. An orange flame—
the Val is burning! A wing goes up and the Val swings over and smacks
the trees a few hundred feet below with terrific impact. Swett streaks
over the spot. It is victim No. 3! He glances nervously in all directions.
He can see no Zeroes on the deck, luckily. But antiaircraft fire is
intense. He realizes it must have been his own antiaircraft fire which
damaged his port wing. Tension begins to relax, slightly. It is hard to
realize he has knocked down three enemy aircraft! But wild fights
continue above. Swett looks ahead; he is halfway across Florida Island,
on a northward course, and getting clear of the thick puffs of antiaircraft
fire.

He checks his instruments and looks at the damaged wing. The engine is running smoothly. The aircraft is a little more difficult to maneuver, as a result of the damage to the left wing, but responds reasonably
well to the controls. Swett pulls up to approximately a thousand feet
and begins to S-turn. If he sees other Wildcats, he'll join up. If he sees
other Vals—there were fifteen or twenty in the dive run on Tulagi—
he'll resume his attack!

He has expended no more than half his ammunition; he will gamble,
again, on the operating condition of his plane. Slowly, cautiously, he
S-turns, reversing course, heading generally south. This is a time for
alert eyesight; he rubbernecks in all directions. All is clear. He scans the
sky for aircraft again.

Off to the right! Dots. Right rudder, right stick. Are they Zeroes?
Swett checks his altimeter. Only 800 feet. If they are Zeroes, it will be
grim. He studies the silhouettes. Vals! They must have completed dives
on shipping in Tulagi Harbor; they're joining up.

Swett notices a few small cumulus clouds. They're perfectly located
for a surprise approach on the Vals ahead. He estimates the number of
Vals at seven. He heads for a small cumulus. He will fly into it, through
it, emerging on the other side, hoping to be in a position to begin a
firing pass. The small cloud approaches, and obscures the view of the
Vals ahead. Swett is still making good speed, with throttle wide open,
and rockets into the milky gray. He carefully maintains even flying
attitude.

The Pratt and Whitney engine roars smoothly through the eerie gray
—nothing visible inside the cloud. He flies on, bursts into the open sky,
and dead ahead, almost in range, is the last of the seven Vals. Swett,

already victor over three Vals, jiggles rudder and stick to move the gunsight rings into position.

Quickly the enemy ahead fills his yellow sight ring. He opens fire—this time with only five 50's, the outboard gun on the left wing being out of commission. Even with five guns the onslaught is too much for the bright gray-green Val ahead. Fragments fly off in all directions as the perfect gunnery concentration rips the enemy aircraft to pieces. A long streak of flame reaches back for the approaching Wildcat, and then, trailing smoke, the Val plunges into the water below, off the coast of Florida Island. Victory No. 4!

A strange realization comes over Swett. The image of the rear gunner is left clearly in his mind. During the firing passes on his first victims, he was hardly aware of the rear gunner. An indication of the tremendous tension and excitement! He maneuvers to close the next Val in line, and marvels at the thought that he had not noticed the rear gunners. Why had he not noticed them?

These thoughts flash through Swett's mind as he cuts through the air over Florida Island, seeking victim No. 5. Miraculously, none of the rear gunners have hit him. He is already moving up on victim No. 5. The rear gunner in this Val once again has little time to act. But this time Swett notices him. He opens on the Val at once. Tracers mark a perfect firing concentration. The distance closes and strikes register all over the Val. In seconds it is ripped apart. Orange flame streaks from the wing roots. The Val wings over and down toward the water. Swett watches the fall excitedly. His fifth victim . . . plunging . . . into Ironbottom Sound! He's an ace—only minutes after seeing the enemy for the first time!

How long can it go on? The next Val ahead is almost within range. The Wildcat is still running smoothly and there's some ammunition left. Automatically, without taking time to occupy his mind with the five victories, Swett maneuvers the blue fighter into six o'clock position for the sixth pass. He clears his tail; no Zeroes.

Now he is directly behind the Val ahead. Once again five 50-calibers roar and spit fire; the Wildcat trembles from the vibration of the firing. Swett is moving in on each succeeding plane so rapidly that rear gunners have no time to prepare for the surprise attack. Tracers mark his line of fire, now slanting into the sixth victim. He's firing at point-blank range. A big flash ahead; instinctively, he dumps the stick, and sweeps beneath—the sixth victim! He has exploded. Swett maneuvers to miss the rain of debris. Six victories! Six victories and twelve enemy airmen.

Swett glances back, makes sure of the kill. He's now moving well away from Florida Island. Ahead, not far away, are more Vals. The engine still sounds good, and Swett estimates he has a little ammunition remaining. Throttle full forward, he heads for the seventh enemy. How long can he get by with these tactics? Why haven't protecting Zeroes spotted the slaughter down under and dived to the assistance of their comrades? Swett has little time to ponder such questions.

The seventh victim is coming within range of his guns. The wing-span ahead widens to fill the 100-mill sight ring. Swett presses the trigger. Five guns are still firing. The Val ahead is caught by a hail of fire. Almost immediately the seventh victim begins to trail smoke. Swett knows he has him. He continues to fire. The nose of the Val dips downward, and the seventh Val victim begins a dive into the sea. Swett banks slightly to the side, streaks by, as the enemy dive bomber disintegrates on hitting the blue water just a few hundred feet below. Seven victims in a few minutes! It has happened so fast, Swett hardly believes it himself. He must have expended practically all of his ammunition. But the Grumman still responds, the engine sounds smooth enough. Perhaps he has enough ammunition for one more. There are other Vals ahead. Swett knows he can't escape the fire of rear gunners forever. But so far his accuracy and fast approach have overwhelmed each victim in turn.

The nearest enemy silhouette is off to the right, ahead. Swett dips his right wing and slices into a turn, overtaking the slower Val. He will fire at a slight angle this time, a deflection shot to the right. Now he watches the enemy's outline in his sight ring, approaching from eight o'clock.

Whang! The forward part of the canopy is shattered! Hits! He is hit! Now, in a split-second look at the Val, Swett sees the twinkle of the rear gunner's machine gun. The enemy gunner has opened on him first!

A crashing thump shakes the cockpit. Swett feels blood on nose and face. The engine runs on smoothly; he can see the enemy gunner ahead, still firing. He automatically ducks his head, glances into the sight ring, still in place, and opens fire in reply. He estimates the distance at 100 feet; it's a duel between him and the rear gunner. Swett sees his tracers streaking toward the Val. And thumps tell him his Wildcat is taking more hits. His white tracers streak straight into the rear cockpit of the

Val's gunner. The distance is 50 feet! The firing continues. Suddenly the enemy gunner slumps. Swett is so close he sees his helmet and goggles. Now the Val begins to trail smoke, and at that instant there is a strange sound.

BRTTT . . . ! Everything is silent. Now it comes to him. His guns are empty. Immediately he kicks right rudder and pulls stick right; the Wildcat stands on its right wing, banking away from the smoking Val. Swett doesn't have time to watch his eighth victim. He knows he's hit, and out of ammunition, and—without altitude—a sitting duck for Zeroes.

He must get back to Guadalcanal. He's near the coast of Florida Island, on a southeasterly course. He keeps his head turning from side to side, and behind, watching for Zeroes. But he's distracted by an ominous sound. A strange noise . . . inside the cowling. Swett's eyes flash to the instrument panel. Engine temperature is in the red! The last enemy gunner did his job well. With a weakening sensation all over, Swett realizes his engine is burning up!

The oil pressure gauge reads zero. The oil has leaked out through a shell hole and friction is turning the engine into melted steel. Swett yanks the throttle back with his left hand. But the engine grows more and more sluggish, knocks louder and louder. He can smell it burning. Ironically, with seven victories under his belt, on his first combat mission, and only minutes away from safety, at Guadalcanal, he has been hit by the eighth Val! He realizes, in despair, the Wildcat will not make it to Guadalcanal. At this instant the engine freezes completely; out front, one of the propeller blades sticks straight up into the air, motionless. He will crash-land in the water!

As if by reflex, Swett's right hand pushes the stick forward, and he begins banking to the right. He is turning toward Guadalcanal, though he must ditch off Florida Island. He has very little altitude and will be in the water in seconds. Ditching procedure races through his mind. He will lower flaps, to lower speed. He operates the flap handle. His right wing begins to drop. The sensation puzzles him. Now he realizes the damaged left-wing flaps do not work. He reverses the flap handle; the right-wing flaps retract.

Only several hundred feet above the water, speed is down to 140 knots, Swett flips off all switches.

As he does, he realizes he is under fire. A surprise! A battery of 50-caliber antiaircraft guns is firing on him from the small island of Tanambogo. Friendly bullets! Swett hardly has time to worry about this danger, as the blue reaches up for him. Speed drops to 130 knots, 120, 110. He pulls back on the stick, and jettisons his canopy, which flies backward in the airstream. He's just over the waves, continues to ease back on the stick. He braces for the shock. Blump! The Wildcat bounces off the water. Swett stiffens for the next impact. In spite of all he can do, the nose dips downward; the Wildcat is almost diving into the sea. A terrific shock and crash, as the Wildcat smashes into the water! Swett's head is thrown into the gunsight, directly ahead. Only his shoulder straps save him. Nevertheless, he's stunned by the blow; his nose is broken and he feels intense pain.

Dazed, unable to think or move rapidly, Swett realizes that water is closing over him. He must get out. But his chute harness is caught on the little yellow handle above his right shoulder, the handle which ejects the one-man raft carried for just such an occasion as this. Swett tugs at the shoulder strap. He cannot disentangle his harness from the handle, and now the water closes over his head. The all-metal fighter starts the plunge into the dark to join the company of Allied and Japanese ships resting on the bottom of Ironbottom Bay. Swett struggles desperately to get the strap loose. He is ten feet, fifteen feet, now twenty feet below the surface! Everything is dark; he is trapped.

Desperate, he breaks loose with one last lunge and brings the raft with him. He yanks the strings of his Mae West. Unable to hold his breath much longer, he struggles to the surface with parachute and raft. A gleam of light! He breaks through and gasps for breath!

(Although not realizing it at the time, the weight of his parachute and flying clothes was holding Swett down. By inflating his lifejacket he considerably speeded up his ascent.)

Swett unhooks his parachute buckle, as he finally gets his breath, still gasping. He has swallowed a considerable amount of water, but at least he is out of the Wildcat, headed for the bottom below. He looks around; he is not too far from shore. He reaches down to his right, and pulls out his .45. He drains the water out of the barrel. Still looking around, he raises his hand above his head and pulls the trigger. The pistol fires. He fires a second shot in the air. Swett returns the gun to its holster and, almost completely exhausted, awaits the reaction.

Nothing happens immediately. He decides to inflate his life raft, and manages to pull himself into it. He tries to relax, though he can feel blood on his face, which continues to pain him. There is still plenty of daylight; Swett hopes someone saw him crash into the water, or at least heard the shots from his .45. Time passes slowly. The water slaps the raft and all is strangely quiet.

And then, as if answering his thoughts, a small picketboat appears between him and Florida Island—heading straight for him. A wave of relief runs through him, since he knows he is bleeding, and weak. The picketboat chugs closer and closer. Swett eyes it carefully. The boat contains a number of people. They are carrying rifles. Obviously those in the boat had spotted the dinghy and are heading for it. When only a short distance away, someone shouts:

"Are you an American?"

"You're damn right I am," Swett replies weakly. The picketboat comes on, and those aboard notice Swett's battered face. They yell encouragement, and now are on him. They haul him aboard and start back to the harbor—Gavutu. They ask about Swett's flight. A short time later they reach a pier, where a Marine colonel, who had seen Swett go into the water, is waiting. The crewmen don't say much, although they look Swett over rather curiously, perhaps admiringly, and help him out of the boat. He offers them many thanks for picking him up. And then he stands up on a firm footing—and feels better.

The most memorable event of Swett's reception by the colonel was a glass of Scotch the colonel poured him, to ease his pain. Shortly thereafter another boat arrived and picked him up, and took him to Tulagi. There a doctor administered morphine. The combination of the mission, his injury, Scotch and morphine made him deathly sick, as it did another rescued pilot—Lieutenant Kenneth Walsh (about whom we will learn more in the next chapter).

Walsh, who had been tail-end Charlie (in fourth position) in Swett's division, had engaged three or four Zeroes, shot down two. He was then hit hard by another Zero, and forced to ditch.

Walsh and Swett discussed the highlights of the big day. Walsh told Swett that Sergeant Jack Pitman, Swett's wingman, had shot down a Zero and a dive bomber, and landed safely back at Fighter 2, his plane badly shot up. Lieutenant Gale Roberts, the division section leader, had been hit by the Zeroes. He baled out at approximately 15,000 feet,

Walsh thought, though his chute failed to open until he had fallen some distance.

Swett and Walsh rested at Tulagi that night, and next day a PBY fetched both back to Guadalcanal. Battered face and all, Swett reported to his squadron. (The doctor at Tulagi had applied sulfa to his face and given him more morphine, but both Swett and Walsh were still very sick.)

One look at Swett and his commander dispatched him posthaste to Koli Point Hospital. He remained there six days.

Swett knew he had scored seven or eight kills, but the mildly irritating part of it all was that everyone seemed skeptical. From the time he was helped ashore, at the pier on Florida Island, and answered the colonel's question about victories with the reply "Seven," he had been the object of strange glances.

Now, in the hospital, his doctor, Commander Olin M. Holmes (from San Mateo, too, and later to be Swett's wife's obstetrician), asked the same question. Swett told him he had downed seven or eight. Holmes, knowing that if the claim was true it was a new record among U.S. fighter pilots, was rightly impressed. But Swett thought he, too, and everyone else still wondered—quite naturally, perhaps.

It wasn't until five days later, when Lieutenant (j.g.) Pete Lewis, of intelligence, returned to Guadalcanal after a five-day trip, the purpose of which had been to confirm or deny Swett's sensational victory claims, that his claim was confirmed. After talking to natives on Florida Island, ground troops, and checking all possible sources of information, Lewis visited the hospital.

"I hope you appreciate the sunburn I went through," he told Swett, with a smile. And then he broke the good news: Swett was being awarded seven confirmed victories! (Not long afterward the Japanese dive bomber which was probably victim No. 8 was discovered on a small island. Both the pilot and gunner were dead. American troops who discovered the enemy aircraft removed a radio deciphering code from the cockpit, as a souvenir, and presented it to Swett, in the belief that it was his eighth victim on that memorable April 7.)

The victory score of American airmen on April 7—a victory achieved in the face of overwhelming numbers of enemy aircraft—was one-sided. Destroyed, according to adjusted American claims, were twelve Val dive bombers and twenty-seven Zeroes, a total of thirty-nine aircraft. VMF 221 destroyed seventeen of these, Swett accounting for seven of the seventeen. (Japanese records, available after the war, admitted the loss of only twelve dive bombers and nine Zeroes, a total of twenty-one aircraft.) Marine losses, though they included seven F4F's, did not include the loss of a pilot, all seven of those shot down having been rescued!

Japanese dive bombers achieved some success in Tulagi Harbor, and off Guadalcanal, but not anything like they had hoped to achieve. They sank 14,000-ton tanker *Kanawha,* though she was not to go down until that night, and an Allied corvette. In addition, destroyer *Aaron Ward* sank while under tow, as a result of hits sustained during the attack.

But if the dive bombers achieved some success, the ferocity of aerial opposition certainly discouraged the enemy.

Moreover, stiff U.S. opposition to massive Japanese raids on Guadalcanal was to continue. In a raid on June 7, defending fighter pilots were credited with twenty-three kills for a loss of five. On the 16th an estimated 120 planes were intercepted by Allied fighters, and in this epic battle enemy losses were better than 50 per cent!

Convinced that the rate of attrition was now unbearable, the enemy scheduled no further raids on Guadalcanal. And the big island, the scene of so many fierce aerial battles, was never again raided by the Japanese in daylight.

For First Lieutenant Swett, recognition for his great flight was yet to come. Back at Espiritu Santo, six months later, Major General Ralph Mitchell assembled the air group and station personnel. The purpose was to present to Swett the Congressional Medal of Honor.

Mitchell read:

For extraordinary heroism and personal valor above and beyond the call of duty, as the Division Leader in a Marine Fighting Squadron in action against enemy Japanese aerial forces in the Solomon Island area, April 7, 1943.

In a daring flight to intercept a wave of 150 Japanese planes, First Lieutenant Swett unhesitatingly hurled his four-plane division into action against a formation of fifteen enemy bombers, and during his dive, personally exploded three hostile planes in mid-air with accurate and deadly fire.

Although separated from his division while clearing the heavy concentration of antiaircraft fire, he boldly attacked six enemy bombers, engaging the first four in turn, and unaided, shot them down in flames. Exhausting his ammunition, as he closed the fifth Japanese bomber, he relentlessly drove his attack against terrific opposition, which partially disabled his engine, shattering the windscreen and slashing his face.

In spite of this, he brought his battered plane down with skillful precision in the water off Tulagi. . . . The superb airmanship and tenacious fighting spirit which enabled First Lieutenant Swett to destroy seven enemy bombers in a single flight were in keeping with the highest traditions of the United States Naval Service.

At that time no other U.S. fighter pilot, in either world war, had ever brought down seven enemy planes on one mission.

PART 2

THE TURNING
OF THE TIDE

5 *Escorting the Heavies to Bougainville*

First Lieutenant KENNETH A. WALSH, U.S.M.C.

AFTER the fearful battle of Guadalcanal ended, early in 1943, American forces began their long advance to the northwest, which in two and one-half years would bring defeat to Japan.

The Solomon Islands are strung out in a general line running northwest-southeast. The largest of the Solomons is Bougainville Island, at the northwest end of the chain, Guadalcanal is the largest island on the southeast end.

From the southeastern tip of Bougainville to the northwestern tip of Guadalcanal it is approximately 250 miles. A line drawn to connect these two big islands (which would run in an almost exact northwest-southeast direction) would traverse the waters of the Slot, now immortal in U.S. naval history as the water passageway between the rows of islands.

Beginning at Guadalcanal, or just north of it, Florida, Santa Isabel, and Choiseul (the latter two islands being over ninety miles in length) comprise the northerly islands. Beginning again at Guadalcanal, the

Russells, New Georgia, Kolombangara and Vella Lavella comprise the southerly island boundary of the Slot.

The American advance to the northwest began shortly after the evacuation of Japanese troops from Guadalcanal in February, 1943, with landings on the Russell Islands, at Munda (on New Georgia), and on Vella Lavella. After these landings Bougainville, the largest of the Solomon Islands, was the logical target. The primary purpose for landing on Bougainville was to secure airfields to be used in attacks on Rabaul, the major Japanese military base in the South Pacific, located on the island of New Britain, in the Bismarck Archipelago, only 150 miles northwest of Bougainville.

The biggest of Bougainville's five Japanese airfields was Kahili, and the air battle which developed preparatory to the U.S. landing on Bougainville was something of a Guadalcanal in reverse. The difference was that the Japanese had five airfields on Bougainville, which was four more than the U.S. Marines had available on Guadalcanal at the beginning, and also that the Japanese were nearer a major supporting base, Rabaul, where hundreds of fighters and bombers were customarily deployed at this period of the war.

They were defending Kahili, just as the Americans had defended Henderson Field in the early days of the battle at Guadalcanal. The air campaign against the airfields of Bougainville actually did not build up to full force until October of 1943. But before that time American air attacks were launched, some by four-engine bombers, escorted by both Marine and U.S. Army fighters. It is with one of these early and fiercely resisted attacks, by U.S. heavies, that we are concerned in this chapter.

Those pilots who took part in the early air raids on Kahili airfield encountered some of the fiercest Japanese fighter opposition of the entire war. As mentioned, the situation was the opposite of Guadalcanal: American bombers, escorted by American fighters, were bombing the enemy airfield. The Japanese fighter pilots rose to defend. Because the Japanese had lookouts on various islands bordering the Slot, they were usually warned of approaching raids ahead of time (just as the Americans had been at Guadalcanal) and were able to scramble a strong fighter force to intercept the attackers.

The mission with which we are here concerned occurred on August 30, 1943, just two weeks after an Army combat team and a Marine defense battalion had gone ashore at Velle Lavella. The aircraft flown by the fighter pilots on this mission was the first single-engine U.S. fighter seriously to challenge the Zero—the Chance-Vought F4U Corsair.

It soon became known to the Japanese as the "Whistling Death," because of its unmistakable sound when diving. Japanese naval intelligence, according to Masatake Okumiya and Jiro Horikoshi in *Zero*, first reported this fighter as one which had been designed for carrier use but had failed to pass carrier-qualification tests, primarily because of unimpressive deck-landing characteristics. However, it was not long before the tremendous fighting qualities of the Corsair became apparent to all.

The Corsair was faster than the Zero in level flight, and could—like most American fighters—outdive the Zero. The Corsair was powered by a Pratt and Whitney 2,000-hp, air-cooled, "Double Wasp" radial engine, the most powerful fighter engine in use at that period of the war. The Marine fighter squadron with which we are primarily concerned is VMF 124, whose commander was Major William A. Millington. In an effort to obtain top performance from the Corsair, VMF 124 had removed all unnecessary weight from the fighter—such as the tail hook (used for carrier deck landings), wing tank CO-2 purging bottles, etc.

At this time VMF 124 had just become the first fighter squadron to operate from the recently completed airstrip at Munda, and had returned only a few days prior to August 30. While at Munda, VMF 124 provided Combat Air Patrol for the landing forces at Vella Lavella, the last steppingstone on the road to Bougainville. Then VMF 124 was returned to Guadalcanal.

On the summer night of Sunday, August 29, 1943, some seven thousand miles southwest of the United States, under the palm trees on now-peaceful Guadalcanal, fighter pilots of Marine Squadrons VMF 123 and VMF 124 were briefed. The New York Yankees, in the American League, and the St. Louis Cardinals, in the National League, were about to win pennants, in the United States, but that was a long way off as pilots of these two squadrons listened to briefing officers explain how they would escort more than twenty four-engined Liberator bombers on a strike at Kahili Airdrome, Bougainville, "tomorrow."

Briefing completed, pilots dispersed to their four-man tents scattered among the palms.

Out in the darkness, dispersed around Henderson Field and auxiliary

Fighter Strips 1 and 2, the dark-blue Corsair fighters which would protect the heavy bombers next day, and engage enemy Zeroes, sat motionless. Only the sound of crickets and the wind that blew in over the waters of Lunga Roads and Ironbottom Sound and rustled the palms broke the stillness. Some of these fast, new American fighters, in action only a few months, would be missing the following night, as would some of the pilots contemplating tomorrow's mission in the tents a short distance away.

Near Fighter Strip 2, west of Henderson Field, under camouflage, stood gull-winged No. 13, of VMF 124. Not far away, with tomorrow's mission on his mind, in one of the tents, sat First Lieutenant Kenneth A. Walsh, of Brooklyn, who had enlisted in the Marines as a private ten years earlier, in 1933. He was, then, a young man caught in the middle of the worst depression in the country's history. Ironically, it was the year in which Franklin Roosevelt and Adolf Hitler assumed leadership in their respective countries.

Seven years later, in 1940, just a year before the United States was engulfed in World War II, Ken Walsh married Beulah Barrinott, of Washington, D.C., and no doubt on this night Walsh's thoughts often made the trip back to the capital city on the Potomac—7,000 miles away. Little did he know, of course, that for the gallantry and devotion to duty that he would exhibit next day he would be awarded the nation's highest honor, the Congressional Medal of Honor.

It had been a long road up from private to first lieutenant, in the corps. He had won an assignment to flight school, survived the rugged ordeal as an aviation cadet, and been commissioned a second lieutenant in the Marine Corps after completing flight training.

Already in the war, he had experienced enough close calls to recognize the face of death, once having had to ditch in the open sea, after a fierce battle with enemy fighters, and having been picked up by a small boat so that he would live to fly and fight again. (This occurred on April 7, on the day Jim Swett flew the memorable mission covered in the last chapter and was also shot down and rescued.)

Walsh, like the other pilots, knew that enemy opposition at Kahili Airdrome next day would be formidable. The Japanese, with five airfields and an estimated 40,000 troops on Bougainville, were certain to vigorously oppose the heavy bombers and escorting fighters. And both carrier-based and land-based fighters were stationed on enemy fields in the Bougainville area. Thinking these thoughts, and others concerned with tomorrow's battle, Walsh finally fell asleep in his tent, in preparation for the day ahead.

The sun rose early on the morning of August 30, 1943, revealing a clear Pacific sky to the east of Guadalcanal. A noncom from the duty section aroused the pilots in Walsh's tent shortly after dawn.

Walsh pulled on his khakis and walked leisurely to the mess hall. Today's mission was an unusually late one. Take-off from Guadalcanal, Walsh knew, was not scheduled until late in the morning. He had time to enjoy Spam, French toast, canned orange juice, and coffee. After breakfast he ambled down to the flight line, where the operations hut was located. The hut was a Quonset, a blackboard set up inside, and this was where pilots of VMF 124 and VMF 123 would get a final briefing for the day's mission.

Walsh already knew it entailed escorting heavy bombers on a strike at Kahili Airdrome. Kahili, the main Japanese base on the biggest island in the Solomons, protected the Japanese stronghold at Rabaul. The Americans had now built airfields on the Russell Islands, at Munda, and only a few weeks earlier had landed at Vella Lavella.

Walsh and the fighter pilots of VMF 124 had been transferred to the forward base at Munda, just a few minutes' flying time from Vella Lavella, to provide protection for the ships landing American men and supplies there. On one day, while American troops and supplies were going ashore at the new American base, Walsh had shot down three Japanese fighters while breaking up an enemy attack on U.S. ships. Just a few days afterward VMF 124 had been withdrawn and brought back to Guadalcanal. Today Walsh would fly from Guadalcanal, over the Russells, over New Georgia (and the Munda airbase), Vella Lavella (where the Americans were working to complete an even more advanced airstrip), over the Shortland Islands, from where the southeastern tip of Bougainville could be seen, and then to Kahili. Kahili Airdrome was located on the southeastern tip of that largest of the Solomon Islands.

Walsh chatted with other pilots until word was passed that final briefing would take place at the Russell Islands, a short hop from Guadalcanal. There VMF 124 would refuel in order to enter the expected battle over Bougainville with as much fuel as possible. With that pilots

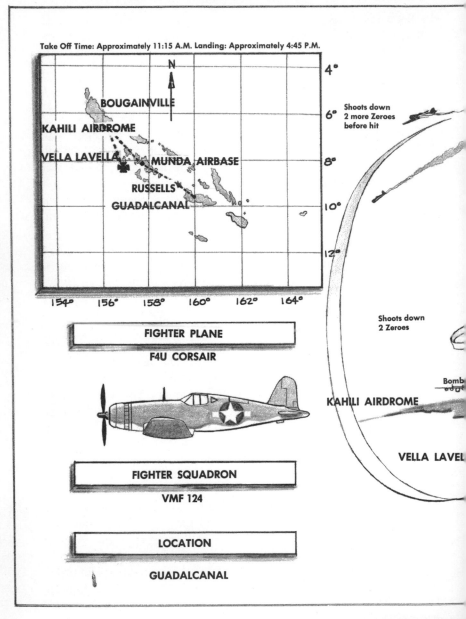

Take Off Time: Approximately 11:15 A.M. Landing: Approximately 4:45 P.M.

BOUGAINVILLE
KAHILI AIRDROME
VELLA LAVELLA
MUNDA AIRBASE
RUSSELLS
GUADALCANAL

Shoots down 2 more Zeroes before hit

Shoots down 2 Zeroes

KAHILI AIRDROME

VELLA LAVEL

Bomb

FIGHTER PLANE

F4U CORSAIR

FIGHTER SQUADRON

VMF 124

LOCATION

GUADALCANAL

MISSION FLOWN

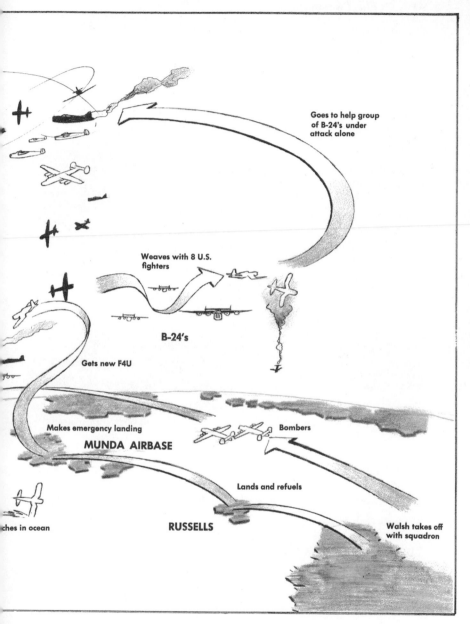

Goes to help group
of B-24's under
attack alone

Weaves with 8 U.S.
fighters

B-24's

Gets new F4U

Makes emergency landing

MUNDA AIRBASE

Bombers

Lands and refuels

ches in ocean

RUSSELLS

Walsh takes off
with squadron

RST LIEUTENANT KENNETH A. WALSH, USMC, AUGUST 30, 1943

dispersed and headed for their aircraft—beneath the palms and camouflage netting surrounding Fighter 2. (Fighter 2 was just west of Henderson Field, Fighter 1 east of Henderson Field—these being the three principal airfields from which Guadalcanal-based bombers and fighters operated at this time of the war.)

Walsh, having donned flying gear, arrived at his revetment to find No. 13 ready and warmed up. It was almost eleven o'clock. VMF 124,

The famous Corsair F4U fighter, known by the enemy as the "Whistling Death," shown in the Solomons. (U.S. Office of War Information Photo)

flying from Fighter 2, was one of two Corsair squadrons which would escort the Liberator bombers.

The three pilots with whom Walsh would be flying (his division) were First Lieutenant W. P. Spencer, his wingman, Captain M. L. Taylor, his section leader, and Captain W. E. Sigler, Taylor's wingman. The Corsairs of these three were not far away. Walsh glanced around the field, at the other planes, to be sure no props were already turning.

About fifteen minutes past eleven he climbed into the cockpit, was hooked up by his crew chief, and pushed the starter button. The 2,000-hp Pratt and Whitney engine bellowed into a steady roar—cleared the smoke out of the stacks. Walsh turned on his radio. All around

Fighter 2 the big three-blade Hamilton Standard's began to spin. Colonel William A. Millington taxied to the end of the runway and a line of fighters snaked along behind him. At 11:30 the Corsairs began to roar down the center of the runway. Near the end, they lifted over the tall palm trees upward into the blue.

In a few minutes VMF 124 was grouped together and headed for the Russell Islands, sixty miles to the northwest. Walsh checked his instruments crossing out over the western tip of Guadalcanal Island. All were functioning properly. His radio worked properly and the engine ran smoothly.

Just before noon the U.S. airstrip on the Russells came into view; VMF 124 began its descent. By shortly after noon all planes had landed safely, and pilots proceeded to a final briefing. Crewmen topped off gas tanks in both wings of the Corsairs. The briefing was not elaborate, since all pilots had been briefed the night before. The Corsairs were to pick up more than twenty Liberator heavy bombers over Rendova Island (near Munda) and escort them northwestward, crossing Vella Lavella, the Shortland Islands, and then on into the target area, Kahili Airdrome.

The bombers would fly to the left of Kahili Airdrome, make a right turn on their bomb run, at which time they would be headed southeast, and, after dropping bombs, would increase speed and streak for home. Enemy opposition was expected to be heavy. It was known the Japanese had more than a hundred fighters in the Kahili Airdrome area. Courses were given, as were instructions in case of separation from the squadron, and pilots were reminded they could land at Munda, or the Russell Islands, if damaged or short of fuel on the return trip to Guadalcanal.

A number of Army P-39's and P-40's also would take part in the escort action. Antiaircraft fire at Kahili would be thick—in fact, there were stronger antiaircraft defenses at Kahili than had been encountered anywhere else in the Solomons. The weather would be excellent, with only a few scattered cumulus to be seen (and this forecast made it certain Japanese coast watchers on Choiseul, Vella Lavella and the Shortland Islands would give defending fighters warning of the American attack).

At 1:30 P.M., after pilots had grabbed a quick bite of lunch, take-off from the Russells began. Pilots were more tense; this time they were heading for battle. In a few minutes VMF 124 was climbing into the northwest at 140 knots. Approximately 200 miles ahead, in that direction, lay Kahili Airdrome. Once again Walsh checked his instruments; everything was functioning properly.

The squadron reached 7,000 feet, 8,000 feet, then 9,000 feet. Radio silence was observed, for the most part, and pilots looked down on the blue waters below. Buraku Island was passed, on the left, and ahead lay the southeasternmost island of the New Georgia group. Soon the 3,600-foot mountain some forty miles southeast of Rendova came into view. Pilots now began to search ahead for the bombers. In the fighter force were some thirty-five Corsairs, of both VMF 124 and VMF 123, and approximately half that many P-39's and P-40's.

All eyes were fixed on the sky in the direction of Rendova Island, and soon the "big friends" came into view ahead. Colonel Millington directed the fighters to a rendezvous point, and on schedule the sleek fighters throttled back to accommodate the slower bombers, and began to S-turn, taking up position. The big Liberators flew in groups of threes, stacked down in string formation. The Corsairs began weaving over the tops of the bombers. They were higher than the P-39's and P-40's. Some of the fighters were on each side of the bombers, and others below them.

Now the unexpected. A strange noise! The engine—losing power! As he continued to climb, Walsh's supercharger was failing. A seal had evidently broken; pressure was lost, and Walsh couldn't maintain position. Disgusted, he realized he would have to turn back. He was losing speed and altitude! Hastily he signaled Spencer, wagging his wings, holding his nose. He pointed to the engine with one hand while holding his nose with the other—then motioned with his thumb that he was going down. Spencer understood.

Now he was dropping back, and he scanned the horizon below. In sight was the new airfield at Munda, from which VMF 124 had operated only a few days earlier! Walsh pushed the stick with his right hand, eased back on the throttle with his left. He began what almost amounted to a dive-bombing run on the airfield. Air speed increased and the altimeter registered a steady loss of altitude. He was in a hurry. His only chance to complete the mission was to land quickly at Munda, obtain another aircraft, and take off immediately. Even then he would be doing well to regain altitude and catch the bombers before they were intercepted by enemy fighters.

The wind screamed on the canopy, outside, and Walsh kept diving toward the airstrip below. He was down to 4,000 feet, lining up for a straight-in approach on the runway. The bombers, with the escorting fighters, were far ahead, above, to the northwest, plodding along through the sky toward Kahili Airdrome.

Now the palm trees were coming closer and closer. Walsh, throttle back, dropped his landing gear and cut power, to avoid being too "hot" when he reached the end of the runway.

Slowed to about 100 knots, Walsh streaked in over the end of the long runway and touched down. He taxied fast in the direction of Operations, and as soon as he could park he jumped out and asked for the commanding officer. Major Jim Neefus came "on the run." Walsh told him he needed a new plane, immediately. Neefus didn't let paper work or technical details slow him down. He told Walsh to take one of the fully armed and fueled Corsairs on standby alert. Walsh ran to the Corsair, strapped in. In two or three minutes he was gunning the engine into a roar at the end of the runway. Barely ten minutes after he had landed he was lifting off the western end of the Munda strip, pointing northwest at full throttle, hoping to overtake his comrades.

The new engine purrs. The six guns of his "replacement" Corsair are loaded with 2,400 rounds of tracer, armor-piercing and incendiary ammunition. He flicks on his gun switches, looks through the sight ring. Everything is in order.

He's climbing at full throttle and 160 knots, and looks northwest but can see no bombers and fighters ahead. Since enemy fighters will probably be circling above Kahili Airdrome, waiting for the Americans (alerted by coast watchers), Walsh decides to gain maximum altitude. He'll approach Kahili alone if unable to catch the other fighters before they reach the target area.

The altimeter registers 14,000 feet, 15,000, 16,000. The supercharger cuts in; this one functions properly. Walsh looks ahead; he still can't make out the bombers, or fighters. Now the altimeter reads 21,000 feet, 22,000, 23,000. Vella Lavella is below, passing behind. In minutes the Shortland Islands will be in sight. Still no bombers ahead. The altimeter reaches 27,000 feet, 28,000. Ahead and far below, the Shortland Islands come into view. The engine is straining; Walsh knows he is close to maximum altitude with the fully loaded Corsair. Still no sight of the bombers. He is approaching the major enemy air base in the Solomon

Islands, alone, which requires him to be fully alert. He looks right, left, and behind, constantly. Now he is crossing the Shortland Islands. The altimeter reads 30,000 feet.

Up ahead, dots! A large number of dots . . . aircraft! The bombers! He eases the stick forward slightly. Maintaining 30,000 feet, and full throttle, he points for the aircraft ahead.

But are these bombers? They appear small for bombers. Walsh strains his eyes. There are some forty or fifty in the formation. Fighters! Where are the bombers? A chill runs down his spine. Could these be Zeroes? His eyes freeze on the dots ahead. They are slightly below. Glancing behind for a split second only, Walsh keeps his eyes on the unidentified bogeys ahead. And now the silhouettes are clearer. It comes to him. Zeroes!

Just at this time Walsh sees, to the left and farther ahead, another force of aircraft. The bombers! They're completing their bomb run on Kahili, and the enemy fighters between Walsh and the B-24's are preparing to go into a diving attack on the "big friends."

Walsh is still far enough away from the enemy fighters to remain undetected, since he is only one small dot. They are a group, and it makes quite a difference. Now he sees that the B-24's are already under attack, by other enemy fighters! He hears excited shouts over the radio. Instinctively he eases stick forward sharply and points his nose at the enemy fighters ahead, beginning a slow left turn which will bring him in on the tail of the unsuspecting Japanese pilots.

The R-2800 engine, at full throttle and diving, begins to roar. Walsh picks up speed and begins to close the distance between him and the large group of Zeroes ahead. He notices heavy antiaircraft fire above Kahili Airdrome. He has little time to watch. He is keeping the enemy fighters in view, and regularly glancing behind, to be sure no enemy fighter slips in on his tail. But he notices a peculiar type of flak, which explodes in the air over the airdrome, leaving long white streamers.

The Corsair is moving up smartly on the fifty Zeroes, and Walsh, tense with excitement, knows full well he is executing a daring, dangerous attack. If discovered before he can sneak in on the enemy's rear, he will be overwhelmed. The last few Zeroes in the formation begin a slight left turn, following the main body, and Walsh points his nose toward the last Zero, which is the farthest right.

Over the radio he hears the voices and shouts of battle, knows the bombers are being hard hit. A wild melee has developed over Kahili Airdrome. Several groups of Zeroes are joining in the fight. Now the last Zero in the group ahead looms larger and larger. The wingspan grows wider and wider in the sight ring. Walsh's right forefinger is on the trigger, his speed is close to 300 knots.

A Captured Tojo, or Japanese Army Type 2 fighter, a "hot" fighter in its day. (Official U.S. Navy Photo)

Range is 1,500 feet, 1,400, 1,300. The Corsair's six guns are bore-sighted for 1,000 feet, now they point directly on the trailing Zero. Now! He pulls the trigger. The roar of 50-caliber guns almost drowns that of the engine. The Corsair staggers and smoke trails from both wings. In seconds, the trailing Zero begins to disintegrate. Fire streaks backward, as does a stream of black smoke. So far, the other Zeroes are unaware of the lone American behind them. Walsh is now almost on his victim. Range less than 300 feet. The Zero wobbles out of formation and begins to go down. It explodes in an orange burst! He has only a second to observe the victory. He is almost within range of the next Zero, slightly left, ahead. He presses left rudder and moves stick left. Tension increases as he continues to challenge the big enemy gaggle, still undiscovered. The dirty-brown Zero ahead looms larger and larger. This time Walsh notices the rising sun painted on each wing. The Zeroes are just a few thousand feet above the bombers; soon the enemy fighters will be on them! Walsh shouts warnings over the mike. The wingspan of the Zero is thirty-five feet; Walsh must wait until the wingspan in his sight ring stretches to a width of thirty-five mills. It gets wider. Walsh maneuvers the nose to line up guns in perfect firing position.

The Zero is in point-blank range. The wingspan fills the sight ring. Walsh presses the trigger button! Hundreds of shells streak toward the fighter ahead. For a second he wonders if he has scored. Now a trail of black smoke! The left wing goes up, the right down. The Zero plunges into a vertical dive. A column of black smoke marks the course of the plane's plunge.

Walsh's gaze at his second victim is interrupted by a flight of Zeroes rapidly circling to his left. He is discovered! They're trying to close his tail. He rams the stick forward. The Corsair dives. But other Zeroes below, now fully alerted, turn to make head-on passes. He jinxes rapidly as one enemy pilot, wings twinkling with 20-millimeter fire, executes a head-on pass. He banks left, and sees a Zero circling behind to get on his tail. They're closing from all sides now. And he is constantly maneuvering to get close to the other F4U's, now not far away.

The bombers are only several hundred feet below; he wonders if they'll open up on him as he plunges toward them. A wild battle has developed; he has broken up the enemy fighter formation, to a degree, though some of the Zeroes begin making passes on the B-24's. The battle grows in intensity; several bombers break out of formation. Walsh continues diving, at least half a dozen Zeroes seek to close him from behind. The action is at such a pitch that only seconds are available for decisions. Plunging through and between bombers, he eases back on the stick.

The F4U pulls up, with high speed, now momentarily out of range of the enemy fighters. Off to the left a Zero approaches rapidly; Walsh slams into a sharp left turn, rolls out, opens fire. A few strikes register on the Zero as he flashes across, left to right, and then plunges downward. Walsh can't follow up . . . other Zeroes begin to close his rear. Over the radio he hears calls of distress from the bombers. Many are being repeatedly attacked. The Zeroes are especially aggressive.

He sees parachutes in the sky; a burning B-24 is going down. It's impossible to line up on a single plane for a concentrated attack; there're too many planes in the air, the fighting is confused. The B-24's divide into three groups, of eight or nine bombers in a group. Walsh looks around anxiously for friendly Corsairs. He continues to clear his tail . . . and look. Seven or eight dots ahead . . . Corsairs! They're weaving back and forth, point their noses in his direction. A hope of support . . . relief! To the side other enemy fighters are climbing up from Kahili Airdrome.

Glancing below, Walsh sees dust on the airfield. More Zeroes are taking off. It's the heaviest fighter engagement of the war for him. Now he's close to the relative safety of the Corsairs, ahead. As they approach, he banks into the famous "Thatch Weave." The Corsairs are trying to protect a group of B-24's at the same altitude . . . now heading home. Several Zeroes attempt a run on the bombers from the side. Corsairs turn into them, head on. The Zeroes break off. Now a bomber is hit by a Zero that sneaks in. Several Corsairs go after him. The bomber trails smoke. Another Zero attempts to break through the fighter screen. A Corsair pilot turns into him, guns blazing; the Zero weaves over into a fatal dive, burning fiercely. Walsh sees a P-40 go down with three Zeroes after it.

The running battle is headed east, the bombers hoping to shake the Zeroes and reach the safety of the first friendly field, Munda. The B-24's are losing altitude gradually, seeking to pick up speed as they descend. Kahili is now miles behind. The Zeroes are staying with the bombers but are more respectful of the Corsairs. Slowly the minutes pass. Walsh, feeling lucky to have survived his attack on fifty fighters, has scored two kills.

The Jap fighters stay with the group, off to the side, and attempt to move in for the kill. The F4U's continue to weave. At this time the radio sounds a desperate call for aid. A group of bombers near Gizo are being hit hard by enemy fighters. They're calling for help. Obviously they have none. Walsh picks up the microphone: "There are more bombers in trouble near Gizo—let's go!" he says. Peeling off, he banks slightly to the right, pushes stick forward, and points his nose toward the Gizo-Ganongga area. He knows the bombers must be in serious trouble, for this is over halfway to Munda, and south of Vella Lavella—a long way from Kahili Airdrome. Jap fighters must have been sticking with the bombers ever since they departed Kahili.

As he rubbernecks, Walsh discovers he is the only Corsair headed for the Gizo-Ganongga area. He thought some of the others would follow. But the others either didn't hear the call or decided to stick with the bombers they were protecting. No Zeroes on his tail, though. Again Walsh finds himself alone, preparing to attack an enemy of unknown strength. The seconds, and minutes, pass slowly. Walsh scans the sky in all directions. He is losing altitude, gaining speed. The big Corsair is slanting downward at full throttle, at high speed. Ahead lies Vella Lavella. The "big friends" can't be far away. He checks his engine instruments; in the green. There's no way of knowing how much ammunition is left. He used short bursts in downing the two Zeroes and figures he has enough ammunition for another fight—if one develops.

Now, ahead, in the distance, he sees dots. Big planes—four engines! B-24's. They're several thousand feet below, and Walsh increases the angle of his dive. Now there are dots off to the side of the bombers. Some of the dots are obviously fighters. They are not attacking the bombers. Others, farther out, appear to be Zeroes. Walsh recognizes several different shapes among the fighters—as he rapidly closes from behind.

He again steepens the angle of his dive. He estimates the bombers to be 5,000 to 10,000 feet below him. Now he can see . . . Zeroes . . . going into the attack! Trying to defend the bombers are several Corsairs, P-40's and two P-39's—some help has already arrived. At least a dozen Zeroes are diving on the bombers. Walsh spots several Zeroes lining up for passes to the rear of the B-24's. He will make a diving attack on their rear, in an effort to break up their attack and knock at least one of them down.

The Corsair is slicing downward through the air at better than 300 knots. Walsh grips the stick handle and trigger. Once again he looks through the sight, getting set for a firing pass. He is fast moving up on the Zeroes below, with his great speed, and must push the stick forward to avoid passing in front of them. The altimeter reads 17,000 feet, 16,000, 15,000. Now he sees there are five Zeroes at six o'clock behind the bombers. He will attack the rear one, hoping the others don't see him until he has completed a successful pass. He is coming in slightly from the left, at seven o'clock. The wingspan of the Zero steadily widens.

Walsh maneuvers to keep it in the yellow sight ring directly in front of his eyes. He glances behind him quickly, to be certain the enemy has not slipped up, unseen, on his rear, and he is clear. Now the wingspan fills half his sight. He hopes to remain undiscovered long enough to get in the first burst. He's once again alone in a dangerous position, and will be in an even more precarious position when discovered. The wing-span is almost filling the 35-mill circle. The five Zeroes, unaware of the lone Corsair behind, are beginning to turn in to the bombers, being about a thousand feet above them. Their orange rising suns are clearly evident.

The rear Zero is within range. Walsh is on him! Fire! Tracers converge on the wing roots of the Zero ahead. Walsh's Corsair staggers, as does the Zero, which almost seems to hesitate in mid-air. Strikes rip into the fuselage and wing roots. Walsh holds the trigger button down. A deluge of shells has converged on the same spot. The enemy's prop seems to slow down and then . . . a big blaze! The Zero literally blows up in front of Walsh's eyes. It completely disintegrates. Victory No. 3! But he is discovered. The other Zeroes turn sharply.

Walsh pushes throttle full forward, hits left rudder and aileron, his right wing rises and he chandelles back up into the blue. By now, however, the other four Zeroes are after him. They—and others off to the side of the bombers—begin to climb. The Liberators are ahead and below, and the other friendly fighters are sticking with the bombers. While glancing down, Walsh marvels at the sight of a parachute below, that of the Jap pilot whose plane just disintegrated. The debris, trailing black smoke, is plunging downward far below.

Suddenly Walsh notices a Zero to his left, behind. The Zero is trying to cross behind. Walsh keeps his eyes on him. He must now circle back from right to left, ahead. Walsh banks to the left. The enemy pilot has obviously come from above, since Walsh has maintained full throttle, and good speed, and the Zero has circled him. He maneuvers for a firing pass at the Zero, and to prevent the Zero from turning sharply left and getting on his tail. Out of a corner of his eye he notices one of the P-39's in a diving, turning fight with another Zero. He can ill afford to watch.

Now the enemy pilot is to his left, slightly above, turning left. Walsh, with good speed, pulls back and left on the stick, pushes left rudder. He'll soon see if he has the speed to close the enemy, turning on the inside. The Corsair moves steadily in, aided by better position.

The Corsair is closing fast off the left rear quarter. The Zero increases its turning angle. Walsh is closing so fast he grips the trigger button and prepares for a deflection shot. He glances behind; no other Zeroes on his tail yet. But he sees the P-39 plunging toward the water below, trailing heavy black smoke. The bombers are calling for help, and other Zeroes are attacking them, but Walsh is doing all he can.

Now the enemy Zero ahead, left, draws closer and closer. Already on the inside, Walsh realizes he'll have time for a short burst. The enemy wingspan fills the sight ring. Walsh pulls the button, once again the F4U opens with all six guns. The tracers reveal a good firing position. They streak into the enemy victim. The Zero staggers. The right wing comes down slightly. Walsh is within a few hundred feet. He maintains his fire. Smoke trails back. The enemy's left wing rises and the fourth victim begins a plunge to the ocean below.

Walsh holds his fire and follows the Zero, to be certain he's mortally wounded. The enemy fighter has not exploded. Walsh is not sure he is fatally damaged. But the Zero streaks straight downward. Walsh follows. Still trailing smoke, the enemy plane passes the altitude of the bombers and continues to plunge downward. Walsh sees no chute. His altimeter reads 9,000 feet, 8,000, 7,000. Still the Zero plunges downward.

Now, disengaging themselves from the attack on the B-24 bombers, four Zeroes peel off and start down after Walsh. Walsh's altimeter reads 5,000 feet . . . 4,000 . . . 3,000. The enemy pilot ahead must be dead; if he's bluffing, he'll have to pull out at any minute. The Zero is only trailing smoke, and it's impossible to know whether he's playing "possum." Walsh keeps his eyes on the brownish-green fighter. It reaches 1,000 feet . . . 500. The Zero continues its slant toward the blue water, closer and closer. Splash! Victory No. 4!

Walsh streaks over the debris on the top of the water. He has no time to mull over his fourth kill. Behind him, on both sides, above, enemy fighters are closing for the kill! These are the four Zeroes who had dived after him as he followed his fourth victim down. Walsh realizes his position is desperate. His ammunition is low. The enemy planes have an altitude advantage. And he has lost speed. Walsh points his nose to the southeast (Munda), applies full throttle. The enemy pilots begin to close the distance. One of the Zeroes behind is close enough to fire. Walsh banks right, then left, to throw off the enemy's aim. But twinkles from the Zero's wings tell him the enemy is firing. Walsh can't turn—Zeroes are on each flank.

Bump!! Bump!! The Corsair is taking 20-millimeter hits! Walsh slams stick left, jams left rudder. The Zeroes, highly maneuverable, stay with him. His situation grows more desperate by the second. He shoves the stick forward and skims over the waves—heading southeast again. The Zeroes, fooled a little by his evasive actions, nevertheless gain slightly, continue to close the distance. Thump! Thump! Thump! The Corsair is being hit again. Now one of the Zeroes, behind and to the right, is beneath him. More hits shake the Corsair! Holes in the right wing . . . a glance at the left wing . . . more holes!

A crashing sound! Hits in the engine! Desperately turning from right to left, moving up and down, and with full throttle, he is unable to shake the Zeroes. They are closing, firing, alternately, and the F4U is steadily being shot up. Now a white stream trails from his cowling. The engine is smoking. He glances at his gauges; a lump sticks in his throat —he is losing power. Fuel pressure is falling . . . he reaches for the wobble pump. He keeps pumping away. And he hears the Corsair take more hits.

He glances frantically to left and right . . . the coast of Vella Lavella off to his left! So desperate has been his plight, he hasn't noticed the island. He's halfway to Munda! But he'll never make it. Smoke now trails from both sides of the cowling. The Zeroes behind, and one below, to the rear, close up for the kill. His speed is falling off; the Zeroes will be able to handle him as they please.

At this desperate moment, off to the left, as if in answer to a prayer, appears a beautiful sight. A P-40 and Corsairs! Can they reach him in time? Walsh sits on the very tops of the waves. His engine is smoking badly, his power is going fast. Munda is at least thirty miles away. His chances of making the closest U.S. airfield are negligible. The Japanese are now distracted, as the P-40 opens fire, out of range, in an effort to save the crippled, lone Corsair. Walsh still hears hits staggering his shattered aircraft. Holes are all over the wings and the engine is fast failing. But the hits are less frequent. Now silence.

Walsh realizes he will have to ditch, even as the Zeroes turn away! The rescuing fighters may have come from recently captured Vella Lavella! Walsh estimates the distance from the shore at a mile. Knowing the Americans landed on the island a few weeks earlier, he hopes to be able to swim ashore or be picked up. The engine begins to cut

out . . . back on, and out again. The Corsair will fly only seconds
longer. Walsh looks at his air speed—150 knots. He decides to drop
flaps. The hydraulic system works; flaps grind down. Speed is reduced
to 120 knots. He's approaching Barakoma Point, on the southeastern tip
of Vella Lavella. He drops down over the waves and eases back on the
stick. He checks his shoulder straps, and rolls back the canopy. He wants
to get out of the Corsair as soon as it hits the water. Now his air speed
drops to 100 knots. Walsh eases back on the stick and the smoking
Corsair slowly settles, still hurtling forward, toward the crests of the
waves.

Thump! The Corsair hits and bounces. Another thump . . . a few
lesser bumps, as the Corsair skims along on top of the Solomon Sea.
Suddenly she mushes in, slows rapidly, and begins to settle. Walsh
quickly unhooks his safety belt, and straps, throws them to the side and
stands up as fast as he can. He steps over the side. Water gushes in over
both sides of the cockpit, the wing having disappeared under the water.
He pushes off the wing and begins to swim, inflating his Mae West by
pulling the strings which release carbon dioxide.

The water is cool, and as the Corsair sinks beneath the waves. Walsh
—for the first time in what seems an eternity—has the time to relax, even
though floating, alone, in the ocean, not knowing how long he'll survive.

But no one is shooting at him, he has ditched successfully, he is
unhurt, and feels relieved! Somehow he's confident he'll be picked up,
since the pilots who saved him must have reported his ditching. And,
Walsh knows, the Seabees are building an airfield at Vella Lavella
(that's why U.S. troops landed there) and knows boats are available
to search for him.

However, it's almost five o'clock. They'll have only a couple of hours
to find him. Meanwhile, he'll swim toward Barakoma Point.

As he begins to swim he realizes how tired he is. He wonders
whether he'll be able to swim the mile. Will unfavorable tides wash him
out to sea? He's completely bushed. If he must swim a mile against the
current, he can't make it!

Unknown to Walsh, on the shore at Barakoma Point, American
Seabees saw the burning, stricken Corsair forced down into the water.
Immediately they organized a search party and a Higgins boat headed
for the spot where Walsh had gone in. Later, just as Walsh was realiz-

ing how tired he actually was, swimming in his inflated Mae West, the Higgins boat rescuers caught sight of the lone figure, bobbing up and down, in the water ahead. They hailed him and told him to relax—they were coming. Walsh, relieved, gave a slight wave of the hand and relaxed, waiting to be pulled in. He had been in the water less than thirty minutes!

The boat pulled alongside him and friendly hands hauled him aboard. They suggested he had had a close call; Walsh thought to himself they didn't know the half of it. But he was thankful for the rescue, and remarked that the Seabees always looked after the Marines. (This was tradition in the Pacific; the Seabees and the Marines got on famously together.) A few minutes later Walsh was ashore. He was to spend the night on Vella Lavella—since he would have to return to Munda by ship.

The Seabees, and U.S. troops in the area, knew he should be checked over, and insisted he go to the hospital. Soon he was in the hospital tent, relaxing as ordered. After the exertions of the day he was physically and mentally exhausted, and didn't kick when told he would spend the night in the hospital.

Shortly afterwards, much to his surprise, another fighter pilot was brought to the hospital tent. He had a broken leg. Walsh talked to him. Had he been on the mission? Yes. What was he flying? A P-39. Where was he shot down? He was shot down by a Zero, while trying to defend a group of B-24's in the Gizo-Ganongga area who had called for help. Walsh smiled. "I saw you go down," he said.

Next morning Walsh and the P-39 pilot left by LST for Guadalcanal. Though the skipper, Walsh, and everyone else expected Japanese air attacks on the southeastern run, the LST was not attacked, and on the following day they reached Guadalcanal safely.

The enemy inflicted losses on American bombers and fighters on August 30. Had it not been for the one-man heroics of First Lieutenant Kenneth Walsh, the Brooklyn-born Irishman who had risen from the rank of private in the Marine Corps to become—at that time—the top Marine ace in the Pacific, American losses would have been far heavier. Interrogators credited Walsh with having helped disrupt the attack of the fifty Zeroes on the B-24's over Kahili Airdrome, then having disrupted Zero attacks on the fleeing B-24's in the Gizo-Ganongga area.

Walsh was officially credited with four enemy fighters for the day. He damaged at least two others. The kills were the seventeenth, eighteenth, nineteenth and twentieth victories of his first tour in the Pacific.

For so spirited a defense of the bombers, even though he had to change planes during the mission, and during which he attacked fifty Zeroes, alone, and for other actions, Walsh was awarded the Congressional Medal of Honor.

However, there was to be no respite in the war for Walsh. Within two days of his arrival back at Guadalcanal he was in combat again. Shortly thereafter his first tour of action in the Pacific ended. He served a second tour in 1945, though the Japanese were more scarce at this stage of the war, and he was able to add only one enemy aircraft to his total. Nevertheless, he ended the war fourth among Marine fighter pilots, with twenty-one confirmed enemy aircraft destroyed.

Today, clear-eyed, active and enthusiastic about the Marine Corps, Walsh is a lieutenant colonel, flying transports between California and the Far East. He has acquired over 8,000 hours of flying time, though the mission on that memorable August day, in 1943, still ranks as the epic flight of his career.

The official citation, awarding him the Congressional Medal of Honor (he was also awarded the Distinguished Flying Cross, with five Gold Stars, and the Air Medal, with thirteen Gold Stars) reads, in part, as follows:

For extraordinary heroism and intrepidity above and beyond the call of duty as a Pilot in Marine Fighting Squadron 124, in aerial combat against enemy Japanese forces in Solomon Islands area. . . . After developing engine trouble on 30 August during a vital escort mission, First Lieutenant Walsh landed his mechanically disabled plane at Munda, quickly replaced it with another, and proceeded to rejoin his flight over Kahili. Separated from his Escort Group when he encountered approximately fifty Japanese Zeroes, he unhesitatingly attacked, striking with relentless fury in his lone battle against a powerful force.

He destroyed four hostile fighters before cannon shell-fire forced him to make a dead-stick landing off Vella Lavella, where he was later picked up. His valiant leadership and his daring skill as a flier served as a source of confidence and inspiration to his fellow pilots and reflects the highest credit upon the United States Naval Service.

6 Trapped by Zekes at Rabaul

FEBRUARY 19, 1944:

Lieutenant IRA C. KEPFORD, U.S.N.R.

THE greatest Japanese base in the South Pacific in World War II was Rabaul.

Rabaul is located on the northern tip of New Britain. Simpson Harbor at Rabaul is one of the finest natural harbors in the entire Pacific, protected by massive hills on three sides, among them five volcanoes.

Ironically, the great enemy base had once been the territory of Japan's World War II ally, Germany. German colonial possessions, including the Bismarck Archipelago, were seized by the Australians and British in World War I.

The Australians administered the former German territory until January 23, 1942, when the onrushing Japanese reached Rabaul.

The Japanese appreciated Rabaul's military potential, its magnificent harbor and strategic location. They set forth to make it the principal Japanese base in the South Pacific, from which their forces would operate against New Guinea, Australia, the Solomon Islands, and even farther southeastward. Rabaul became headquarters of the enemy's

Southeastern Fleet and Eighth Army. A hundred thousand men were sent there, among them 75,000 Army troops.

Around Rabaul, on the northern end of New Britain, five military airfields were constructed: Laukani, Vunakanau, Rapopo, Keravat, and Tobera.

Rabaul's importance as a naval base was second only to Truk, the main Japanese fleet base 695 miles to the north. From Rabaul came practically all of the striking forces which fought the battles for control of Solomon waters for the better part of a year.

From this harbor, and the airfields surrounding it, the Japanese launched most of their air and naval strikes against Guadalcanal and against American forces island-hopping along the Solomons, after U.S. forces had achieved victory on Guadalcanal, in February, 1943, and begun their advance.

By late 1943 U.S. air power was strategically disposed to open a major offensive against the enemy's principal South Pacific base. American troops had successfully completed a landing on the coast of nearby Bougainville, at Empress Augusta Bay, though the Japanese were entrenched on both ends of this long island. An air base—Torokina Field —was operating on Bougainville. In addition, numerous American air bases were in operation farther down the Solomons chain, to the southeast. To the west, General Douglas MacArthur's forces were advancing along New Guinea, and had hopped Cape Gloucester, to the western tip of New Britain.

The American air offensive on Rabaul opened in earnest in the last months of 1943, and from then until February 19, 1944, the heaviest series of aerial encounters of the Pacific war up to that time took place. The Japanese threw in hundreds of extra fighters in a desperate attempt to check the American air offensive.

The air battles exacted a heavy toll from the defenders, and in January, 1944, the reorganized 2nd Carrier Division of the Japanese Navy, under Rear Admiral Takaji Jojima, was ordered to dispatch its planes to Rabaul to bolster the tottering defenders (the 26th Air Flotilla). They arrived on January 25.

The 2nd Carrier Division's Air Staff officer was Masatake Okumiya, one of Japan's greatest fighter pilots and most aggressive combat leaders. The more than one hundred planes of the carrier division flown from Truk to Rabaul strengthened the enemy's defenses considerably, bringing to over 300 the number available for the defense of Rabaul. And the carrier reinforcements flown in were the best of Japan's carrier fighter pilots.

American air attacks on Rabaul were continued throughout January, the enemy often sending up as many as seventy-five or a hundred defending fighters. American forces included fighters, dive bombers and torpedo and heavy bombers. The torpedo bombers concentrated on shipping in Simpson Harbor, and on some raids were highly successful in spite of the bitter opposition encountered. On January 17 five Japanese ships were sunk by SBD's and TBF's. The U.S. attackers lost twelve aircraft in the air battle, one a TBF which struck a Japanese ship after its torpedo run.

A week later, on January 24, another sizable force of torpedo bombers, escorted by fighters, attacked shipping in Simpson Harbor. The torpedo bombers carried 2,000-pound bombs, with delayed action fuses, and once again five Japanese ships were sunk. Just after this attack planes of the enemy's 2nd Carrier Division arrived at Rabaul.

Nevertheless, the continuing fierceness of the aerial assault, the success of the dive bombers and torpedo bombers, forced the enemy to withdraw most of his ships from Rabaul by the end of January.

It was in this month, in the intensified battle for Rabaul, that many of the top United States aces were shot down. Lieutenant Robert M. Hansen, U.S.M.C., credited with twenty-five kills, was killed in a crash pulling out of a strafing run on Cape St. George. Major Gregory Boyington, U.S.M.C., with twenty-two kills in the Pacific, was shot down off Rabaul, and taken prisoner.

One of World War II's great Navy aces, Lieutenant Ira C. Kepford, was among the handful of U.S. fighter pilots stationed on the newly won base at Bougainville at the time of the Rabaul offensive. Kepford and his comrades of VF 17 had been at Bougainville only a short time (they arrived January 24) when the assault on Rabaul reached its climax. Already VF had lost a number of its pilots in the battle, operating under far-from-ideal conditions.

Japanese troops were still sniping at the pilots from the jungle. The fliers were living in hastily assembled tents in a sea of mud. And under these conditions duty often consisted of two flights to Rabaul a day!

It was a grim contrast from Kepford's recent college days at Northwestern University, where he had joined the Navy. He had been blocking back on Northwestern's football team, and was inducted at half-time ceremonies during the Northwestern-Purdue game, in 1941.

At Bougainville the Muskegon, Michigan, athlete was confronted with living conditions far different from those of college life. Bougainville was the end of the American supply line, and American pilots had to make out with delicacies such as ram's tongue. Needless to say, the reaction of Navy pilots, who rated "chow" by carrier standards, was less than enthusiastic.

A captured Japanese fighter being examined by Marines at Kolombangara in the Solomons. (Navy Department Photo)

Bougainville was dusty and dirty—or rainy. It seemed always to be hot. The coral dust was a problem for pilots and crew chiefs, and caused trouble in the big engines of the F4U Corsairs, which VF 17 pilots were flying. Pilots wore only a pair of shorts, a summer flight suit, and tennis shoes.

In spite of these difficulties, VF 17 was to compile one of the outstanding records among fighter squadrons in World War II. And Kepford, the Northwestern halfback, was to emerge from his tour of duty the fifth-ranking World War II ace of the U.S. Navy.

His most memorable mission, and the one which almost cost him his life, was to occur on February 19, 1944. It is to that mission that we now turn our attention.

The duty officer shook Kepford awake early on Saturday morning, February 19. He was flying the day's first mission. He pulled on a light-weight flying suit and white tennis shoes. After a quick breakfast at the chow tent, he walked to the palm-surrounded briefing shack.

Leading the day's mission was the executive officer of VF 17, Lieutenant Commander Roger Hedrick, who conducted the briefing. Twenty planes would participate in the day's first mission, would strafe Rabaul and surrounding military installations. Hedrick expected Japanese fighter opposition to be heavy, especially since the Japanese had received reinforcements in recent days (the 2nd Carrier Division).

One of the targets to get particular attention was the concentration of antiaircraft guns on the volcanic slopes on the upper end of the harbor, and near Lajunai Field, which jutted into the harbor.

The weather officer forecast good weather. The squadron would be split into two groups, one to do the strafing and a smaller force of four fighters to act as top cover. Kepford was assigned to top cover.

An ammunition truck hustled Kepford to squadron headquarters, where a second briefing took place, to ensure close co-operation among the divisions of the squadron. After that, the ammo truck delivered pilots to their aircraft, each wearing a Mae West, pistol, and emergency medical kit—strapped under the left arm. (Parachutes were left overnight in the planes.)

Leading the four-fighter division which would act as top cover was Lieutenant Merle ("Butch") Davenport. Kepford had been Davenport's wingman but had graduated and was now second-in-command of the division, flying No. 3 position. Ensign Don ("Red") McQueen, of Chicago, was flying his wing.

The squadron's call name was "Hog," the leader of the flight was always "Big Hog." Kepford was flying F4U 29, and, therefore, was known on the radio that morning as "Hog 29."

The dark-blue Corsairs taxied out to the end of the runway and began taking off into a clear sky. Soon twenty F4U's were airborne, climbing at 170 knots over the hills and palms of Bougainville, course 320 degrees. It was 8:00 A.M., and the sun, behind, was rising, basking the ocean, to the left, in shimmering sunshine. The sun was so bright that,

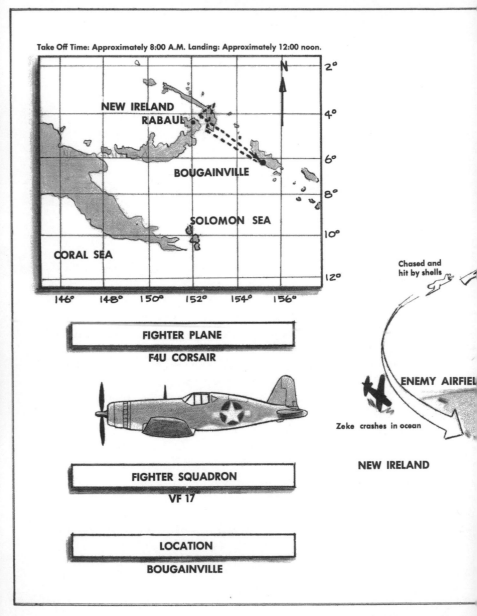

Take Off Time: Approximately 8:00 A.M. Landing: Approximately 12:00 noon.

NEW IRELAND
RABAUL

BOUGAINVILLE

SOLOMON SEA

CORAL SEA

N

2°
4°
6°
8°
10°
12°

146° 148° 150° 152° 154° 156°

FIGHTER PLANE

F4U CORSAIR

FIGHTER SQUADRON

VF 17

LOCATION

BOUGAINVILLE

Chased and
hit by shells

ENEMY AIRFIEL

Zeke crashes in ocean

NEW IRELAND

MISSION FLOWN BY:

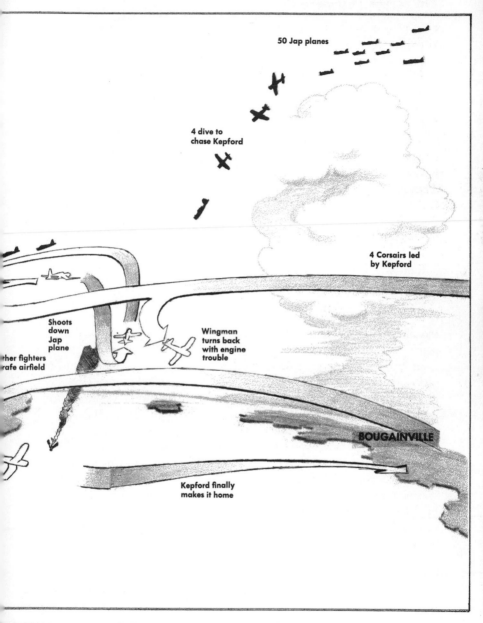

50 Jap planes

4 dive to
chase Kepford

4 Corsairs led
by Kepford

Shoots
down
Jap
plane

Wingman
turns back
with engine
trouble

ther fighters
rafe airfield

BOUGAINVILLE

Kepford finally
makes it home

LIEUTENANT IRA C. KEPFORD, USNR, FEBRUARY 19, 1944

looking backward, the sky was a blur. Ahead, a bright haze reduced visibility in the direction of Rabaul. The light painted the tips of the waves silver.

The squadron continued to climb into the northwest, blowers cutting in at 17,000 feet. Shortly the coast of New Britain appeared ahead, and pilots began to tense—for the attack was expected to precipitate a lively fight.

The Japanese had lost over 300 aircraft since the American aerial offensive against Rabaul had begun, in December, and while these were heavy losses, substantial reinforcements had arrived in recent days. They were capable of sending up a considerable interception force, which might already have been done—since they made good use of Bougainville coast watchers. The coast of New Britain, ahead and below, was now quite near.

Kepford glances at his wingman. Red McQueen is flying oddly. Kepford eyes his F4U closely. His engine is sputtering, puffs of white smoke shoot backwards from the stacks. The engine is running erratically; McQueen is falling behind, every so often, and unable to close the distance. Now Kepford eases back slightly, to look into his wingman's cockpit.

As he does, he can see McQueen motioning to him. He appears to be saying he thinks there's coral dust in the carburetor. He won't be able to continue to the target, must turn back! Worse, Kepford must turn back too—no singles are allowed to participate in attacks on Rabaul.

Hedrick is informed of the malfunction; Big Hog directs McQueen to return to the base. Kepford would have shepherded him home under normal circumstances. However, as the big blue Corsair turns away, and down, headed back for the American airfield on Bougainville, Kepford asks permission to accompany the bombers to the target area. McQueen, he feels, is in no danger of attack. Hedrick grants him permission to stay with the squadron, but only until it is over the target area. Now Kepford banks into position with Davenport and his wingman; the division is down to three planes. And this is the division to act as top cover.

The coast is below, the target just beyond. Kepford will stay until the last minute. He scans the sky in all directions, to see if anything is developing. The sky is apparently quiet, and now he must turn back. This is the target area.

He catches the attention of Davenport and his wingman, waggles his wings, and gives the traditional good-by kiss with his hand. Then he curves into a sweeping right turn, disappointed in being forced to abort from the mission only minutes before the strafing begins.

As he turns right, New Ireland, the long island above Rabaul and running northwest-southeast, lies straight ahead of him. Kepford, a lone American fighter in an area where many enemy fighters are likely to appear at any moment, just can't turn back and forget the whole thing. He will sneak over New Ireland, and see what's below. (Meanwhile, his comrades prepare to dive on Rabaul—in strafing runs on that air and naval base.)

Kepford is also interested in getting a few peeks at the Buka Island base of the enemy, just a few miles from the northern tip of Bougainville. Alone now, continuing to bank slowly to the right, Kepford constantly rotates his head right to left, behind, and up and down, searching the sky for bandits.

Throughout flight training, from the beginning as a cadet and all through the rest of his training and experience, instructors had drummed into every trainee's head the advantage of constantly scanning the sky. It is the cardinal rule for fighter pilots—the advantage lies with the pilot who spots the enemy first and has time to prepare an attack, or avoid one, as the circumstances dictate.

As Kepford looks around him, on all sides, vigilance is rewarded. Ahead, below right, Kepford's eye catches the motion of something moving just above the water. He looks more closely. A dark object . . . moving toward him, from one o'clock, just above the surface of the water.

It's an aircraft . . . a float plane. The silhouette is not American. Bandit! It's a single-engine enemy float plane, very large, dark, flying straight toward Kepford.

A quick glance behind him, and Kepford pushes the stick forward, slides off to the left slightly. He will use his superior altitude to execute a 180-degree turn to the right, as the enemy approaches below, and will dive straight down on him in a vertical pass. The enemy aircraft comes on, apparently completely unaware of Kepford's presence—a grave oversight. Kepford will wait until the enemy is about to cross under him, then roll over into the dive and, if all works well, will fire straight down, and the enemy pilot will fly into his line of fire.

The dark enemy silhouette comes on. The enemy is almost directly below. Kepford steps on right rudder and wings over into a vertical dive. The F4U dives with increasing velocity; Kepford eases back on the throttle. Now his gaze is fixed on the two yellow circles on the sighting glass. The enemy should appear at any moment, just above the cowling, flying into the Corsair's line of fire. Kepford's dive continues. Suddenly the dark silhouette streaks out from under the nose of the F4U, is in Kepford's sight circle. In range!

Kepford squeezes the trigger. Tracers streak straight down as the staccato of six guns violently shakes the Chance-Vought fighter. The enemy aircraft flies straight through the line of fire, the Corsair's guns ripping holes all along the top of the fuselage! Kepford is almost on top of him. The enemy floater is badly hit. No time to watch. Kepford must pull out—or hit the water. He yanks back on the stick, blood drains from his head, and his line of vision races forward over the ocean, the cowling once again pulling out in front of the stricken Japanese below.

The ocean rushes up, the Corsair curves through the bottom of its arc and levels off. Immediately Kepford glances back. The dark-colored enemy aircraft, banking slightly, is streaming smoke. In another second the Japanese smashes into the ocean! Kepford looks at the spot, easing back on the throttle (having gained tremendous speed in the dive) and sees a slick on the water. It was a quick victory.

He banks into a sweeping right turn, and heads south. He picks up the mike and presses the transmitter button: "Big Hog from Hog 29. Scratch one. Returning to base." As Kepford hauls back on the stick, to begin his climb on the return flight, he hears a reply over the radio: "Prove it!" He realizes, with chagrin, that no one has seen him down the enemy plane. Wing cameras are not reliable in conditions such as exist at Bougainville. Therefore, he may have no film to corroborate his victory claim.

His altimeter registers gains in the southward climb. He continues to search the sky in all directions, looks back in the direction of Squadron VF 17, can see nothing. He scans the sky behind; all clear. He looks right and left. He looks ahead, raises his head . . . and freezes!

Dots . . . above . . . many dots! His heart beats faster. The dots could be enemy fighters. If they are, they're between him and Bougainville, have a tremendous altitude advantage, and greatly outnumber him! The situation couldn't be worse. Kepford strains his eyes. There are at least ten, no, fifteen, twenty planes! He continues on course. The dots grow larger. Now there are thirty, forty dots! He must identify them. He studies the formation, the silhouettes. The fighters aren't friends . . . Zekes!

Kepford's only hope to escape enemy eyes is to be as unobtrusive as possible, and hope the enemy doesn't spot him. Pushing stick forward, throttle all the way forward, he noses down toward the waves, angling slightly away from the oncoming gaggle. The Zekes are now unmistakable in the bright sunshine, continue to fly straight ahead, as if they do not see him. Will his luck hold? Kepford nervously picks up the mike and radios VF 17: "Bogeys at five o'clock to your position!"

Hedrick immediately replies: "Where?" Kepford: "Repeat, five o'clock to your position."

There is suddenly no more time to talk. Four Zekes peel off and start down. Kepford knows he's been discovered. He can't take on the four, even if he would accept four-to-one odds. There are thirty-odd Zekes above, any one of which could get him in the end, since all have an altitude advantage. He'll run for it. He stands the F4U on its left wing—at full throttle—and turns away from the diving Zekes.

He's now headed north, away from his base. The big engine ahead roars, and sweeps him along over the waves . . . but the Zekes are gaining. Diving from considerable altitude, they are coming on fast. One is far ahead of the other three. He closes so fast he only has time for a short burst. Then he skids out in front . . . for an instant. Kepford opens fire at once. Hits register on the enemy's tail. He has shattered the Zeke's stabilizer! The Zeke falls off to the side. The other three Zekes spread out behind. Kepford sees one to his left, behind, and can see two off to the right, behind, all a dirty green.

They're boxing him in, to prevent him from turning back to the side. Whichever way he turns he will turn into one or more of the Zekes, who will have a shot at him. The Zekes continue to gain. Now tracers streak by on the right! The enemy fighters are already firing. His stomach feels weak; unless he can shake his pursuers he's certain to be splashed in minutes. He glances at the throttle quadrant. A copper wire and notch prevent the throttle from going farther. That copper wire is to be broken only in an emergency. It injects water into the engine, adds power, but lasts only minutes. This is an emergency! Kepford thrusts his left arm forward, the full weight of his body behind it. The copper wire breaks. The engine seems to pause, then screams, and Kepford can feel the extra surge of power. He knows it is temporary, but it is his only chance.

The F4U vibrates heavily, rockets across the coast and over the trees. Kepford is roaring northward across New Ireland, directly away from his base. The Jap pilots hang in there, close. He glances behind to the right, and then to the left. He can't be sure . . . whether they're still gaining. Tracers streak by his wing. Whump! Something slams into the Corsair from behind. They're definitely in range!

The engine howls and vibrates, the air-speed indicator registers a gradual increase. His wings waxed and polished, to give him a few extra knots, his engine on emergency power, Kepford is doing well over 300 knots straight and level. But the Japs stay in there, behind, as if they are tied on.

Whump! Whump! More hits. Kepford feels the Corsair shudder as a result of the hits. He's desperate . . . almost frantic. He zigzags in an effort to throw the enemy pilots' aim off. Ahead, he sees the water. He has crossed the island, is headed northwest. If he can't turn back soon, the chase can only end in his destruction or ditching.

He glances back again. The Zekes are still there. He can see three. But are they closing? He thinks not. He's holding his own! And they're no longer hitting him! He looks at the pad on his right knee, his navigation pad. He jots down the time and notes the amount of fuel remaining. He will fly on northwest a little longer, but soon he must turn back. It's impossible right now. The enemy is too close. A turn in either direction would bring him into the firing line of an enemy fighter, and with that advantage the enemy pilots would shoot him down. He will have to continue straight ahead, until he can lengthen the distance between them.

Earphones come to life. Big Hog is calling. Hedrick wants the position and direction of the Zekes!

"Still five o'clock from you," Kepford replies. Then he adds:

"Many bogeys—this looks like it!"

Hearing this call, other pilots of VF 17 realize Kepford is up against the wall. Many fear it may be his last transmission.

Kepford, too, is almost convinced his position is hopeless. He breaks out in a heavy sweat. Looking back, he can see the Zekes in almost the same position. The big Pratt and Whitney has been on emergency power for what seems like ages. That means his emergency power is about expended, after which he must turn into the enemy and give him a firing opportunity. His hands begin to tremble on the stick, his feet are jumping on the rudder bars.

For the first time in the war Kepford is completely racked with fear. He is trapped, getting farther and farther from his base every second. The engine now begins to heat up. It is throwing oil back over the canopy, a yellowish film. Engine gauges reflect higher and higher temperatures.

Strangely, seized with fear and shaking all over, perspiring heavier than ever before in his life, Kepford's thoughts flit back to the past. He thinks about his family, remembers seeing his mother's face. He thinks about his father, the day in the far-distant past when his father took away his air rifle.

His thoughts go back to the campus at Northwestern and to his brother, now a Marine sergeant. He thinks of friends, and then of Lieutenant Commander Tom Blackburn, the squadron commander.

His feet—in tennis shoes—are soaking wet. Kepford looks down groggily at his feet. The white Keds have turned green! For a moment he can't understand it. Can his tennis shoes really be green? They are. It puzzles him, even in the desperate situation. Then he realizes that perspiration from his body, so profuse, has completely discolored them!

He glances at his knee pad. The engine has just about spent its maximum power. He glances behind again. He double-checks. The enemy fighters are slightly farther behind. He is leaving them! The Corsair is widening the gap. The emergency power is too much for the enemy fighters.

But he must decide what to do next; his emergency power is giving out. He must turn one way or the other, and fight his way out. His engine gauges reflect the continuing strain on the engine, climb higher. Kepford hopes the high temperatures are only the result of emergency power. If any of the enemy's hits are responsible, the engine might quit at any moment.

Another glance behind. The Corsair is definitely stretching the distance. The two enemy fighters to the right are still in position, but farther back. So is the lone enemy fighter to the left, behind. Kepford begins to fake a little, to see if he can fool the Japanese. He banks slightly to the right, the enemy immediately following. Then he slips out of the turn as smoothly as possible. The Japanese take a moment longer to straighten out from their turns. They lose just a little in the game. Kepford fakes to the right again, and invisibly rudders left, sliding out of the turn unobtrusively. The Japanese lose just a little more ground, in the cat-and-mouse maneuver.

Kepford decides to ease back slightly on the throttle. He is out of firing range, and emergency power is used up. He comes back on the manifold pressure about two inches and the engine seems to run just a bit more smoothly. It is still rough and vibrating, however, and Kepford is shaking as much as the engine.

He must turn, and head for home. He can't fly north forever. He looks behind, decides to reverse course to the left. There are two enemy planes to the right, and if he turns right, they'll both be on him, cutting him off in the turn. To his left there is only one enemy plane. He will take his chances with one. Another consideration is the torque of his engine. It will enable him to turn left quicker than right, since he will be turning against the propeller. There also is the chance that one or more of the pilots behind him, opening fire in a turn, just above the waves, might not keep his eye on the water carefully enough and dip a wing into the sea. It will have to be a sudden, violent turn.

It is time to turn, now or never. He kicks left rudder hard, pulls the stick back into the sharpest turn his body can stand. The F4U stands vertically on its left wing and racks up a blood-draining arc to the left. Specks dance in front of his eyes; his vision dims—the first sign of a blackout. Vision grows dimmer. He pops the stick forward slightly, lessening the pull of gravity, and the blood flows back into his head just enough to regain vision.

Now he pulls the stick in again. The dull-green Zeke on the left, behind, follows, banking sharply in behind him. Twinkles appear on the leading edges of his wings. He has opened fire! Tracers streak by the banking F4U. The enemy pilot is attempting to turn inside him. The next few seconds will tell. Kepford holds the stick in, tracers shoot past

and out into the sky ahead. The Corsair shudders on the verge of a
stall as he racks it around.

The enemy pilot continues to fire, and to turn, only barely above the
tops of the waves. Kepford can see him out of the left corner of his
eye, guns winking fire. It is a tight spot. The Corsair is almost 180
degrees around. Now . . . a splash behind! The left wing of the enemy
fighter hits the water! The right wing comes on over . . . the enemy

A Japanese Jill torpedo bomber attacking a carrier. Aircraft was
destroyed shortly after this picture was taken. This is approximately
the altitude at which Kepford flew while trying to escape off Rabaul.
(Navy Department Photo)

fighter is cartwheeling! The Zeke's guns, continuing to fire, throw
tracers up into the sky, and all around. The enemy fighter literally
cartwheels along the surface of the ocean, its wings breaking off.

A wave of relief sweeps over Kepford. The enemy fighter which
should have shot him down in the turn has crashed into the sea. Kepford looks back. He can see the debris of the wrecked Zeke in the
water. The F4U is straight away, headed back for New Ireland again,
having successfully executed a 180-degree change of course.

Kepford looks to his left, and behind. Are the other two enemy fighters following? Apparently not. They're either staying behind, with their comrade in the sea, or realize they can't catch the Corsair. In the turn to the left Kepford has increased the distance from the two Zekes trailing him on the right.

Kepford looks at his fuel gauges. He must throttle back and lean the mixture if he is to make the base at Bougainville. He flies on for several minutes, constantly scanning the sky, almost limp as a result of the close call. He glances at the engine gauges. They're still in the red, but the engine runs surprisingly smoothly. He eases back a little more on the throttle.

Up ahead, on the horizon, he sees the shore of New Ireland. If he can get safely over the island, he'll feel more secure.

Meanwhile, back at the base on Bougainville the other pilots of VF 17 have landed. The word is being passed: The last thing heard from Kepford was an excited transmission that many bogeys were attacking him, and that that looked like it.

The airstrip resembles a T, the strip itself being crossed by a taxiway. Where the taxiway crosses the runway is a large tree, and under it sits Kepford's crew chief, Moore, and his ordnance man, Dineen. They sit there, waiting, in spite of suggestions from other crewmen that they give up No. 29 as lost. Kepford is long overdue, he had been heard transmitting that last, desperate message. There's no point in sitting there dragging it out—they're told. But Moore keeps repeating:

"Mr. Kepford will get back."

Kepford roars over the coast of New Ireland, headed southeast. He is crossing the island, low, on the tops of the palm trees. His main worry now is fuel. Emergency power (full throttle) has used up a tremendous amount of fuel. He has the mixture control on very lean position, which causes the engine to run rough and hot. Kepford figures he has less than a fifty-fifty chance to make it back to Bougainville. However, the engine is running, and there is nothing to do but try.

Now he is approaching the opposite shore of New Ireland. The blue Solomon Sea is ahead, and just 200 miles away the base! Minutes seem to drag by. The sun is still bright, and everything at the moment is a strange anticlimax.

The Corsair grinds along, over the Solomon Sea, the loud roar of the engine becoming monotonous. The sky is clear and the white glare of the sun almost blinding; Kepford is flying into it, on his return.

There is no radio chatter, the other pilots have long ago landed at the base. Kepford is alone in a blue sky that arches over him on all sides, in brilliant sunshine, as he flies battered No. 29 homeward, low on gas, and almost in a complete daze.

Up ahead, Bougainville! The long island at last is in view. Kepford's gasoline is dangerously low, but he thinks now maybe he'll make it. He is staying to the right of enemy positions on Buka and northern Bougainville, will turn slightly left shortly, to approach the U.S. base on the western coast, approximately halfway down the long island.

After what seems a long interval Kepford catches sight of Empress Augusta Bay! He has only a few gallons of fuel left. The airfield is not far away but he has been unable to contact the tower, by radio, and no one knows he is approaching. Therefore he must circle the base and get the green light from the tower, clearing him to land.

He is just over the water and approaches the base from the sea. He circles left. Down below he can see the airstrip. He can see activity on the base, though no planes seem to be taking off. He continues a slow left turn, and now, from the tower, he sees a green light. It is just in time. He doesn't have enough fuel to tarry. He drops wheels, turns onto the base leg, and then turns another 90 degrees onto the approach. He slows the big Corsair to about 100 knots, eases back on the stick, and waits for her to bump the dusty runway. She bumps and settles and rolls, Kepford keeping her straight with rudder. He slows enough to taxi, and approaches the intersection of the runway and taxi strip—and the big tree.

Kepford is acting mainly on instinct, being almost completely dazed. His crew chief and armorer are up and staring at the Corsair, slowing to a normal taxiing speed. They recognize No. 29, dash for the battered gull-winged F4U and jump on the wings. Moore looks Kepford in the eye with a grin and gives him "thumbs up." Kepford doesn't have it in him to reply with a similar gesture. He is shaking all over as the tremendous tension begins to run out. Tears are streaming from his eyes.

The two crewmen notice holes in the wing, in the flaps, and through the elevators. Watching Kepford, they realize he has been through a considerable emotional strain, try not to make him self-conscious. As

Kepford taxis mechanically to his revetment, and cuts switches, a few friends and fellow pilots race up to the battered Corsair.

Kepford climbs from the cockpit, weak, shaky, and suffering from shock. He hardly recognizes fellow pilots as he walks to the squadron tent. The skipper and the flight surgeon, Lieutenant Lyle Herrmann, meet him at the squadron tent. A glance at Kepford, and Blackburn knows he is in no condition to be interrogated.

The skipper orders all other personnel, including pilots, out of the tent. Kepford insists on telling the intelligence officer what happened, though Blackburn and Herrmann urge him to relax.

Herrmann pours him four ounces of medicinal brandy, but Kepford is still in a state of shock. Herrmann insists that he take two large pills, and Kepford takes them. The flight surgeon also insists that Kepford get something in his stomach. He is given fried meat and coffee.

Then, still early in the afternoon, Kepford—exhausted physically and emotionally—is put to bed.

He slept all that afternoon, that night and most of the next day. And when he awoke, his tennis shoes were still green!

Though Kepford could not know it at the time, his sighting of the large formation of enemy fighters, just off New Ireland, was one of the last such spectacles of its kind to be observed by American pilots at Rabaul. The last day the Japanese scrambled a major force of fighters to oppose the American aerial offensive, which had begun in December, was February 19, when fifty enemy fighters intercepted American torpedo planes, dive bombers, F4U's, P-40's and F6F's.

The American pilots exacted a heavy toll—shooting down twenty-three Japanese planes. Next day remnants of the decimated fighter forces at Rabaul were withdrawn to Truk, where, ironically, carrier pilots of Task Force 58 had just wrecked over three hundred Japanese planes—intended reinforcements for Rabaul.

The Americans did not immediately realize that the Japanese had pulled back the bulk of their fighter strength from Rabaul, that the important enemy complex of bases was virtually abandoned, and that the long and bitter aerial struggle had been won.

The Japanese lost approximately four hundred aircraft in their defense of Rabaul, not counting the more than three hundred knocked out at Truk.

The battle had not been as costly for the Americans, though it had cost this country some of its greatest aces (and had almost cost the life of Lieutenant Ira Kepford). One of the most significant results of the victory at Rabaul was the impression it left on Japanese pilots, and on the air staffs. The strain on the higher staff officers at Rabaul was almost unbearable, as they saw the weight of the American attack increase, almost day by day, and witnessed the futility of Japanese resistance.

Despite the most strenuous efforts and the commitment of carrier fleet pilots, it became apparent to Japanese fliers that even their country's best Army and Navy squadrons couldn't stop the crushing American day-and-night aerial offensive. To many, the tremendous weight of the American attack, the increasing numbers of U.S. planes seen, the improved performance of the American aircraft, convinced them the war was lost.

One Japanese air staff officer who served at Rabaul, Masatake Okumiya, has written that when the battle was finally over it was clear to the Japanese who had watched it from the beginning that a great gap existed between the industrial potential of Japan and the industrial potential of America. This produced a growing spirit of defeatism, reaching into the highest military circles. The Rabaul air battle, more than any other fighter battle fought from land bases during the war, broke the back of Japanese air power.

The once-powerful Japanese bastion at Rabaul was to be bypassed. In February, with Rabaul in its death throes, New Zealand infantry landed on Green Island, little more than a hundred miles from Rabaul itself. On March 6 a 5,000-foot coral airstrip was completed on Green, and a week later American fighters arrived.

On March 20 the 4th Marine Regiment landed on Emirau Island, in the St. Matthias Group, northwest of Rabaul. This completed the encirclement of the vulnerable Japanese base and cut it off from Truk, more than six hundred miles to the north.

Thereafter the mighty Japanese air and naval base, from which so many fleets had sailed toward Guadalcanal in that bitter campaign, and from which so many heavy air raids had been mounted against the Americans in the Solomons, slowly strangled to death.

Kepford's use of water injection, for an extra burst of power, was one of the earliest demonstrations of the value of this device. Shortly afterward, in May of 1944, the Navy issued a release to the press entitled: "Top-Scoring Navy Fighter Pilot Credits Water-Injection Device on Plane's Engine with Saving His Life."

The Navy had only recently obtained the water-injection device (the Army Air Forces also utilized it) and there was still some debate over its merits at the time of Kepford's memorable flight. The hair-raising experience the native of Harvey, Illinois, came back to relate, as a result of water injection, was therefore eagerly awaited confirmation of its value.

The Navy described Kepford's historic use of water injection as follows:

> The twenty-five-year-old pilot, whose home is in Muskegon, Michigan . . . found himself in a position that is a nightmare to every combat pilot.
>
> He was only fifty feet over the water and three Zekes were close on the tail of his plane—two on the right, astern, and one on the left. If he pulled up, he would be at the mercy of the Zekes; the same if he turned right or left.
>
> . . . It was then that the pilot flicked the water-injection switch. The resulting spurt of speed carried him far enough ahead so that he left the streaks of tracers. . . .

Kepford ended the war with seventeen confirmed aerial victories. He was awarded two Navy Crosses, the Silver Star, three Distinguished Flying Crosses, and the Air Medal. On the day of his memorable mission the U.S. fighters attacking Rabaul caused considerable damage and suffered negligible losses.

The Navy's fifth-ranking fighter ace was discharged from the Navy shortly after the war ended, in 1945, and married Esther M. Kraegel, of Superior, Wisconsin.

In search of a job, he answered a newspaper advertisement of the Rexall Drug Company. The company, after giving him various tests, hired him. Today he is president of the eastern division of the company, in Stamford, Connecticut, and also president of the Liggett Drug Company. He is one of the top fighter aces who has disproved the phony theory that war heroes seldom amount to much.

PART *3*

THE U.S. CARRIER OFFENSIVE AND VICTORY

7 Hellcat at the Turkey Shoot

JUNE 19, 1944:

Lieutenant (j.g.) ALEXANDER VRACIU, U.S.N.R.

ONE of the Navy's greatest days in World War II was June 19, 1944, the date of the now legendary "Marianas Turkey Shoot" when U.S. Navy fighters and antiaircraft gunners of the ships of Task Force 58 shot down 346 enemy aircraft.

These were fighters, dive bombers and torpedo bombers from a Japanese fleet that included six carriers, the first time the enemy had committed his main fleet to battle since the Battle of Midway, two years earlier. It had been provoked into action by the U.S. invasion of Saipan, in the Marianas.

The resulting battle is known as the First Battle of the Philippine Sea and is still the subject of controversy. Although the Japanese lost three carriers, and other ships, and almost four hundred aircraft, some believe Task Force 58 could have won a greater victory—and destroyed most of the enemy's fleet.

The critical decision of the battle was whether the massive U.S. fleet protecting the amphibious operation at Saipan should have steamed west to meet the enemy (whose approach was known) sooner than it did. On the night of June 18, as a result of submarine sightings and a radio intercept, Admiral Marc A. Mitscher, commanding U.S. carriers aboard *Lexington,* proposed to turn his ships west, to bring them within 200 miles of the enemy by 5:00 A.M. on the 19th.

That would have allowed the potent U.S. carrier force to strike the enemy a devastating blow that morning. However, the decision of Admiral Raymond A. Spruance, over-all commander of the fleet, was that the carriers should remain close to the landings on Saipan, the protection of which was the fleet's primary obligation. This was the safe course to follow and Spruance's decision has been supported in most of the postwar memoirs and evaluations by the Navy's highest officers.

Nonetheless, in retrospect, knowing what we know now, it is probable that, had Mitscher been allowed to steam west on the night of the 18th, the result would have been the most spectacular carrier victory of the war, on the 19th.

As it turned out, carriers of Task Force 58 found themselves waiting for the enemy's air attack on the morning of the 19th—an attack which developed on schedule and resulted in a great defensive victory—the above-mentioned "Turkey Shoot."

One can readily understand Mitscher's desire to close with the approaching enemy fleet on the night of the 18th. He and then Captain Arleigh Burke, who, also aboard *Lexington,* shared Mitscher's sentiments, had read reports of Japanese fleet movements with growing anticipation. At last the enemy's main fleet had come out, and if Task Force 58 could utterly devastate it in full engagement, the war might be appreciably shortened.

As it turned out, the Japanese fleet, or most of it, managed to escape and was left to fight another day. It came out in full strength, for the next and last time, in the Battle of Leyte Gulf, in October, of which we will hear more about in the chapter involving the Navy's highest-scoring fighter ace of the war, Commander David McCampbell.

The enemy had ample military justification for committing his fleet in June—in an effort to smash the U.S. invasion of the Marianas. The Marianas are part of a chain of islands which stretch almost due south of Tokyo for over a thousand miles. They are the steppingstones to the south, to the great naval base at Truk, and to the Carolines. In the hands of an enemy, they would provide air bases and a staging area for further advances north, up the island ladder to Japan itself.

Saipan was the first U.S. invasion target in the Marianas. Guam and Tinian were to follow. The following year, as the island-hopping march toward Tokyo continued, Iwo Jima, to the north in the Volcano Islands would similarly be invaded, and six Marines would earn immortality by raising the flag on Mount Suribachi, on February 23, 1945.

The invasion of the Marianas, in 1944, was viewed by the Japanese as a critical test for the Imperial Navy. The commander in chief, Admiral Soemu Toyoda, had decided, before the landings on Saipan began, to commit the Japanese fleet if the Marianas were invaded. Opinions in higher echelons of the U.S. Navy were divided—as to whether or not the enemy fleet would make an all-out stand in the Marianas.

On June 13 the U.S. submarine *Redfin* reported heavy enemy fleet movements into the Sulu Sea. Two days later coast watchers in the Philippines reported a major enemy fleet, composed of battleships and carriers, headed toward San Bernardino Strait. Another submarine report confirmed this, and still another told of another fleet 200 miles east of Surigao Strait—apparently heading for the Marianas. The last two submarine reports, from *Flying Fish* and *Seahorse,* were instrumental in convincing Mitscher the Japanese were committing their fleet.

As a result of the impending fleet action, the invasion of Guam—scheduled for the 18th—was postponed, and Mitscher's carrier force was beefed up by the addition of ships from the actual landing operation at Saipan and by the recall of carrier forces then raiding enemy airfields on the Volcano and Bonin islands.

By the night of the 17th-18th, it was clear the enemy fleet was steaming toward Saipan, and when, in the early morning hours of the 18th, Burke awoke Mitscher to inform him of the latest submarine report from *Cavalla,* to that effect, Mitscher concluded a carrier strike might be possible late that afternoon if Task Force 58 proceeded west immediately.

But the dangers involved in leaving the vicinity of the largest amphibious operation of the war, and in risking a night engagement, were considered too great by Spruance and Admiral Willis Augustus Lee, commanding the battleship force. Even that night, when Pacific Fleet Commander Chester Nimitz reported that monitoring stations had picked up a broadcast from the Japanese fleet commander, Admiral

Jisaburo Ozawa, indicating the enemy's fleet was now 355 miles to the west-southwest, Task Force 58 was not ordered to close the distance.

And so it was that dawn on the 19th of June found the massive naval force of Task Force 58, comprising some fifteen carriers and an estimated 900 aircraft, waiting expectantly for an attack from the enemy's approaching carriers. It was to come, that day, as expected.

On flying duty aboard *Lexington,* Mitscher's flagship, was a fighter pilot destined to end the war as the Navy's fourth-ranking fighter ace, Lieutenant (j.g.) Alexander Vraciu, of East Chicago, Indiana.

Vraciu had been a flying enthusiast before enlisting in the Navy. He qualified for a civilian pilot's license before joining the service in June of 1941—just six months before Pearl Harbor. Within a month of the country's entry into the war, the Navy ordered him to Corpus Christi for flight training as an aviation cadet.

But it was to be almost two years before Vraciu would shoot down his first enemy aircraft, in October of 1943. He completed cadet flight training in August of 1942, two months after the Battle of Midway and at the onset of the long struggle for Guadalcanal, but he was not sent overseas at that time.

Instead, he went to Melbourne, Florida, for further flight instruction in carrier flying. It was in 1943 that he was ordered to San Diego and shipped out from that bustling World War II port for combat duty. He was fortunate in being assigned to the wing of the late Lieutenant Commander Edward H. ("Butch") O'Hare, skipper of Fighting Squadron 3. At Wake Island, on October 5, Vraciu shot down his first enemy plane and on another mission at this time he helped sink a Japanese tanker— winning air medals for both actions.

But the enemy caught up with O'Hare. An enemy bomber got him at night, and for Vraciu O'Hare's death was a bitter blow. He had learned his flying and fighting trade from O'Hare, whom he admired in many ways and on whose wing he had flown. Vraciu reacted intensely to O'Hare's death; he resolved to shoot down ten of the enemy for Butch. From then on he hated as few fighter pilots did, and was out to repay the debt. He paid the largest installment during the Marianas Turkey Shoot on June 19, 1944, about which we shall now learn.

Pilots aboard *Lexington* had been aware of the impending battle for days. They had been disappointed when *Lexington* and other Task Force carriers did not steam west during the night of the 18th, toward the approaching enemy fleet, in order to launch a dawn strike. No strike went off next morning. And search planes had found nothing. It was nine o'clock.

Vraciu was one of twelve VF 16 fighter pilots on the alert. The squadron commander, Lieutenant Commander Paul Buie, would lead any scramble, Vraciu leading the second division (the second four-plane unit). But there had already been an aerial battle that morning. Japanese fighters based on Guam swarmed into the air at approximately 7:15. They were met by fighters from *Belleau Wood,* orbiting above Guam for that very purpose, and by fighters scrambled by other carriers. The score had been impressive: thirty-five enemy aircraft had been destroyed for the loss of one Hellcat! It was an omen of bigger things to come.

Though search planes had not located the Imperial fleet, it was nevertheless within range and had already launched an all-out strike at the U.S. fleet. At approximately 9:50 radar screens on various ships began to reflect the images of a large raid. At four minutes past ten, general quarters was sounded aboard *Lexington,* and as the warning bell sounded throughout the ship, Vraciu and the other pilots on alert dashed for their fighters. There was no question about it. This was it.

On the flight deck the scene was action in color. Engines were beginning to roar as plane handlers in blue hurried chores. Plane directors were dressed in yellow, hookmen in green, chockmen in purple, fire fighters in red, and there were two monsters in asbestos suits. It was, as Theodore Taylor so ably described it in *The Magnificent Mitscher,* "controlled frenzy."

In a few minutes Buie was roaring off the end of *Lexington,* now plowing through the sea at close to 30 knots, into the wind. After Buie had cleared, and three others, Vraciu, making an "end" speed of 90 knots, pulled back on the stick and dragged the F6F off the end of the flight deck.

Soon the twelve F6F's from *Lexington* were climbing into the west, Buie far out front and the others strung out behind. Vraciu had difficulty keeping up; his engine was throwing oil and Buie had a new engine, which could outperform his own. The skipper was going hell-for-leather for the enemy, as he should have been, but he was pulling away from Vraciu in the process.

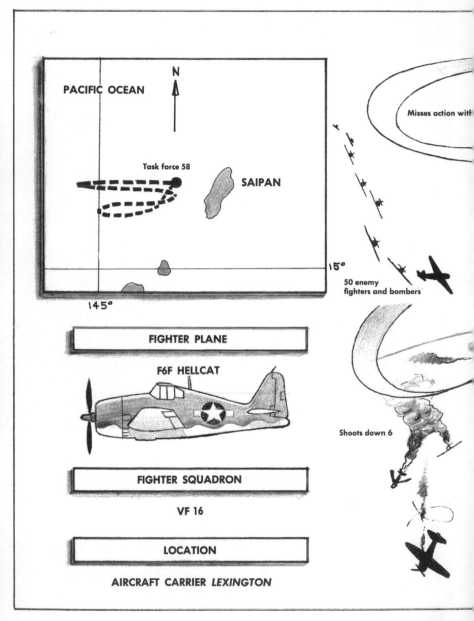

PACIFIC OCEAN

N

Task force 58

SAIPAN

Misses action with

50 enemy
fighters and bombers

15°

145°

FIGHTER PLANE

F6F HELLCAT

Shoots down 6

FIGHTER SQUADRON

VF 16

LOCATION

AIRCRAFT CARRIER *LEXINGTON*

MISSION FLOWN B

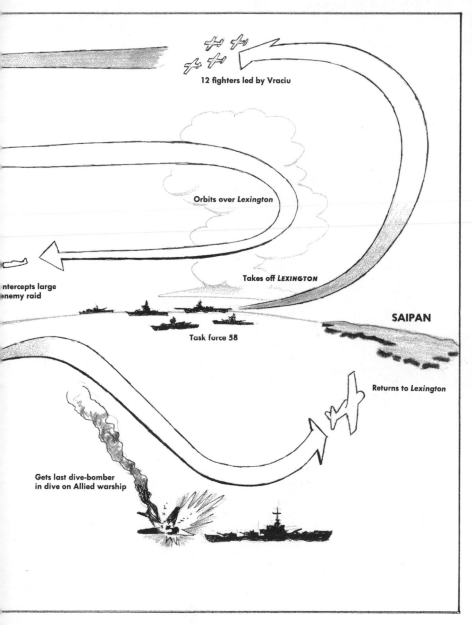

12 fighters led by Vraciu

Orbits over *Lexington*

Takes off *LEXINGTON*

Intercepts large
enemy raid

SAIPAN

Task force 58

Returns to *Lexington*

Gets last dive-bomber
in dive on Allied warship

EUTENANT (J.G.) ALEXANDER VRACIU, USNR, JUNE 19, 1944

Apparently some of the other Hellcats couldn't keep pace either. Vraciu noticed the skipper had lost his wingman, and several others were dropping back. He found himself with several additional fighters, which gave him six in all. Buie pulled away steadily, out front, as the fighters of many carriers streaked into the west, the morning sun at their backs.

An F6F Hellcat fighter getting the launching officer's signal to take off from the deck of U.S.S. Lexington. *(Official U.S. Navy Photo)*

The sky was full of contrails. It was a clear day, with a westerly wind and a bright sun as the blue-gray F6F's bit their way up into the higher altitudes. Radar scanners had indicated the enemy's altitude at 24,000 feet, and the defending fighters were straining to reach that height. First reports had indicated the enemy was 100 miles west, bearing 260 degrees.

At this moment the first interception of the enemy was made, not by *Lexington* fighters, but by those of Commander David McCampbell's VF 15, from *Essex*. (During the day this squadron destroyed over sixty enemy aircraft.) After the first interceptions there was a lull in the battle.

Vraciu, meanwhile, had seen no enemy planes and no action. He now experienced trouble with his supercharger. As he reached 20,000 feet and attempted to put the engine in high blower, it cut out every time he pushed the throttle handle forward.

Dismayed, and disappointed because he had been unable to intercept the enemy, Vraciu reported to the fighter director aboard *Lexington*. He was ordered to orbit near the carrier with his six fighters. The F6F's circled their floating base in a wide arc, and waited. Vraciu had time to check his instruments, guns and gunsight. The engine gauges were normal. The engine was smooth and running cool, though it wouldn't shift into high blower. Vraciu could see other fighters orbiting above other ships in the distance. He continued circling . . . for ten, twenty, twenty-five minutes.

Another large enemy air armada is now on the way, unknown to Vraciu at the moment. Aboard *Lexington,* below, the radar screen detects the ominous spots. Suddenly, as the F6F's orbit above *Lexington,* the fighter director breaks in over the radio: "Vector 265!" Vraciu knows by the tone of voice that this is something big.

He banks into a 265-degree heading and quickly pushes the handles which charge his six 50-caliber guns. He checks the gunsight, which is operating properly, and glances behind to see if his comrades are in proper formation. To the side he can see other Hellcats pointed in the direction he is flying, obviously vectored by other carriers to the bogeys approaching from the west.

For ten minutes the Hellcats streak westward . . . down below fighter directors warn the enemy gaggle is very close. Vraciu estimates he is twenty-five miles west of *Lexington*. At that instant he sees them! Three unidentified specks in the sky ahead! "Tally-ho!" he yells into the mike. He is not sure of the identity of the three strangers. They're slightly below the Hellcats ahead. And this can't be the enemy armada.

Vraciu, known for keen eyesight, scans the sky, up and down. The three specks are ten miles in the distance. He looks all around them, then he takes a long look at the air space beneath them. Faintly . . . specks . . . dots . . . a mass of dots! It must be fifty. Vraciu again calls in over the mike: "Tally-ho, eleven o'clock low!"

Now the tempo of events picks up. Other carrier interceptors spot the Japanese and rush to meet them. The enemy planes are dangerously close to the U.S. carriers. There is not a minute to lose.

Nerves tingle as the Hellcat pilots watch the silhouettes of the oncoming enemy planes grow larger and larger. They come closer and closer and still the two opposing forces continue on converging courses; the Americans want to intercept as far away from ships of the fleet as possible. Vraciu is so close he can see that the enemy planes are painted a light color, not the usual dirty greenish-brown. There are Judys, Jills and Zeroes in the enemy gaggle . . . dive bombers, torpedo bombers and fighters! He reports this to *Lexington*.

Japanese Navy's Raiden fighter (Jack), which made its debut in the battle for the Marianas. (Official U.S. Navy Photo)

Now the distance between the several groups of Hellcats and the big enemy formation closes and the Hellcats begin to rack into tight turns as they arrive overhead and prepare to make deflection or six-o'clock passes on the enemy planes, which are at about 17,000 feet.

Vraciu spots one of the enemy planes off to the side. He stands on his left wing and carves an arc, reversing his course, and rolls out on an approach from the rear port quarter of the enemy. He checks the sky above for the three enemy fighters; they're nowhere in sight.

The big gaggle is so close to the fleet every Hellcat races to a target and the sky is soon filled with individual actions. Now the enemy aircraft ahead is almost in range of Vraciu's guns. But . . . off to the right, another Hellcat, moving up on the enemy's tail! Vraciu has spotted him just in time. The two pursuers are on converging courses! Vraciu slaps his stick right and down. The Hellcat sticks its nose down and with added speed roars beneath most of the enemy aircraft. Vraciu pulls clear, and turns back toward the melee.

He sees a Judy to the left of the enemy gaggle and slices in behind, pouring on throttle and closing the gap fast. This time he is determined to get the job done; the Judy widens in his gunsight glass and the victim ahead comes within range. Vraciu's finger is on the trigger. His canopy is smeared with oil, his vision obstructed, and he wants to make sure of this one. He is on him. . . . 300 feet, 200!

Now! He squeezes the trigger. The shock and thunder of the Hellcat's six guns silence the engine. Shells converge into such a close pattern that the Judy immediately begins to fly to pieces. Vraciu has only a second or two left, being so close. The F6F's guns throw a murderous stream of shells into the Judy's fuselage.

It's too much. The dive bomber in the sight circle erupts in a fiery explosion. Vraciu manages to steer clear of the smoke and bits of wreckage. In the excitement he shouts into the mike, triumphantly: "Splash one Judy!"

But the enemy is close to the fleet. No time is to be lost. Vraciu pulls the stick into his belly and back out and then back in. He clears his tail and then picks out two more Judys flying side by side. He will make another dead-astern approach. And this time he will try to knock down two on one pass. Checking the sky behind, and finding his tail clear, he dips the stick and starts down on the enemy gaggle, now so low that some of the dive and torpedo bombers are letting down in preparation for the attack on the fleet.

The air is full of calls and shouts, as other F6F's maneuver desperately to knock the enemy planes out of the sky before they can deliver their bomb loads on the U.S. carriers. The Judys and Jills, meanwhile, seek to avoid the U.S. fighters so they can carry out their attack.

The two Judys ahead fly on. Vraciu will first close the one on the right. He rams the throttle all the way forward. The big Hellcat roars and steps up on the Judys from behind. The rear gunner this time sees the F6F approach, however, and twinkles from his 7.7 machine gun catch Vraciu's eye. Responding, Vraciu opens with his six guns. The rear gunner continues his fire but the accuracy and volume of Vraciu's shooting immediately dooms the Judy, which staggers and begins to fall off on the right wing.

Vraciu keeps up the fire. A long trail of black smoke stretches backward. As the second victim wings over, the Jap gunner in the rear cockpit is still firing away. He goes down still firing; the burning Judy plunges to the sea at the bottom of a vertical column of smoke. Without a moment's hesitation, Vraciu slips left, with left rudder and stick, and is on the other.

The battle everywhere is fast and furious. Two enemy torpedo bombers reach *Lexington* at this time, drop torpedoes intended for Mitscher's flagship. *Lexington* nimbly dodges them. But *South Dakota* and *Indiana*, in the battleship force farther west, are not so lucky. *South Dakota* takes a bomb and *Indiana* receives a suicider.

But most of the Japanese planes have failed to penetrate the fighter defense. Vraciu is working on victim No. 3 as the battle reaches a climax. Following up his second kill, he is now within firing range of the third Judy, to the left. A short burst produces quick results; the Judy instantly catches fire. Flames and smoke streak backward.

Vraciu follows with another short burst at point-blank range, and watches the burning enemy bomber wobble out of formation and take the fatal dive. Three victories in a matter of minutes! But the attackers continue on course. Vraciu takes time to radio *Lexington*: "Don't see how we can possibly shoot 'em all down. Too many!"

With that sentiment he plunges back into the fray. He had pulled up to radio *Lexington;* now he leans forward in a dive at a fourth Judy!

The Judy ahead is breaking away from the formation. Vraciu curves in behind him, once again closing from the rear. Neither the enemy pilot nor the tail gunner seems to have caught sight of the F6F swooping down from the rear. In seconds, Vraciu is only several hundred feet behind his fourth victim. Carefully lining him up in the gunsight circle, Vraciu again squeezes the trigger.

The effect of his fire is even more devastating than before. The Judy immediately bursts into flame and wobbles wildly to the right. Victory No. 4! It is deadly accurate gunnery. Out the side of his eye Vraciu sees most of the Judys pulling to one side or the other, preparing for runs on the ships of the fleet, now clearly visible ahead and below. The Jills, down low, begin shallow glides, preparing to drop torpedoes at selected targets. Vraciu immediately turns away from his fourth burning victim, now out of control. With full throttle he points his nose at three Judys about to wing over into dive-bombing runs on a ship below.

Vraciu wonders if he can reach the three in time. The distance is short, but the first of the three Judys is almost over the ship target ahead. The Pratt and Whitney strains, and the F6F steadily closes. The blue-gray Hellcat is on the last of the Judys, but the first is over the target.

Five-inch flak begins to dot the sky as Vraciu readies his aim to open fire on the third plane. He squeezes the trigger. Aim is accurate. Shells instantly strike the Judy and, as he closes the distance, pieces of the dive bomber's engine fly backward. As the fifth victim disintegrates, he can see the first of the three Judys diving on a big ship below.

Still at full throttle, he banks away from the fiercely burning Judy and aims at the second in the three-bomber formation. Down below, Vraciu sees the first Judy still diving. The Judy ahead now wings over into his dive-bombing run on a destroyer. Vraciu stands on a wing and starts down after him. He'll risk antiaircraft fire, in an effort to bring down the dive bomber in a vertical dive. It's a dangerous feat.

The wind screams as the big F6F plunges straight down at ever-increasing speed. Ahead, the diving Judy is zeroing in on the U.S. destroyer. Vraciu sees five-inch bursts all around him, and as the altitude decreases the flak gets thicker. He will have to finish the job in seconds. The heavy fighter rockets straight down. He is rapidly overtaking the Judy. At terrific speed, he glances through the gunsight glass and waits . . . seconds. Now! The F6F's guns thunder and tracers streak straight down into the enemy dive bomber. Vraciu hangs on for a few seconds, wondering how long he can fire. At that instant he blinks at a bright explosion—where the Judy had been. The enemy's bomb must have detonated. Vraciu yanks back on the stick, blood draining from his head, and pulls out of the screaming dive.

As he levels out, and draws away from the destroyer, he glances behind to see what's happening below. The first Judy in the formation is now directly over a U.S. battleship, farther away. Vraciu watches, frozen, to see if the enemy pilot will succeed in crashing into the battle wagon. He picks up the mike and radios *Lexington*: "Splash No. Six! One more dive bomber ahead—diving on a battleship." However, the curtain of iron thrown up by the battleship's antiaircraft guns explodes the dive bomber. A bright flash at a thousand feet! Vraciu breathes a sigh of relief.

Climbing for altitude again, he scans the sky for other enemy planes. Almost miraculously, the sky seems completely cleared of the enemy. In every direction he sees only Hellcats. The enemy formation has been received by the fighters of many carriers.

Still, there must be some of the enemy left; Vraciu looks down on the surface below to see if any Jills are closing the ships just above the water. He can find no enemy planes, either directly on the water or in the sky in any direction. The big enemy gaggle has been wiped out, probably to the last plane. Vraciu himself hasn't done badly: six dive bombers and twelve enemy airmen sent to a watery grave. This was a day Butch O'Hare would appreciate!

On board the carriers below, radar screens show the sky cleared of enemy aircraft. Judys attacked *Lexington, Enterprise* and *Princeton,* but all escaped injury. The fleet is in good condition. Losses suffered by the enemy are staggering. The air battle had raged up and down the line of ships, and the attackers were slaughtered as in no other interception of the war.

Jubilation reigns aboard many of the ships as Vraciu turns toward *Lexington,* the sky now clear, and prepares to land. Some pilots are already putting down on their carriers. Many have great tales to tell. Air Group 15, aboard *Essex,* destroyed more than sixty aircraft. VF 16, from *Lexington,* accounted for forty-four, for a loss of four. Vraciu's total of six is high for the squadron.

Now Vraciu is approaching from his assigned sector, and as he reaches the outer screen of ships around *Lexington,* American antiaircraft gunners open fire on him.

Startled, Vraciu jinxes immediately, turns away from the fire. His "IFF" is operating normally. Why have the ships fired on him? IFF is a radar device designed to identify him as a friendly aircraft. Rather than take further chances, Vraciu detours around the fire, and heads straight for *Lexington.* Over the radio he offers some philosophy to the antiaircraft gunners—too strong for print.

Soon he is approaching *Lexington,* which plows through the seas into the wind, undamaged, taking aboard Hellcats. Vraciu prepares to come down, circling to the left, banking into the landing approach, tail hook extended. He is now to be the center of one of the great human-interest moments of the war. Ahead, the landing signal officer gives him the "cut," and Vraciu pulls throttle back all the way, feels himself settling toward deck. The oil-spattered fighter bangs the deck, bounces, and then the tail hook engages. Vraciu is snapped to a stop. The cable is disengaged. He taxies to the parking area, canopy back, looking up toward the bridge, a grin on his wind-blown face. Mitscher looks down from the bridge. Vraciu holds up six fingers. Mitscher gets the message.

Vraciu cuts the engine, unbuckles belt and harness, and climbs out on the wing. His crew chief and other deck personnel rush to his side. They beam when he relates how the six enemy aircraft had fallen before his guns. Another well-wisher hurries up to the twenty-five-year-old ace. It is the small, tanned face of Marc Mitscher that catches Vraciu's eye.

A smoking Hellcat landing safely aboard Lexington *after an air battle.* (Official U.S. Navy Photo)

By now, photographers and other pilots are crowding around. Mitscher comes right up to Vraciu and congratulates him personally for flaming six Japs. He shakes the smiling pilot's hand feelingly, then steps to one side. Vraciu answers questions for the others.

The photographers go to work, and Vraciu's "flight of six" becomes history. Comparatively unnoticed, to the side, Mitscher enjoys the scene. Then, embarrassed, he asks to pose with the young flier, with a qualification:

"Not for publication. To keep for myself."

The carrier pilots of Task Force 58 had missed their best chance to destroy the enemy fleet by not being in position to launch a dawn strike that morning. However, the enemy was not to get away unscathed. By three o'clock that afternoon it was apparent the enemy's offensive punch had been spent. Admiral Spruance signaled Mitscher he was free to go after the enemy fleet. Mitscher immediately conferred with Burke and other senior officers.

The carriers, it was decided, would launch a strike at the fleeing enemy fleet. The decision was reached only after much soul-searching; there was a grave risk that the attacking planes could not complete the return trip to their carriers before darkness set in. Never had a major air strike been launched with the knowledge that many of the planes might have to find their way back to their carriers in darkness. But this was the only chance to hit the enemy fleet. Mitscher ordered the strike.

By 4:30 that afternoon the first deckloads of fighters were away. Mitscher was launching everything he had. A few minutes before sunset, far to the west, Task Force 58 pilots spotted the first ships of the enemy fleet. The enemy had lost most of his fighters in the day's operations, but launched what he could as American dive bombers and torpedo planes went in to the attack.

The failing light was perhaps the enemy's best defense, although carrier *Hitaka* was sunk and many other ships were hit. The loss of *Hitaka*, along with two carriers sunk by U.S. submarines, brought Japanese carrier losses in the battle to three, a major naval disaster.

The drama of the day, however, was not yet over. Night settled over the Pacific, and aircraft from the U.S. carriers straggled east, searching for their ships in the darkness. Mitscher had made the decision to carry out the strike, though he knew a night recovery might turn into a disaster. Therefore, as he walked the bridge and glanced at his watch, the tension mounted. At 8:30 the first returning planes were sighted. But to the south there was lightning, and some pilots, mistaking this for the fleet, turned south.

The fuel supply of most of the planes was extremely low. In the sky above, returning pilots who had already spotted ships of the fleet were unable to identify them in the darkness. The ships were blacked out, according to standard operating procedure, designed to protect them from submarine attacks. Mitscher now made one of the stirring decisions of the war, one which will long be remembered in naval history. As returning planes began to stray southward, and mill about, pilots thoroughly confused by an inability to identify the ships below, Mitscher was in agony. In Flag Plot with him at the time was Captain Burke. He looked Burke in the eye and calmly said, "Turn on the lights."

Suddenly the entire task force burst into light as if to say to heck with the enemy submarines. Searchlight beams fingered the sky, cruisers threw up star shells, and the fleet was visible for miles and miles away. And the planes began to land.

Of 216 planes launched, about a hundred managed to make it back to the carriers, though all but sixteen pilots and twenty-two crewmen were rescued from what had threatened to be the Navy's worst carrier aviation disaster.

The Vraciu story had a happy ending. For his gallant performance on June 19, the Indianan was awarded the Navy Cross. The citation was for "extraordinary heroism" and said, in part: "With his Task Force under attack by a numerically superior force of enemy aircraft, Vraciu struck furiously at the hostile bombers and, despite vigorous fighter opposition, succeeded in shooting down six and contributing to the breaking-up of a concentrated enemy attack.

"His outstanding leadership, superior flying ability and daring tactics maintained in the face of tremendous odds contributed materially to the success of our aerial operations . . ." it continued. At the end of the war Vraciu's total number of confirmed kills was nineteen, and there were additional victims he did not claim as victories. The Japs were never to get their hands on the U.S. Navy's fourth-ranking fighter ace, though he bailed out twice, ditched on two occasions, and was aboard two torpedoed carriers. It just wasn't in the cards, it would seem, for harm to come to Vraciu.

That he would be hard to get was demonstrated during the first attack on Truk atoll by the Navy's carriers, on February 16, 1944. Unassisted, he took on four enemy fighters and shot all down. For this feat he was awarded the Distinguished Flying Cross, one of two he received during the war, the other being for the destruction of three enemy bombers at Kwajalein.

The Japanese finally shot him down, but were denied the satisfaction of capturing him. It was during the reoccupation of the Philippines, when he was one of a strike force of F6F pilots strafing enemy airfields around Manila, in support of the U.S. landing at Mindora. The date was December 14, 1944. The Hellcats dropped their bombs and completed strafing runs. Vraciu had destroyed three enemy aircraft, headed down for one more pass at the field—Clark Field. He opened fire on another parked plane amid bursts of antiaircraft fire on all sides.

Pulling up after the pass, he sickened as he noticed a dollar-sized hole in the engine cowling—a shell hole! A glance at the oil pressure gauge confirmed his worst fear—his engine was losing oil. It would seize in a matter of a minute or two at best, when the oil had drained out and the engine had become a mass of hot metal, friction heating up the moving parts.

Vraciu, remembering instructions given pilots by the *Lexington*'s intelligence officer, turned his fighter's nose into the west, toward the hills, not toward the carrier. Philippine guerrillas were active only a few miles to the west, in the hill country, and he hoped to make contact with them after crash-landing or bailing out.

He watched the oil pressure gauge nervously as the dying Pratt and Whitney engine pulled him into the western sky. The temperature gauge was rising steadily and oil pressure dropping. In a minute or two, at 200 knots, he would be between five and ten miles away from the field.

The prop turned slower and slower; he had to pull back on the stick to keep the Hellcat's nose up. Soon she was mushing along, losing flying speed each second. Vraciu looked down . . . there was no suitable place to ditch. He would jump.

He had bailed out before—once over San Diego when a fellow pilot trainee cut off his tail in an SNJ. He had also ditched on two occasions, so he had been mentally prepared for either. He climbed out onto the wing; for some reason he held on for a few seconds, looking down, reluctant to release his grip on the cockpit. Then he dived off into the Philippine sky, and, not having been able to gain more than 2,000 feet altitude, hit the ground only seconds after he pulled the ripcord.

He landed near the village of Bam Ban, and at this moment the enemy's chance to capture the ace who had sent nineteen sons of Nippon to glory in little over twelve months were excellent. But they missed him by a hair. Vraciu floated down just a few hundred feet beyond a garrison of Japanese troops. Guerrillas had seen him bail out and watched him fall. They hurried to him before the Japanese could reach the scene. The first native at his side thrust a straw hat on his head and, with a quick change into pants provided, he became unidentifiable among the crowd.

There was no time to lose; the native group hurried off into the west, into thick fields of bamboo. This was the escape route into the hills the Japanese could not follow. The paths through the thick bamboo were not known to anyone but the natives, who had stretched strings about a foot above the ground. They held back sharpened bamboo canes, bent back, which would snap forward as spears when the strings were broken.

Thus Vraciu progressed only slowly through the death-laden field, and the group moved only a few feet at a time, as a Pygmy, able to check the strings, led the way.

Having missed the enemy's troops by only minutes, and having heard that the Japanese had seized a number of the residents of the town of Bam Ban, killing some of them in an effort to learn his whereabouts, Vraciu then led a party of 150 northward, to meet Americans who had landed at Lingayen Gulf, on Luzon.

This required many days of marching, and when the ordeal was over, and the party had made contact with American troops at last, Vraciu was a major in the guerrilla forces and had succeeded in picking up valuable information concerning enemy supplies, tanks, etc., which he immediately turned over to a U.S. general.

Not long after the Marianas Turkey Shoot, Vraciu returned to the United States, to enjoy a week's leave at home, in East Chicago, Indiana. The enemy's best pilots had been no match for the American ace, but he was conquered with a glance in his home town.

As he was one of the war's heroes, a celebration and parade were staged in his honor. As he proceeded through the city, in the parade, with the cheers and well-wishes of townsmen ringing in his ears, he noticed a pretty girl on the porch of one of the houses he was passing, apparently not too interested in the parade, or in Vraciu. There was something about her. Vraciu could not drive on. He stopped the car— it was a convertible—got out and boldly ran up to the porch and introduced himself. He came back next day and managed a date for that evening!

She was Kathryn Horn, a senior at Indiana University home for the summer (it was August). Before Vraciu returned to the West Coast, to ship out on his last combat tour, she was his wife. As this book goes to press, Commander and Mrs. Vraciu are the parents of five children, making their home in San Francisco, California. Vraciu, still in the Navy, has continued his flying, his last assignment being aboard carrier *Midway* in the Seventh Fleet.

8 *A Strike at Formosa*

OCTOBER 12, 1944:

Lieutenant CECIL E. HARRIS, U.S.N.R.

THE second-ranking Navy ace to emerge from World War II typifies the citizen-soldier with which this country has fought its wars since the Revolution. A reserve officer again in service today, having been called back to duty during the Korean conflict, his story is, in a sense, the American story.

Cecil Elwood Harris was born into a Crespard, South Dakota, farm family, in 1916, and was twenty-three when Hitler's soldiers invaded Poland in September, 1939, touching off World War II. Harris had attended Northern State Teachers' College, in South Dakota, for three years and was teaching school in a small town in that state when he saw the world going up in flames. He enlisted immediately in the United States Navy Reserve as a seaman.

In six months he was appointed a reserve aviation cadet, and four months later—five days after his twenty-fifth birthday—the Japanese attacked Pearl Harbor. So he became one of that generation of Americans who put aside civilian life to take up arms against the professional soldiers of the dictators.

Harris took elimination flight training at the naval reserve base in Minneapolis, Minnesota, and reported to the naval air station at Corpus Christi, Texas, for additional training. His cadet class—its pilots desperately needed—was speedily graduated on February 11, 1942, near the darkest point of the war.

In the spring of 1942 Harris became a part of the Navy's Fighting Squadron 27, and received further training with the Advanced Carrier Training Group, Atlantic Fleet. He saw his first combat duty during the American landings in North Africa, flying support from a carrier. Then, early in 1943, he was ordered to the famed aerial battle area at Guadalcanal, where he shot down two Japanese planes—the first of an even two dozen confirmed victories he was to score in World War II. It is perhaps a measure of his modesty that few people, even many who serve with him or under him today, are familiar with the record of the Navy's second leading ace.

After achieving his great record in World War II, Harris returned to his civilian teaching career and the small schoolhouse in South Dakota that had captured his affection, only to have it interrupted again by United States intervention in the Korean conflict, when the Navy recalled him to active duty. As was the case with so many of World War II's veterans, men already trained, whose skills were needed immediately, Harris received "preference" over younger men who—in fairness— should have supplied the manpower for that conflict.

Interestingly, Harris and Joe Foss, who shot down more enemy planes in the Pacific than any other Marine pilot, both hail from the inland state of South Dakota, far from any ocean, and within whose boundaries no carrier ever sailed.

During World War II the South Dakota schoolteacher displayed a coolness and effectiveness in the face of superior numbers which won for him nine medals, six of them major awards and all of them resulting from performance in combat.

In this chapter we are concerned with a mission Harris flew when mighty Task Force 38 struck Formosa. But aside from this mission, several other equally daring missions merit brief mention.

For example, he won the Navy Cross for a flight fifteen days after the one we will relate in detail. His action was described in the Navy Cross award citation:

For extraordinary heroism as a Fighter Pilot in Fighting Squadron 18 (U.S.S. *Intrepid*) on Luzon, Philippine Islands, October 29, 1944.

Quick to intercept two successive flights of Japanese fighter planes preparing to attack our bomber and torpedo squadrons as they completed a strike on Clark Field, he boldly led his division in a swift assault on the enemy planes . . . shot down one enemy plane from each flight, and put the other to rout. . . .

Intercepting a superior force of enemy fighters . . . he engaged in a fierce dogfight . . . successively knocking down two enemy planes . . . and assisted essentially in the utter defeat of the entire enemy formation without the loss of any of our planes from enemy action. . . .

The reader will note that no American planes were lost in the action described above, though Harris shot down four enemy aircraft. He will be more impressed to learn that, in all his combat throughout the war, no enemy bullet touched his fighter. This, his fellow pilots agree, was due to a remarkable flying touch and not to good fortune in avoiding dangerous situations.

A month before Harris flew the mission to be described in this chapter, he shot down four enemy planes in a savage aerial battle, for which he was later awarded a Gold Star—in lieu of a second Silver Star.

On another occasion he shot down three enemy aircraft in defense of the fleet, shooting down one well inside the fleet formation, in the face of very heavy antiaircraft gunfire, a feat for which he was awarded the Distinguished Flying Cross. In the Battle for Leyte Gulf he won a Gold Star, in lieu of a second Distinguished Flying Cross.

He won another Gold Star, in lieu of another Distinguished Flying Cross, for a mission over Central Luzon, in the Philippines, in which he destroyed three enemy aircraft, probably a fourth, in a fierce engagement which cost the enemy eleven planes.

Among the other medals he received was one for action against major units of the Japanese fleet- during the Battle for Leyte Gulf, when he bombed and strafed an enemy battleship, damaging her severely, and diverted enemy aircraft fire from vulnerable torpedo and dive-bombing planes to himself.

All this, achieved by a shy, mild-mannered farm boy, turned school-teacher, turned fighter pilot. All this from a man members of his squadron remember as "the most popular guy in the outfit."

The day with which we are here concerned is October 12, 1944 (two days prior to a memorable mission of another great ace, treated in the next chapter). A somewhat detailed account of the three-day fleet action involved will be found in the succeeding chapter. For the purpose of understanding this mission, it should be pointed out here that the action of Task Force 38 on October 12, 13 and 14, 1944, was part of the preparatory campaign for the invasion of the Philippine Islands. The air strike against Formosa, on which eighteen Japanese air bases were located, was designed to cripple this major staging base for the dispatch of reinforcing Japanese aircraft to the Philippines.

Task Force 38 was the most powerful fleet assembled by the United States in the Pacific up to that time and contained four separate carrier groups. On this day Harris was aboard carrier *Intrepid*, a part of Carrier Group 2 (38.2).

October 12 was the opening day of the three-day aerial strike against Formosa, and, with the possible exception of the Battle of the Philippine Sea, the enemy reaction constituted the heaviest series of air attacks launched by the Japanese against American naval forces with land-based planes. Earlier in the war, it should be noted, Japanese land-based planes had been highly effective in attacks against Allied ships. They quickly sank the two principal capital ships of the British Far East Fleet, off Malaya, and had—on several occasions—dealt severely with American warships.

American commanders were not unaware of the impressive Japanese aerial strength on Formosa. Therefore, it was decided that the first aerial strike on that Japanese island fortress would be a massive fighter sweep.

Among those taking part in this dawn strike were pilots of Air Group 18, aboard *Intrepid*. Included in the group were VF 18, the fighter squadron whose pilots flew F6F Hellcats; VB 18, the dive-bombing squadron; and VT 18, the torpedo-bomber squadron. With such pilots as Harris, VF 18 had by this time already earned the nickname of "Two-A-Day 18."

The typhoon which had threatened the Pacific Fleet earlier in October was gone and forgotten the night of October 11, 1944. The 27,000-ton U.S. carrier *Intrepid*, and sister carriers *Hancock*, *Bunker Hill* and *Independence*, of Carrier Group 2, parted the surface waves of the Pacific on a northwesterly course under a bright, starlit sky on the approach to Luzon Strait, a 200-mile stretch of water separating Luzon and the southern tip of Formosa.

Aboard *Intrepid* the flight officer of VF 18, Lieutenant Cecil E. Harris, was making up the squadron's schedule for the dawn fighter sweep. Ordinarily, the third ranking officer in the squadron would have been flight officer, but no one had objected when Harris was assigned this duty. The soft-spoken pilot, now twenty-nine, had demonstrated only the month before a remarkable flying ability, shooting down four enemy planes on one mission.

There would be sixteen fighter pilots from VF 18 taking part in to-morrow's sweep, and when Harris had selected the sixteen who would fly, he posted the list of names on the squadron bulletin board. Those not scheduled to fly were disappointed—fighter sweeps were the most sought-after assignments.

Since Task Force 38 would arrive before dawn at a predetermined launching position some fifty to ninety miles east of Formosa, Harris and Lieutenant Commander Ed Murphy, the squadron CO, informed pilots that take-off would be before daylight. Those in command knew the fleet had been shadowed by the enemy, that an enemy air attack was to be expected. A predawn launch, in addition to clearing the decks of the carriers, enabling them better to defend themselves, would also make it possible for pilots on the dawn sweep to arrive over enemy air-fields at daybreak, in time to catch enemy aircraft on the ground.

On the flying schedule Harris posted on the bulletin board he was listed No. 9 in the sixteen-plane formation, leading the third division of four Hellcats (F6F's).

As blacked-out ships of the fleet moved nearer Formosa, on Wednes-day night, Harris and the sixteen fighter pilots who would fly the fighter sweep the next morning, and the "spares" who would go along, got to-gether for an informal briefing. Questions were asked about Formosa, and, from every source of intelligence, the expectation was that enemy opposition would be formidable. There was an air of the unknown about the strike on the big island, because this was the first fighter sweep of the war to be launched against it.

Across from the wardroom on *Intrepid's* starboard side, on the first deck below the hangar deck, Harris was awakened by bugle reveille over the loudspeaker at approximately 4:00 A.M., October 12. He crawled

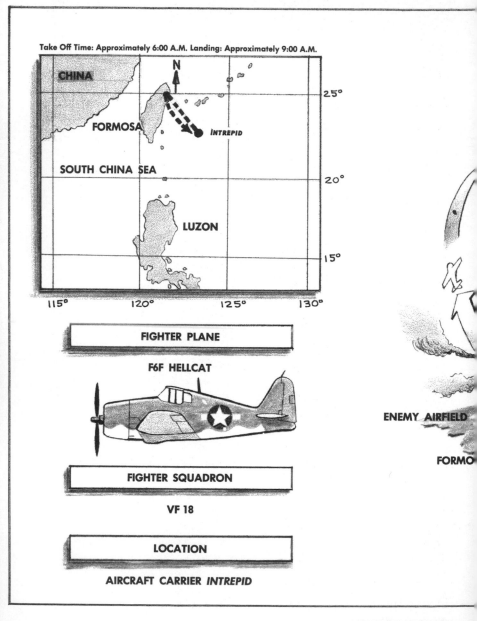

Take Off Time: Approximately 6:00 A.M. Landing: Approximately 9:00 A.M.

N

CHINA

25°

FORMOSA

INTREPID

SOUTH CHINA SEA

20°

LUZON

15°

115°   120°   125°   130°

FIGHTER PLANE

F6F HELLCAT

FIGHTER SQUADRON

VF 18

LOCATION

AIRCRAFT CARRIER *INTREPID*

ENEMY AIRFIELD

FORMO

MISSION FLOWN BY:

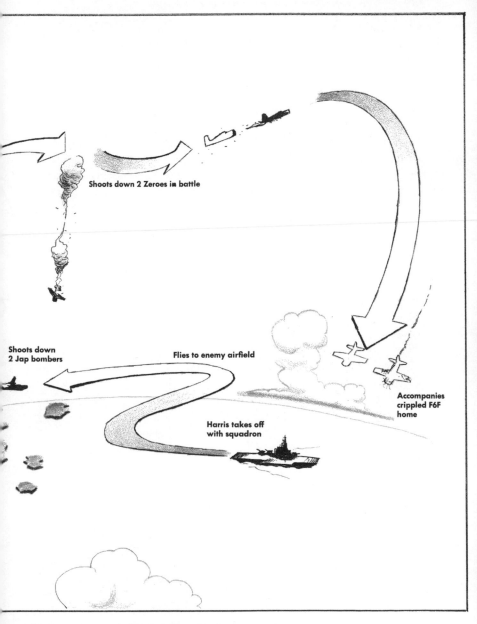

Shoots down 2 Zeroes in battle

Shoots down
2 Jap bombers

Flies to enemy airfield

Accompanies
crippled F6F
home

Harris takes off
with squadron

LIEUTENANT CECIL E. HARRIS, USNR, OCTOBER 12, 1944

out of the lower bunk, shaved, donned his khakis and Marine-type shoes, and in ten minutes was in the wardroom eating breakfast. Carrier pilots enjoyed good food, and though the milk was powdered, Harris had eggs, bacon, toast, coffee and juice.

Over the loudspeaker system the bugle sounded "Flight Quarters," and Harris and other pilots of VF 18 hastened to the fighter ready room just above the hangar deck. Briefing began minutes later. The roll was called, and the sixteen pilots who would take part in the mission were all "present," as were the spares. The intelligence officer warned that some of Japan's better pilots would be encountered over Formosa. Harris outlined the route of the mission, telling the pilots they would do their own navigating. The weather officer forecast good weather for the day —a welcome pronouncement for pilots flying from carriers.

Lieutenant Commander Murphy pin-pointed the enemy airfield the squadron would hit. It was on the northeastern coast of Formosa. That meant a northwesterly course to target and a southeasterly course returning to *Intrepid*. He warned pilots to maintain strict radio silence, and stick together. Wingmen were reminded to stay close to their leaders. The squadron would climb to an altitude of 15,000 feet. Each section was asked to cover the rear of other sections.

Now the chaplain led the pilots in prayer, asking a "safe return." Over the loudspeaker system came the familiar announcement: "Pilots man your planes—on the double!" Harris bounded out of the squadron ready room, up the ladder to the flight deck, and into his big Hellcat. *Intrepid* was launching the fighter sweep with two catapults, and Murphy would be the first off. After his division, the second division (eight planes in all), Harris and his division would be launched.

Intrepid was now headed into the wind, plowing through the seas at a good clip. The sky was just beginning to whiten in the east. The deck now came alive with the spinning three-blade props of Hellcats, crewmen scurrying back and forth while pilots, inside their cockpits, checked instruments and switches. Now Murphy was ready. He braced his head on the head-rest and revved up the engine. Suddenly the catapult thrust him forward, his weight pressing against the back of the seat. The carrier deck suddenly ran out, he felt a slight mush, and began to maneuver quickly with rudder and stick, and the Hellcat inched upward in a slow climb.

Murphy's F6F and that of his wingman, after a short turn to clear the bow of slipstream, climbed straight out in front of the carrier. Two more planes followed. Then came the first two planes of the second division, then the last two planes of the second division. Harris was maneuvered onto the catapult by deck crewmen. When the launching officer suddenly came down with outstretched arm, the catapult rammed him forward as if a gigantic hand had yanked him ahead, and soon he was over the water at full throttle, now beginning a slow climb.

In the lead, Murphy continued to fly straightaway. When Harris' division and the last and fourth division of four planes were airborne, Murphy banked into a 180-degree turn and flew back to the carrier. As he did, each of the Hellcats turned in behind him, and by the time Murphy's Hellcat passed over the carrier, flying in the opposite direction, the squadron was assembled. Then Murphy banked into the northwest—toward the target, Formosa.

The Hellcats are climbing at 150 knots. The squadron is flying "finger-four" divisions, the four divisions themselves making up one "finger-four" squadron. Murphy's wingman is on his right, a section is behind and to his left. Slightly behind and to the right of the lead division is the second division. The second division leader's wingman is to his left, and the second section in the division is to the right and slightly behind.

Behind the second division, well to the left, is Harris' division, with Harris' wingman, Franklin Burley, on his right and behind, and his second section, led by Lieutenant (j.g.) Bill Zeimer, to the left and behind. The fourth division is to the left, and behind Harris, with the division leader's wingman on his right and slightly behind, and the second section in the last division to the left and behind the lead section.

Intrepid is now a small silhouette, falling farther and farther behind. Harris looks out on each wing. His crewmen waxed them only the day before, to give him that extra few knots speed. With waxed wings, and emergency water injection, Harris has a speed advantage over enemy fighters which could be vitally important in an engagement. Harris and the others flip on gun switches.

VF 18 continues its climbing northwesterly course; other groups of Task Force 38 planes, over an expanse of many miles, from many different carriers, drone upward on climbing courses, heading for other targets on Formosa.

There is radio silence, a silence almost eerie, combined with the roaring engine up ahead, and the sight of the squadron in formation, moving closer and closer to enemy territory in the dim light of early morning. It's more than twenty minutes since the squadron left the carrier. VF 18 is leveling off at 15,000 feet; the first stage of the superchargers go into action.

Ahead, in the distance, Harris sees the eastern shore of Formosa, green, beautiful hills and mountains. Now the earphones vibrate with an order from Murphy. He tells Harris to take his division down to have a look at the target airfield, near the coast. Harris acknowledges the order, pushes stick forward. The four blue Hellcats of the third division point their noses downward and begin to gain speed. The twelve Hellcats remaining in the squadron continue on course at 15,000 feet. The green shoreline becomes clearer, and the mountains and hills grow larger and larger.

Harris sees the open space near the shore, ahead, which must be the airfield. He banks slightly to point his nose in that direction, and continues on course. His wingman, Burley, to the right and his second section to the left are in position. He wonders whether the division will have the benefit of surprise, or whether the Japs have picked them up on radar and have already scrambled fighters to intercept them.

Now the shoreline comes closer. Harris' altimeter needle continues to drop as he descends. He must be low to get a good look at the enemy field. He can already make out a large runway, lying southeast-northwest. On the eastern edge of the field is a major industrial plant of some kind.

He constantly rubbernecks, knowing his division is in the most precarious position of any in the squadron—approaching an enemy field at a low altitude, where Japanese fighters are most effective. (It is a legitimate fear, which events are to justify.)

The coastline of Formosa is immediately ahead, and Harris is down to several thousand feet. His division is in good order, and he is scanning the field. Above, Hellcats of Two-A-Day 18 are approaching the field to the north, preparing to circle to the left. Harris, a little ahead of the rest of the squadron, sets course to pass north of the field also, and circle to the left.

The four Hellcats cross the coastline at a high throttle setting, and with the advantage of the long decline are registering approximately 250 knots. Harris dips his left wing and begins to circle the field. Now he is at the southern end and has a good view of a number of Japanese aircraft parked below. He banks into a turn and pulls out on a northeast heading. He will shove the nose down and pass directly over the field, carrying out a strafing run. This will test the enemy's flak. The engine responds to full throttle, and he pushes the stick forward.

The best way to feel out an airfield's defenses, Harris knows, is to make a sudden strafing run on it. Above, Murphy and the other Hellcats will be able to locate the position of the antiaircraft guns on the field, while acting as top cover. The four Hellcats now begin to pick up speed. They are only about two thousand feet above the tops of the green trees.

"Bandits!"

Harris is startled. It's his section leader, Zeimer, shouting over the radio. He's spotted five enemy bombers.

Harris looks desperately ahead and to both sides, but can't see them. He tells Zeimer to lead the division down on them, and Zeimer makes a violent pull-up, presses into a blood-draining bank to the left. The four Hellcats, turning as tightly as possible at this high speed, are now over and behind the bombers, which are heading southwest. Harris sees them now! Five . . . land-based . . . twin-engined. The enemy leader has four bombers stacked back on his right. Orange meatballs on the wings are clearly visible. The bombers appear to have taken off only moments before, since they are almost on the deck. The Hellcats, with their superior speed, are rapidly closing the gap, with Zeimer in the lead and Harris' section close behind.

Harris feels the tension of the kill. The division, now almost on the trees, is in a precarious position, though, if enemy fighters are nearby. He scans the sky quickly, but sees no enemy fighters. Looking through the sight ring, he sees the silhouettes of the bombers grow larger and larger. Zeimer is maneuvering perfectly to be in a position to open fire on the enemy bomber which is last in formation and farthest to the right. Harris kicks left rudder and moves stick slightly left, and eases out to the left. He watches Zeimer, ahead, almost within firing range.

The bombers are caught from behind by surprise. A few seconds more and the Hellcats will be pouring shells into them. The seconds drag. Now! White smoke streams back from the wings of Zeimer's Hellcat as the six 50-caliber guns send streaks of shells into the trailing brownish-green bomber on the right. In seconds Zeimer's fire is tearing holes in him, and smoke is streaming back. A splash of flame! The enemy bomber has exploded and disintegrated.

The tempo of battle now picks up. Zeimer whips his Hellcat onto the tail of the fourth enemy bomber, now the last in line, and opens fire almost immediately. Harris, eyes focusing through the yellow sight ring on the gunsight glass, sees the wingspan of the bomber ahead of Zeimer's steadily widening. He holds back his finger for a few seconds. Now the wingspan fills the sight circle.

Thunder and vibration! The six guns shake Harris' Hellcat. His aim is deadly. The bomber is taking fatal hits. The enemy bombers make no move; it is happening so fast that those not hit are not yet aware of the Hellcats. Harris' guns literally tear the bomber apart, and he watches the enemy victim wing over and dive for the earth below.

Instantly he applies left foot and stick and pulls in behind the next bomber, ahead. He is almost on him, and opens fire immediately. By now Zeimer's second victim is trailing fire. Grayish-black puffs fill the sky, as Japanese enemy antiaircraft guns, not far below, open up on the four Hellcats. Harris maintains fire; the bomber ahead is already badly hurt. Pieces fly back, smoke begins to stream from the fuselage. Without warning, a flash . . . the bomber has exploded, and Harris rockets through the debris and smoke, emerging with the front of his canopy and his wings covered with oil—from the exploding bomber.

Ridiculously easy, so far. But things become more grim. Harris has no time to appreciate the two kills he scored so rapidly. Someone shouts over the radio: "Zeroes!" Enemy fighters are up above . . . they have the altitude advantage. Harris looks up and behind, in a desperate effort to spot the enemy fighters. He sees nothing. He is in a vulnerable position. The lone remaining enemy bomber is forgotten.

An enemy Zero, streaking down from above, opens fire on Zeimer. The Hellcat staggers from the enemy shells. Now Harris gets his first glimpse of the Jap fighters. The Zero pilot firing on Zeimer dives between Zeimer and his wingman. Harris glances back at his wingman . . . in position. He looks back at Zeimer . . . his Hellcat is trailing smoke. Zeimer will have to get out fast if he is to parachute, since they are at low altitude. Even while clearing his tail, looking for the enemy, he keeps an eye on the stricken Hellcat. A chute now blossoms—Zeimer. As he floats down to enemy territory below, his wingman, Lieutenant (j.g.) Egidio Di Batista, fastens on the tail of the Zero pilot who shot down his section leader. The Hellcat's guns are in range. The Zero spurts flame and wings over into a fatal plunge. Zeimer is avenged.

An enemy Zero-type fighter under attack by a U.S. fighter over Truk in 1944. (Navy Department Photo)

Harris sees an F6F smash into the ground below, quickly followed by a Zero. He can't tell where the Hellcat came from. Ahead is Zeimer's wingman, Di Batista, and, on Harris' right and slightly behind, his own wingman, Burley. He must protect Di Batista, and get the three planes together, but before he can pull abreast of him, he sees a dot, above, plunging downward. The dot, now growing larger and larger, the unmistakable silhouette of a Zero, is at ten o'clock, diving on Di Batista, at twelve o'clock. Harris grabs the mike button and yells:

"Zero's diving on you from above and behind!" Up above, the Hellcats flying top cover have seen the Zero and yell the same warning.

Harris, left hand all the way forward on the throttle, pulls back on the stick. Di Batista is at approximately 1,500 feet altitude, and the enemy fighter is leveling out for a firing pass from astern. Before the American can get out of the line of fire the Zero is at six o'clock. At the same time Harris is getting the enemy in his sight ring, and fast closing on him. The three fighters, strung out in line, roar over the rolling green hills at full throttle. Will the guns of No. 2 or No. 3 score first? Harris opens fire. His aim is true, lucky for Di Batista. But the enemy's 20-millimeter fire is scoring on "DeBat," as fellow pilots know him. Harris' guns have taken a heavier toll. The Zero, pierced by many 50-caliber shells in the fuselage and wing, curves out of the line of fire, in a steady decline, straight ahead. Harris, withholding fire, watches intently as the Zero heads straight for the trees. He clears his rear, and looks above. Now the enemy pilot goes straight into the trees, and the Zero bursts into flame as it spreads forward over the earth below. Victory No. 3 for Harris!

Once again, however, before Harris can scarcely think about it, the radio crackles. Di Batista . . . he's hit, hurt badly. The Zero Harris shot down scored heavily before going down. Harris tells Di Batista to turn left and head for *Intrepid*. He and his own wingman will go with him all the way. Di Batista is pessimistic; he may have to ditch on the beach. Harris urges him to make for *Intrepid*. "We'll keep you covered," he promises. Di Batista reports his engine hit, the hydraulic system damaged, and controls fouled up. But he'll try. Harris knows it will be close. Now Murphy, high above, who sees the three Hellcats heading for the coast and *Intrepid*, calls to say he has the Hellcats in sight. He promises to come to their aid.

At full throttle, closing on Di Batista, Harris welcomes the news. Just then he spots a number of Zeroes above. Will Murphy get to them in time? The rest of the Hellcats, at high altitude, move to engage their attention. But several are diving on the three Hellcats now seeking to return to *Intrepid*. Harris pulls up behind Di Batista, and prepares to defend his rear. The coast is still several miles ahead, and the three Hellcats are climbing into the southeastern sky. But the Zeroes are not finished yet.

Harris spots an enemy fighter behind him, above, and several others behind him. Enemy pilots are quick to go after cripples, and they won't neglect Di Batista. The nearest enemy behind, with an altitude advantage, is in position to dive on Di Batista; Harris can't turn directly into the Zero for a head-on pass, for that would leave Di Batista unprotected and expose his other two planes to heavy odds—since more than twenty Zeroes are in the area. He'll play possum! He'll maintain position behind Di Batista, let the enemy begin a firing pass—as if he were undetected.

In this way Harris will be able to stay with Di Batista until the last minute, and he'll delay making a 180-degree turn. This strategy, however, will require split-second timing; if he allows the diving Zero to approach too closely, he's liable to fall victim to the enemy's guns himself. (The Zero is so hightly maneuverable that once the enemy is behind him he might not be able to shake him off.)

Realizing the dangers and the disadvantages involved, Harris will take the chance—stick with Di Batista and attempt to trick the enemy pilot, above, behind. He continually glances back. The enemy comes on, approaching closer and closer, overhead. Harris checks Burley, to the right . . . in position. The coastline approaches ever so slowly. The Zero behind is gaining. Now he is but a few thousand feet behind, above. Harris flies on . . . straight and level. Will the enemy pilot take the bait?

The Zero now goes into an ominous descent. Harris looks hard. He is coming down. And Harris flies on, straight and level. The enemy pilot is now diving, increasing his speed. Other Zeroes are preparing to follow the lead Zero, now rapidly approaching from the rear. Harris sweats. He hopes he can pull it off.

The wingspan behind him is now rapidly approaching his level and pulling out. He can maintain straight and level flight only a few seconds longer. And, true to his expectations, the enemy fighter behind is pulling directly in behind him, not DeBat. The Zero comes on. He is almost within range. Now Harris slams left stick and rudder. The Hellcat shudders into a violent, vertical left turn. Harris, with Burley following, apparently leaves the crippled DeBat alone, flying straight ahead, now down to approximately 900 feet.

What will the enemy pilot do? As soon as he is out of the bank, Harris glances back. Has the enemy pilot followed him or will he follow the cripple? A glance gives him the answer. The Zero is steadily walking up on the rear of the stricken Hellcat! Instantly Harris slams stick right and hits right rudder. The Hellcat drains blood from his head as he banks—just as violently—back to the right. Harris sticks his nose down, and, at full throttle, streaks for the Zero, now at three o'clock.

DeBat and the Zero are down to about 500 feet. The enemy pilot now senses what is happening. Two Hellcats are moving on him from the left. They had not run away. The Zero, not far above the trees, streaks for the deck to escape.

The two Hellcats, separated by a few hundred feet, begin to close the gap, from behind. DeBat, momentarily relieved, continues on at low altitude. The lone Zero and two pursuing Hellcats, only a few hundred feet high, roar southeasterly at maximum power. If the enemy pilot knew one of the Navy's most accurate gunners was behind him, he might be tempted to bail out. But he is game; he is making a run for it.

The Hellcats close the gap slowly. Harris' eyes once again fix upon the enemy silhouette through the gunsight glass. The wingspan widens. It stretches past the inner circle, approaches the sides of the outer circle. The Jap pilot is on top of the trees, at full throttle, but the Hellcats are gaining. Now the Zero is squarely in Harris' sight. His right forefinger closes the stick trigger, and, for the fourth time today, the Hellcat's guns thunder and spit a salvo of shells—a hundred a second streak after the enemy fighter. In seconds the deadly pattern rips holes in the victim and before the pilot can take evasive action, a telltale stream of black smoke streaks backward.

Harris is almost at point-blank range. The Zero has taken too many hits! A wing goes up and the brownish-green enemy fighter seems to slide downward, to the right. Harris withholds fire, watches the enemy fighter head for the trees only a few feet below. Suddenly a wing tears loose as the Zero hits the trees. A splash of fire marks the crash. The two Hellcats rocket over the fatal spot, as Burley yells over the radio: "You got another one!"

Harris looks at "Chink" Burley, off to his right, and realizes his wingman deserves much of the credit for the victories. He has stuck with him all the way and protected him from surprise attack. The enemy respects a section of two American fighters, but a lone fighter, and especially a crippled one, is considered choice game.

Harris hits left rudder and stick. Di Batista is still on course for *Intrepid*, and is now well out to sea. Harris and Burley have just crossed the coast, eyes glancing backward into the sky, to see if other Zeroes are following. The deadly shooting of Harris, and the quick work he has made of the leading Zero, apparently discourages the other enemy fighters. They remain behind, at a respectful distance. The three Hellcats roar on over the ocean, heading home. They now need but a few minutes' grace to be well away from the enemy island.

Harris continually scans the sky. Above, and behind, he sees a group of fighters. He studies the silhouettes closely. He realizes an attack by a large force of Zeroes, coming from a high altitude, would be difficult to turn back. With good shooting, and strategy, he has already saved DeBat from one Zero possessing the all-important advantage of altitude, but the same strategy would fail with ten or fifteen.

He nervously eyes the planes. So does Burley. A sense of relief comes over him as he recognizes the silhouettes . . . Hellcats! Now, over the radio he can hear Murphy, calling *Intrepid,* and DeBat. The squadron is following him home. DeBat reports considerable difficulty with controls, though he's managing to stay on a southeasterly course. Every few minutes that pass means the carrier is that much closer. Harris wonders if DeBat can safely land the crippled fighter which he is having trouble controlling in straight and level flight.

Now, ahead on the water, Harris spots dots, the outer screen of Carrier Group 2. As the Hellcats come closer and closer, the dots on the sea become ships, and the whole fleet spreads out over the horizon. It is a majestic sight, and a welcome one to every pilot who has ever flown, alone, over the ocean on a combat mission.

In a matter of minutes the three Hellcats, and the squadron above, are bearing down on *Intrepid.* She turns into the wind to prepare to take them aboard. DeBat will be given landing preference. But can he control his shot-up fighter well enough to execute the exacting carrier landing? The big ship is plowing ahead, directly into the wind, and ready to take the Hellcats aboard. Over the radio DeBat reports more trouble. Each time he slackens his speed he loses control of his aircraft. Since he can't land at cruising speed, and must slacken his speed for a deck landing, DeBat is in a dangerous dilemma.

He again tries to slacken speed, and once again finds he's losing control of the aircraft. He reports the critical situation to the air officer aboard *Intrepid.* The danger involves not only DeBat and his damaged Hellcat, but the carrier as well, for an out-of-control Hellcat and its high-octane gasoline are a serious menace to *Intrepid* and the more than two thousand men who sail her.

DeBat gets his orders. He will bail out into the ocean! Other Hellcat pilots watch as he climbs to gain altitude. Destroyers surrounding *Intrepid* are alerted that a stricken Hellcat will be abandoned, that a pilot will parachute into the ocean. It's a tricky undertaking for DeBat; he must slip out of his parachute quickly, once in the water, and inflate his Mae West, and then be picked up at sea. Moreover, he must make a successful jump from a crippled and hard-to-control aircraft.

Japanese Jill torpedo bomber passing U.S. carrier's seaboard quarter after dropping "fish." (Navy Department Photo)

Other pilots in Two-A-Day 18 circle the carrier slowly and watch the drama unfold. DeBat slowly circles and climbs above *Intrepid*. He reaches the desired altitude and approaches the big carrier from the rear, off the port quarter. The eyes of many a seaman on more than one ship, and in many fighters, watch as DeBat slides the canopy back and climbs out. The damaged Hellcat, however, does not behave properly. As DeBat jumps, the tail assembly of the erratic fighter hits him. In spite of this, DeBat, conscious, pulls the ripcord and fellow pilots watch the parachute billow open well above the sea. The damaged Hellcat dives crazily for the ocean, and as Harris watches it, plunges into the water and is enveloped by the all-encompassing sea.

All eyes in the squadron follow the descending parachute, and injured pilot, who flops into the water under the big white chute far behind *Intrepid*. DeBat manages to get away from his chute and inflate his jacket and is seen to be floating on the surface. Behind him, not far away, a destroyer approaches as pilots of the squadron relay directions below. The destroyer has the injured pilot in sight, and Harris and others turn for *Intrepid*. In a few minutes they are touching down, and as the hooks trailing from each Hellcat's fuselage engage the big cables stretched across *Intrepid*'s rear deck, they are jerked to a sudden halt.

As soon as Harris was down, crewmen rushed up to his plane and asked about the mission. How many enemy aircraft did he shoot down? Harris quietly replied that he had destroyed two bombers and two fighters. They looked over his Hellcat. Oil on the wing and canopy, which came from the second bomber destroyed, but not a nick, not a shell hole! As usual—and as was to be the case on every future mission throughout the war—Harris had evaded every bullet.

Harris credited Chink Burley with having made his victories possible, and reported to the ready room below. Interrogated, he reported his division shot down four twin-engined enemy bombers and three Zeroes, in a running fight with twenty, having been jumped by the enemy from behind and above.

By now word had been passed that DeBat was picked up successfully by the destroyer, and though suffering a broken leg, he would recover. In other words, Harris' division destroyed seven enemy planes, including four twin-engined bombers, for the loss of one pilot, even though the division was surprised by enemy fighters from above.

Interrogation officers listened to Harris' story with awe, for just a month earlier, on September 13, he had destroyed four enemy planes on a mission. He had done it a second time in thirty days! (What intelligence officers did not know was that Harris would—on the 29th of that month—shoot down four enemy planes again, for the third time, over Luzon, in the Philippine Islands.)

However, Harris was not impressed with his efforts on this day as were some of his fellow pilots. In fact, in a few hours he was again

A Navy fighter, having crushed through barrier and into a parked plane, continues over the side of carrier heading for the sea. (Official U.S. Navy Photo)

taking off from *Intrepid,* escorting bombers on another raid on Formosa. His commanding officer, however, realized the skill he had exhibited in protecting DeBat against superior numbers of Zeroes on the return flight. He recommended Harris for the Silver Star, a recommendation approved. The citation accompanying it read in part:

> For conspicuous gallantry and intrepidity as a Fighter Pilot in Fighting Squadron 18 . . . on Northern Formosa, October 12, 1944 . . . he braved intense enemy aircraft fire . . . to execute an attack upon an important airfield installation and, during the same flight, valiantly engaged in a terrific aerial dogfight with numerically superior aircraft . . . succeeding in shooting down four of the hostile craft . . . in two instances saved two of his teammates during the action. . . .

Altogether, on that day, Task Force 38 sent three strikes against Formosa. United States losses were heavy—forty-eight planes. But enemy losses were over three times that number. Samuel E. Morison reports, in *Leyte,* the twelfth of his admirable fourteen volumes on naval operations in World War II, that the Japanese admiral commanding the defense of Formosa, watching the destruction of his fighters by Navy pilots above the island, was thoroughly dismayed, and described his defending planes as "so many eggs" thrown at the strong wall of enemy formations.

The sad part of the story yet to be related is that, shortly after Harris shot down his third "foursome," the gallant carrier *Intrepid* was struck by two Kamikazes. Harris, who had just taken off from the flight deck when the suicide aircraft struck the carrier, circled the stricken ship. For hours he watched the burning carrier fight for her life. He managed one small consolation during the ordeal. Enemy planes approached and Harris, turning on a Zero which might have been a Kamikaze, shot down his twenty-fourth victim of the war!

With the battering of *Intrepid,* Fighting Squadron 18, which achieved one of the greatest records of any Navy fighter squadron in World War II and produced the Navy's second leading ace, was temporarily withdrawn from combat.

Back in the United States, Harris re-formed a fighter squadron and prepared for further combat. Pilots received the new F8F fighter and were preparing to return to duty in the Pacific when, on August 14,

Japan surrendered. Had not that Japanese Kamikaze hit *Intrepid*, thus removing this famed fighter squadron and Lieutenant Cecil Harris from the combat zone, there is little doubt that the farm boy from South Dakota, who became a schoolteacher and then a hell-for-leather fighter pilot, would have scored many more aerial kills. And, chances are, no enemy bullet would have found his fighter—so phenomenal and precise was his shooting and flying ability.

9 Hornet's *C.A.P. Breaks Up an Attack*

OCTOBER 14, 1944:

Lieutenant CHARLES R. STIMPSON, U.S.N.R.

Stimpson, left, with Lieutenant James Swope, U.S.N.R.

LEADING up to history's greatest naval battle, the Battle for Leyte Gulf, Task Force 38—the most potent assemblage of warships in history—struck the enemy on Okinawa and on other islands in the Ryukyus, at Formosa, and on airfields at Luzon.

This interdiction strike, on scores of airfields, was designed to hinder enemy aerial reinforcements to the central Philippines, especially around Leyte, which was to be invaded on October 20, 1944.

Task Force 38 was comprised of four large, self-sufficient carrier groups and assembled for this mission shortly before dark, October 7, 1944, 375 miles west of the Marianas. The task force ships fueled from nine oilers on the 8th and assumed a northwesterly course toward Okinawa.

An idea of the magnitude of the force can be gained from a listing of its principal ships. The four groups were designated 38.1, 38.2, 38.3 and 38.4.

Group 1 included aircraft carriers *Wasp* and *Hornet*, light carriers *Monterey*, *Cowpens* and *Cabot*, heavy cruisers *Wichita*, *Boston* and *Canberra*, and fifteen destroyers.

Group 2 included carriers *Intrepid*, *Hancock*, *Bunker Hill*, light carrier *Independence*, battleships *Iowa* and *New Jersey*, light cruisers *Houston*, *Vincennes*, *Miami*, *San Diego* and *Oakland*, and seventeen destroyers.

Group 3 included carriers *Essex* and *Lexington*, light carriers *Princeton* and *Langley*, battleships *Washington*, *Massachusetts*, *South Dakota*, and *Alabama*, light cruisers *Sante Fe*, *Mobile*, *Birmingham*, *Reno*, and fourteen destroyers.

Group 4 included carriers *Franklin* and *Enterprise*, light carriers *San Jacinto* and *Belleau Wood*, heavy cruiser *New Orleans*, light cruiser *Biloxi*, and twelve destroyers. In all, the task force contained seventeen carriers!

This magnificent array of aerial and surface striking power closed Okinawa on October 10, 1944. On that day it launched the first of the massive attacks on Japanese airfields lying on the island route from Japan to the captured southern territories.

The carriers launched 1,396 sorties at the Ryukyus (including Okinawa) on the 10th, destroying approximately a hundred enemy aircraft, four cargo ships, two submarines, twelve torpedo boats, a submarine tender, and smaller vessels. The cost to the carriers was twenty-one aircraft, five pilots and four crewmen.

This was an impressive aerial strike, but it was the preliminary to a larger effort—the three-day air offensive against the larger island of Formosa.

Admiral Soemu Toyoda, Commander in Chief of the Combined Japanese Fleet, at Tokyo, was in Formosa when news of the October 10 carrier strike on Okinawa was received. He and his staff rightly guessed the American task force would turn its attention to nearby Japanese bases, and at least one enemy admiral correctly predicted Task Force 38's next strike would be on Formosa.

The Japanese were not surprised by the effort to block reinforcements to the Philippines, nor were they surprised at our landing, a few days later, on Leyte. On the contrary, the Imperial Japanese Navy was expecting the landing and was prepared to throw in everything it had in one great gamble to win a decisive victory, and repulse the Philippines landing.

Admiral Toyoda realized the importance of resisting the carrier strikes on Okinawa and Formosa. The Formosan air-base complex played a vital role in maintaining the aerial lifeline between Japan and the Philippines. Therefore, as soon as he received word of the October 10

Part of Task Force 38 as seen from U.S.S. Hornet, *shortly before action described in this chapter.* (Navy Department Photo)

strike on Okinawa, he ordered all-out aerial attacks on the American task force. In addition, he ordered Japanese carriers *Zuikaku, Zuiho, Chitose, Chiyoda,* and converted battleship carriers *Ise* and *Hyuga,* to transfer all their operational aircraft to defensive land bases.

For the defense of Formosa, the Japanese commander could count on approximately 230 operational fighters on the island, and could look to the reinforcements from Kyushu and the carriers.

On the night of October 11, Task Force 38 was steaming northwest at better than 20 knots, headed for a position from which the carriers would launch the first strike in a three-day effort to eliminate Japanese air strength on Formosa. The military objective was to wreck airfields and installations to such a degree that Formosa would be incapable of acting as a staging base for Japanese planes bound for Leyte.

Before dawn on the morning of October 12 (as related in the preceding chapter), less than a hundred miles east of Formosa, the first strike on Formosan airfields was launched—a fighter sweep. During the day three major strikes were delivered by the four carrier groups, each group having been assigned to a certain area of the island. Damage inflicted on ground installations was heavy. American pilots encountered stiff enemy opposition, and at the end of the day no less than forty-eight American planes had been lost.

The Japanese lost over a hundred defending fighters on this first day of the "knock-down, drag-out fight between carrier-based and shore-based aircraft" (as Admiral William F. Halsey described the battle), and, in addition, admitted losing forty-two aircraft in attacks on ships of Task Force 38 that day. The enemy attacks were successfully fended off by defending fighters and antiaircraft guns of the fleet.

The second day of the classic battle began at dawn on October 13, and by the end of the day's activities almost a thousand sorties had been flown by American pilots. American losses were less than those of the day before, but carrier *Franklin* took a crashing, flaming bomber on her deck, and heavy cruiser *Canberra* was the victim of an enemy torpedo, causing near-fatal damage. Thus the enemy's assault on the fleet achieved its first tangible results on its second day.

It is with the third day of this aerial slugfest, October 14, that we are concerned here. Aboard *Hornet,* in Carrier Group 1, was Lieutenant Charles R. Stimpson, of Santa Barbara, California (now of Walnut Creek, California), who would fly one of the most memorable missions flown by a Navy fighter pilot in World War II.

Only one major strike was launched at Formosa on the 14th, consisting of 146 fighters and 100 bombers. All the sting had not been taken out of the Japanese defenders, for twenty-three American planes were lost. However, enemy losses were much greater, the total for the three days having risen to almost five hundred aircraft. In addition, Task Force 38's strikes had resulted in the sinking of some forty ships, damage to many others, and heavy damage to enemy defense installations.

Hornet's Fighter Squadron VF 11 took part in the morning strike at Formosa, and among those who flew on that mission was Lieutenant Stimpson. As he touched down on *Hornet's* deck, after the last strike on Formosa, Stimpson had yet to achieve a kill in the three-day operation. The six victories he had scored at Guadalcanal, earlier in the war, were his only victories.

As he climbed out of his big fighter on the flight deck and headed for the squadron ready room below, he was disappointed that he had missed out in a chance to add to his six victories in the three-day aerial battles. Any number of fellow pilots had scored more than one kill over Formosa in these battles, but not Stimpson. And with the task force due to depart the area shortly, his chances of adding to his victory total seemed slim indeed as morning turned into afternoon. Stimpson lunched in the wardroom and *Hornet* plowed through the Pacific on a northeasterly course, in good weather.

Routine orders came from above: Stimpson and seven other fighter pilots of VF 11 were to take off and fly combat air patrol above *Hornet.* Lieutenant Jimmy Eldow Savage would lead the eight-plane flight, with Lieutenant N. W. Dayhoff the leader of the second division of four planes. Stimpson would fly as leader of Dayhoff's second section.

Quickly the eight pilots prepared for take-off. Up above, on deck, crewmen readied eight big F6F Hellcat fighters. A short briefing was held below, though the mission was routine—*Hornet* maintained a combat air patrol above at all times in combat zones—and soon the eight pilots were scrambling into their cockpits, as the big carrier's bow sliced slowly up and down, through the waves and into the wind.

One by one the fighters, engines roaring, lined up for take-off. Each pilot revved his engine, checked controls, and waited for the signal to release brakes. The carrier was making better than twenty-five knots, and this—added to the speed of the wind—created a gale for crewmen working hurriedly and nimbly on the decks.

After the warm-up signal—an upraised arm whirling round and round—"release brakes" came next, and pilots, at full throttle with their left hands, released both brakes and roared off into the wind. It was an orderly take-off, for no scramble was involved, and one by one the big blue Hellcats lifted off the end of the carrier and climbed into a bright autumn sky, broken by a layer of scattered clouds at 8,000 feet.

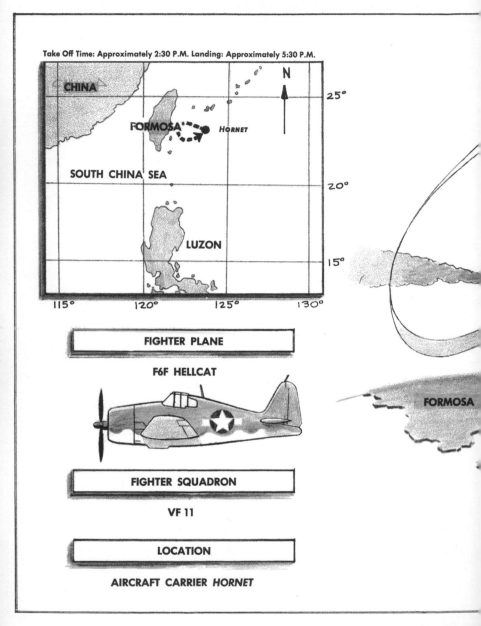

Take Off Time: Approximately 2:30 P.M. Landing: Approximately 5:30 P.M.

CHINA

N

25°

FORMOSA *HORNET*

SOUTH CHINA SEA

20°

LUZON

15°

115°   120°   125°   130°

FIGHTER PLANE

F6F HELLCAT

FIGHTER SQUADRON

VF 11

LOCATION

AIRCRAFT CARRIER *HORNET*

FORMOSA

MISSION FLOWN BY

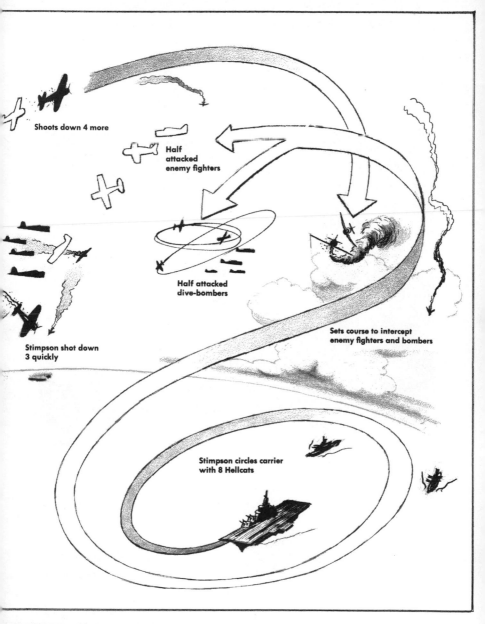

Shoots down 4 more

Half attacked enemy fighters

Half attacked dive-bombers

Stimpson shot down 3 quickly

Sets course to intercept enemy fighters and bombers

Stimpson circles carrier with 8 Hellcats

LIEUTENANT CHARLES R. STIMPSON, USNR, OCTOBER 14, 1944

Stimpson looks at his altimeter: 1,000 feet. Down below, *Hornet* gets smaller and smaller, tracking the surface with a white wake. Lieutenant Savage, the flight leader, gathers the big Grumman fighters together. The Hellcats are climbing at better than 150 knots, circling the carrier below. Savage is in radio contact with "Ginger Base"—the fighter director on board *Hornet*. Ginger Base orders the Hellcats to climb to

Pilots on U.S.S. Hornet *relax in the Ready Room.* (Navy Department Photo)

approximately 20,000 feet, and await further instructions from the fighter director, who is constantly monitoring radar scanners and is in radio contact with ships of the outer screen.

The eight fighters knife into broken clouds at 8,000 feet, three-blade props pulling them up through the cumulus, then out of it. The climb continues. Through breaks in the clouds the fighters keep the carrier and screening vessels in sight at all times. Now pilots check their guns, which are electrically charged—a great improvement over guns in earlier fighters, charged by hand. Stimpson, therefore, merely flips the switches and all six 50-caliber machine guns are "charged" for simultaneous firing. He leans forward and looks through his gunsight; the two electric, yellow light rings are centered on the glass.

The flight passes 10,000 feet. The climb continues . . . 11,000 feet, 12,000 feet. Stimpson cuts in his blower, maneuvers rudder pedals and stick to stay in formation. He glances back at his wingman, Ensign F. J. C. Blair, who is in position off to his right. Fifteen minutes have passed since the eight Hellcats lifted off the deck of Hornet; it is 2:45 P.M.

Halfway across the world American fighter pilots opposing the Luftwaffe are just beginning to realize that war in Europe will not end in 1944. The Germans, badly beaten in Normandy, are re-forming their lines, and the Allied advance toward Germany is grinding to a halt. And German aircraft factories are to produce more planes this year, despite Allied bombing, than in any other year of the war.

Likewise, Japanese factories are producing an increasing number of aircraft in the year 1944, despite American bombings. This is to be reflected in a minor way this very day, for in spite of the fact that aircraft of Task Force 38 have destroyed almost five hundred enemy aircraft, Japanese air power on Formosa has not been wiped out, but has been replenished.

The eight Hellcats continue their climbing turns. Ginger Base is relatively quiet. Now altitude reaches 20,000 feet; the Hellcats level off, S-turning above the carrier. The armada of American warships below is an inspiring sight, even to the pilots who are treated to the spectacle day after day. Stimpson checks his instruments. Fuel pressure, oil pressure, engine temperatures—all in the green. The big prop whirls, out front, at cruising pitch, pulling the fighter through the sky at better than 200 knots. Up above everything is blue, and visibility excellent. Stimpson checks the time; it is three o'clock.

Combat air patrol will circle the carrier for two or three hours. Hornet is now making good speed, on a northeast heading, gradually drawing away from Formosa, to the left. Constantly glancing behind and from side to side, Stimpson checks the open sky; no unidentified aircraft on any quarter. His engine runs smoothly, everything appears quiet and anticlimactic. The afternoon of this last day of the Formosa strike wears on.

And then things change with a start. Ginger Base cracks a warning: "Bogeys fifty miles out—bearing 300 degrees—vector 300 degrees!"

The air is instantly charged with excitement. Lieutenant Savage kicks left rudder and left stick, and points the blunt nose of his Hellcat northwest, increasing throttle. The other Hellcats follow. Stimpson peers ahead, tensing in anticipation of battle. His eye catches the wagging wings of his section leader.

Lieutenant Dayhoff is trying to attract his attention. Stimpson eases up closer, being careful not to jam his wingtip into the wingtip, or prop, of Dayhoff's fighter. Now he's quite close, can see Dayhoff pointing to his earphones. Radio out!

Dayhoff motions to Stimpson to take over the division. Stimpson nods, guns his throttle, and pulls ahead. Dayhoff drops back and takes position on Stimpson's left. Thus the second of the two divisions of the CAP is now led by Stimpson, his wingman off to his right, the section of two planes led by Dayhoff farther back, left. It's the finger-four formation.

Up ahead, Lieutenant Savage pushes stick forward, picks up speed, while gradually descending, in an effort to get as far away from the carriers as possible before intercepting the enemy. Every pilot knows *Hornet* is his home, that if the enemy gets to her, and sinks her, he'll be forced to find another carrier, or ditch. So the farther out the Hellcats intercept the better chance they'll have to save the carrier.

Savage is in constant contact with Ginger Base aboard *Hornet*, which steadily grows smaller and smaller to the southeast.

All eyes focus forward—through the canopies, and to right and left, ahead, but the bogeys are not in sight. Now the flight leader's voice crackles over the radio: "My compass is out. Stimpson, take over the flight!" It's the second change of flying position; Stimpson pushes throttle forward, pulls his division into the lead of the eight-plane formation. Savage drops his four-plane division back, to the left. Only a few minutes before Stimpson was second-in-command in Dayhoff's division. Now he is flight leader, leading the interception mission.

Hornet is out of sight. Stimpson estimates he is forty miles out from the carrier, on a northwest heading. Being in the lead position, he scans the sky constantly; still no enemy in sight. Over the radio he hears preparations being made for the launching of additional fighters to support the eight already on their way to intercept the enemy. Stimpson hopes the others will scramble fast enough to somehow catch up. He would feel better if he knew reinforcements were close behind.

Ginger Base calls to say Stimpson's Hellcats should be in the vicinity of the enemy. Heads turn. The sky is searched; no enemy is sighted. *Hornet* insists the bandits should be seen at any second, crossing right to left. Stimpson and the other American pilots fix their eyes on the sky at one o'clock and two o'clock. Stimpson wonders if he has missed them. The eight Hellcats roar on into the blue northwest sky.

"Tally-ho!" yells Savage. With a start, Stimpson strains his eyes. There they are! Two o'clock! Small dots . . . three groups . . . At the bottom are enemy dive bombers. Stimpson estimates the bombers at eight to twelve. At least twenty fighters above! He radios this estimate to *Hornet*. The enemy fighters are obviously protecting the bombers, who are seeking the ships of Task Force 38. Stimpson glances at his altimeter. The Hellcats are down to 17,000 feet, and are slightly above the bombers which are crossing from right to left. He radios *Hornet* the disposition of the fighters, says he is going in to the attack.

The enemy, apparently, has not yet sighted the Hellcats, now drawing closer, and the Japanese formation passes to the left, ahead. This will give VF 11's eight a chance to close in from the rear; Stimpson hopes to catch the enemy in this vulnerable position, before sighted. Every pilot feels the drama as the Hellcats move in, closer and closer.

His strategy works, as the enemy aircraft angle slightly to the right, making it easy for the Hellcats to turn in behind, on a six-o'clock approach. Stimpson identifies the fighters, now clearly in view, as Hamps, Zekes and Tonys. The bombers are stacked up in threes behind the lead element. Higher, the fighters also are stacked, from front to rear, in threes.

Stimpson reports these details to Ginger Base, describing his approach on the approximate level of the lowest of the enemy fighters. He will attack the fighters, on the same level, while Savage's division goes after the dive bombers, which carry the seeds of destruction for the American ships.

The enemy's fighters will outnumber the Hellcats by perhaps five to one, but he will risk the odds, in the hope Savage's division can decimate the dive bombers. It is a daring attack. Stimpson is dividing his force in the face of a numerically superior enemy.

Tension heightens as the silhouettes of the Japanese planes grow larger and larger. Still the enemy has not reacted; the Americans are steadily closing, undetected.

Stimpson moves his left hand forward against the throttle; already all the way forward. The distance is closing slowly, agonizingly, and every second seems a minute. Stimpson fears the enemy will spot him, now coming on directly from behind, at any moment. The element of surprise would be lost. He presses the mike button, calling Lieutenant Savage: "You get the bombers and I'll take the fighters!" Then he warns all pilots to hold their fire. Becoming visible under the wings of the enemy planes are attachments. Now it's obvious. The fighters carry extra fuel tanks! Luck! This will make them vulnerable targets, especially if the element of surprise is not lost.

Stimpson fixes his eyes on an element of three Hamps, dead ahead and at his altitude, maneuvers left rudder and stick, to bring the one farthest to the left into the electric yellow sight rings of his gunsight glass. Only seconds away, now, he glances around, and behind, and sees Ensign Blair on his right, in perfect position. He snaps his head back, sighting through the gunsight, tensely watching for the first sign the enemy has detected him. That would be falling extra fuel tanks, which the enemy pilots would release as soon as they spotted the Hellcats. The wing tanks do not drop.

The wingspan on the Hamp farthest left, in the three-plane formation, grows wider and wider. Stimpson's finger grips the trigger on the stick as the wingspan passes the 50-mill ring, stretches out farther, touches the inner sides of the 100-mill ring.

He is within range, presses the trigger! The Hellcat vibrates. The six guns belch fire and a deafening roar. Tracers point a fatal path to the Hamp on the left. The Hellcat continues to thunder and shake. The deadly fire pours into the startled victim and 50-caliber shells smash the airframe to bits, even as they crash into wing tanks, which burst into orange flame. The entire enemy fighter is enveloped in yellow and orange flame. Instantly Stimpson kicks right rudder and pulls right stick, to maneuver into position behind the middle Hamp. As he does, he passes to the right of the stricken Hamp, now falling off on his left, leaving a trail of black smoke and debris, plunging toward the water below.

The Americans are achieving complete tactical surprise. Stimpson's wingman, Blair, has taken aim at another unsuspecting enemy fighter, now receiving the full fury of Blair's guns. The other section of the four-fighter division, led by Dayhoff, has selected two other enemy aircraft—Judys—and both Dayhoff and Ensign J. A. Zink, his wingman, are opening fire on them. As Stimpson opens on his second victim, Dayhoff and Zink open on the Judys. Soon both Dayhoff and Zink's victims are burning fiercely.

Below, Savage's division is diving on other Judys. Thus all four pilots of Stimpson's lead division have scored kills in the opening moments of the battle, a battle that now grows fiercer.

Savage is leading only three Hellcats in a diving attack on the Judys —one of his fighters has been forced to turn back! So it is seven Hellcats against twenty fighters and twelve dive bombers.

Now Stimpson is easing up on the second Hamp. The enemy fighters are slowed by the extra tanks, while the Hellcats are at full throttle. In a matter of seconds the wingspan of the second Hamp is touching the 100-mill ring. The brown-green aircraft seems to stand still. Stimpson is in range. He squeezes the trigger button!

Tracers mark a converging path once again, and shells instantly strike the leader of the Jap formation. Shells are blasting from the muzzles at a rate of better than a hundred per second, and both planes seem to stagger, the enemy's from hits and Stimpson's from the vibration of the guns. The enemy's wing begins to wobble slightly, and then . . . flash! A ball of flame follows the explosion. The Hamp literally disintegrates, falls away in a death dive.

Instinctively Stimpson pushes right rudder, dips his right wing, and curves toward the remaining Hamp, to the right, ahead. Suddenly he realizes he is almost on him, and chops his throttle all the way. Still, he is overtaking the third Hamp, which now—at last—seems to sense that something is wrong. Stimpson rushes up on him, even though the prop windmills with the throttle back. The Hamp begins to pull up, right, but Stimpson is on him. As his left wing lifts, Stimpson follows the maneuver and curves in behind. Hanging on him, he opens fire! Can he stay behind long enough to bring him down?

Tracers streak into the Hamp. Stimpson sticks with him, in the turn, firing. A slim yellow streak of flame trails behind. The distance closes to a hundred feet. Still firing! The Hamp explodes! Stimpson yanks back on the stick, but barely misses the burning enemy fighter as he rockets straight through smoke and debris from the explosion.

His heart pounding, Stimpson glances around. Blair is off to his right, behind, and no enemy fighters have jumped him as yet. It has happened so fast, it is hard for him to believe . . . three kills without having been fired on!

But the enemy is now alerted; the task becomes more difficult, and more costly, for the seven valiant American pilots.

Not far away Lieutenant Dayhoff, whose radio malfunction caused him to turn over his division to Stimpson, is turning into a Zeke. His wingman, Zink, follows in a left chandelle. Suddenly a Zeke passes in Zink's line of fire. The ensign opens with all guns. The Zeke takes hits, flies on. Zink follows him with his eyes for a moment. He bursts into flame and explodes! Zink's second kill!

His satisfaction is interrupted. Two Zekes, from above, slice down in a firing pass on him and Dayhoff. Zink maneuvers frantically to evade the line of fire, escapes. Dayhoff pours shells into one Zeke, but catches heavy enemy fire. His Hellcat falls off into a vertical dive. There is no indication he is conscious at the controls. Zink, shocked and helpless, follows him down, diving toward the ocean. Now there are but two U.S. fighters left, above, to hold off the enemy fighters. Meanwhile, of the three Hellcat pilots below, Lieutenant (j.g.) S. E. Goldberg is missing.

The greater numbers of enemy fighters—Hamps (improved Zeroes with self-sealing tanks), Tonys (faster than the Zeroes, with inline engines), and Zekes (improved Zeroes)—turn their revengeful attention on the remaining American fighters. Several of the enemy's dive bombers have successfully been shot down, others damaged, but now the Americans are forced to defend themselves against determined attacks by enemy fighters, which close on all sides.

With Dayhoff and Zink out of the battle, and Goldberg missing, only four American pilots are left. Now Goldberg's wingman, Ensign Tadeus L. Lepianka, is raked by heavy enemy fire, which shreds his Hellcat from stem to stern. Lepianka reports he is wounded, and turns to a heading toward *Hornet*.

There are three Hellcats left—Stimpson, his wingman Blair, and Savage.

Savage is engaged in a desperate battle with several Zekes, which jumped him as he headed for the dive bombers. On the first pass, Savage destroys one Zeke, from a 15-degree deflection gunnery run. Several others jump him, from above, and he manages to evade their fire. He closes from astern on another Zeke, opens with all guns, and shoots him down. Now he is attacked by other Zekes.

Stimpson also has his hands full. After destroying the three Hamps he has regained some altitude. He spots a Zeke, below, diving on a Hellcat. Could it be crippled Lepianka? Fearing for the Hellcat pilot, Stimpson wings over in a vertical dive and streaks for the Zeke. Blair follows at a distance. Stimpson points his guns ahead of the enemy; the Zeke below will have to fly through their path. It is a daring pass. The Hellcat gains speed and the wind whistles by. Stimpson is looking almost straight down, the Zeke flying perpendicular to his course. Now the sleek enemy fighter is approaching a position directly below his nose. Just before the enemy fighter is directly below, Stimpson, eyes on the sight ring, which he maneuvers into position, presses the trigger. The six guns throw a hail of shrapnel straight down. Stimpson has timed it beautifully. The enemy fighter streaks directly into the firing pattern and, caught by surprise, is raked from engine to tail by the shells. Stimpson begins to pull out of his dive, watches the enemy fighter. His daring pass is rewarded. The Zeke, ahead only a short distance, explodes. The burning pieces float down over the blue water. Victim No. 4 for Stimpson!

He looks around. Even before he can relax, and enjoy the satisfaction of kill No. 4, he spots another enemy fighter slightly above. Having dived on the last victim, Stimpson has plenty of speed, slices into a bank to approach the Zeke from behind. This enemy pilot, thoroughly alerted, sees the approaching Hellcat, rolls on his back and split-S's. Stimpson must decide whether to follow. The Hellcat can outdive the Zero, because of its greater weight. But as the odds are heavy, he hesitates to get below so many enemy fighters.

In a calculated decision, Stimpson lets the Zeke get away, pulls back on the stick. The altimeter needle winds to the right as he regains altitude. Blair, still faithfully following, is behind. He has shot down a second Zeke in the swirling battle, but has managed to stick on Stimpson's tail through it all.

Only seconds pass before Stimpson's visual searching uncovers more action below. Just as he levels out after regaining altitude he sees a Tony, below, right, on the tail of an F6F. Instantly, once again, Stimpson shoves stick forward, noses down. He banks into a steep turn to curve out on the Tony's tail. The enemy pilot is so intent on his intended victim that he neglects to clear behind him.

Stimpson's Hellcat gains speed and closes the distance. The Tony is still following the Hellcat, now very close behind. Stimpson must fire quickly, if he is to save the American. From above, and to the side, still diving, Stimpson zeroes in. He is a little far, but maybe not too far, and, leading the Tony, he pulls the trigger. Tracers shoot out front of the Jap, then move backward. The shells begin to strike and take effect. Black smoke begins to trail the brownish-green, slim-nosed enemy fighter. The damaged Tony turns away, Stimpson still firing. Now the Tony plunges straight down, leaving a heavy black smoke column.

Lieutenant Savage, the Jap pilot's intended victim, looks back, and is relieved. Victim No. 5 for Stimpson! But neither Stimpson nor Blair nor Savage has time to consider the victory. They are all under attack. Blair is engaging a Zeke, maneuvers into a slight angle approach from behind—approximately 20 degrees. He opens on the enemy, maintains fire, and in short order Stimpson's wingman has scored another kill.

Now Blair turns in to Stimpson in a defensive maneuver—as another enemy fighter dives on him. Stimpson and Blair immediately go into the Thatch Weave. (This is named after Navy pilot Jimmy Thatch, and enables two fighters to protect each other's rear by weaving in and out, so that each is in a position to fire on an enemy plane on the tail of the other.)

Stimpson and Blair cross in this defensive maneuver, then pull out to the side, and turn, for another approach. And from a distance off Blair's side, Stimpson sees a Jap closing Blair's tail. Tony! Blair continues the weave; he is turning back in. Stimpson points his nose directly at his wingman. They approach from a thousand feet. Stimpson grips his gun trigger, again, squints through the sighting glass to the rear of Blair's tail. Soon the F6F flashes through the sight ring, and then, close behind, the Tony. Fire! Stimpson still has ammunition, the 50-caliber guns spurt a stream of shells into the Tony.

Stimpson sees strikes on the cowling, engines and wing roots. They rush together. Smoke begins to trail from the Tony. Stimpson flashes by, turns to continue his weaving pattern with Blair. The Tony wings over and starts down, but is not afire. There is no time to follow the Tony's descent. A number of enemy fighters are watching the pair of Hellcats.

A Zeke dives on Blair's tail. In firing at the Tony, and driving him off Blair's tail, Stimpson was pulled rather wide. Now he must hurry back again, to protect Blair. His wingman is banking back toward him, and Stimpson, now alarmed at the nearness of the Zeke on Blair's tail, holds his breath. The leading edges of the Zeke's wings twinkle.

Now the distance closes, and Stimpson is fast coming into range. He can see that Blair has been hit. At last Blair crosses in front of Stimpson, and the Zeke is in range. Hoping some ammunition remains in his guns, Stimpson presses the trigger. The 50-calibers explode into action once again, and the tracers mark a path of revenge toward the Zeke. The accuracy of fire tears the enemy aircraft apart. Almost instantaneously the Zeke's left wing explodes, near the root, and Stimpson's seventh victim careens wildly, in a half-spin, downward, burning, smoking.

Stimpson kicks rudder and stick and slices into a curve to close Blair. He feels a sickening sensation. Fire is streaming from his wingman's belly tank! He grabs the mike button and yells for Blair to drop his tank and dive for the deck. Only he and Savage remain, undamaged, of the seven American pilots who engaged the enemy. (And Savage, having hit a third Jap fighter after his two victories, is headed for *Hornet.*)

Stimpson looks at Blair. He's diving toward the water below. Stimpson covers him from above. Now another of the enemy fighters above, a Zeke, dives after the stricken American fighter. Wondering when his ammunition will be exhausted, Stimpson banks in behind the Zeke. Blair is descending fast, the flames are spreading to the lower part of his engine. Stimpson, even as he follows the Zeke, knows Blair can't make it back to *Hornet.* Now he closes from an angle on the Zeke, who apparently has not seen him. For the last time in the day's bitter battle, Stimpson squints through his sight ring. When the Zeke's silhouette is large enough, he presses the trigger, and several tracers streak in front of the Zeke! Erratic firing, the strange vibration, tell him he is running out of ammunition. It is just enough, though, for the Zeke banks sharply away, frightened off by Stimpson's fire. Had the Zeke stuck to Blair's tail, there was little Stimpson could have done about it.

Now Blair is approaching the water. After the bitter fighting, all the narrow escapes, Stimpson's one hope now is to save his wingman. Glancing to his rear, he is relieved to see no other enemy fighter pilots are diving after the burning Hellcat. A breather at last.

Stimpson picks up the mike button and calls Blair. No answer. Blair is obviously preparing to ditch. Stimpson points his nose lower and watches the burning Hellcat, helpless, wondering if Blair can pull it off, and get out. The flames are now streaming back from his engine and lower fuselage. The Hellcat rapidly heads for the water. The sea is rough. The Hellcat is going in! It smashes into the waves with terrific impact. Anxiously, Stimpson circles the sinking Hellcat, straining his eyes to see if Blair gets out. The big fighter sinks beneath the waves, and Stimpson sees no one get out. He circles and circles. A floating belly tank; nothing else. The Hellcat is now completely out of sight, below the water. He refuses to take his eye off the spot, until he is no longer sure of the exact spot where the Hellcat sank. Nevertheless, he still hopes Blair got out, since he obviously made a controlled landing.

Sick over the ditching of his wingman, though hoping he got out somehow, alone just over the waves, out of ammunition, with no friendly Hellcats in the area, Stimpson pulls back on the stick, at full throttle, and turns to a southeasterly course toward *Hornet*. It is five o'clock—two and a half hours since take-off.

Stimpson calls Ginger Base. No reply. He flies on, carefully checks instruments and engine temperatures. In the desperate fight, in which he used maximum power most of the time, he could have overtaxed his engine. But the big Pratt and Whitney up front roars smoothly, and the Hamilton-Standard prop spins away, pulling him closer and closer to *Hornet*. Slowly the altimeter climbs. Stimpson reaches 5,000, 6,000 feet. Heading 120 degrees, he calls the carrier again. At a higher altitude, nearer the carrier, this time his transmission is answered.

"I'm returning to the carrier," Stimpson reports. "My wingman has been shot down." Ginger Base acknowledges his report and checks his heading. Ahead Stimpson spots a destroyer, one of *Hornet*'s outer screen. He will pass directly above the destroyer, on the way toward *Hornet*. His eye suddenly fixes on the temperature gauge. With a start, he notices the gauge is in the red. The engine is running hot! He looks through the canopy toward the cowling, to see if oil is seeping from the engine, but there's no sign of oil. He listens carefully to the engine . . . running smoothly. Yet engine temperature is up. Stimpson decides he will ditch near the destroyer, ahead, if his engine cuts out or catches fire. He will maintain throttle setting, however, in a bid to get back to *Hornet*. He closes the destroyer rapidly. The lone Hellcat crosses it (without drawing friendly enemy aircraft fire—always most unwelcome by fighter pilots returning from battle).

Stimpson watches the engine temperature gauge. It remains steady, but abnormally hot. The minutes drag by. It is 5:25. Then up ahead . . . on the horizon . . . can it be? A longer look. *Hornet* ahead! The big carrier is preparing to take him aboard, turns into the wind for his landing. The engine is still running hot, but Stimpson now knows he'll make it down!

He is completely depressed by the loss of his wingman and wonders if anyone has taken off to search for Blair. Now the Hellcat becomes a larger and larger speck to deck hands aboard *Hornet*, looking northwest, waiting for their seven Hellcats to return. Only Lieutenant Savage and Ensign Zink have returned undamaged, of the seven who met the enemy. The reinforcements never joined the battle. Ensign Lepianka, badly wounded, managed a miraculous landing, his Hellcat shredded by enemy shells. After a quick examination, his fighter was jettisoned as worthless.

Stimpson is down to a few hundred feet, is approaching the rear of the carrier. He watches the flags in the hands of the landing signals officer standing near the rear of the flight deck. He drops flaps, eases off on the throttle, and gets down to about 110 knots. The deck of the carrier rises up and seems to rush toward the fighter. Hook down, he gets the flag signal to cut his gun and yanks the throttle back with his left hand.

A bounce! Another bounce and a jerk! The cable catches him; the Hellcat is abruptly jerked to a stop. Crewmen release the cable and motion to Stimpson, and he begins to taxi toward the parking area. As he approaches, several fellow pilots and crewmen race up to the side of the plane. He can sense the excitement, and as soon as he cuts the gun, and begins to crawl, exhausted, out of the canopy, they are asking him questions. They are surprised because Stimpson is so depressed. They ask how many victories he scored.

"Five and two probables," he says, matter-of-factly. Exclamations greet his answer.

Curiously, Stimpson thinks very little of his victories. He walks to the ready room, below. He broods because he was the leader of the flight, a flight that has lost three pilots and had another badly wounded. The intelligence officer in the ready room senses his depression, tries to cheer him up, but to no avail. As soon as he is interrogated, however, a message comes from the bridge. Captain A. K. Doyle, skipper of *Hornet,* asks to see him. Stimpson hurries to the superstructure, climbs the ladder to report to the captain.

As soon as he enters the captain's quarters, Doyle congratulates him on his victories. But even this does not dispel Stimpson's obvious gloom. Doyle senses his mood. He knows Stimpson is second-guessing his own tactics in the attack.

"Well, son, remember you saved our ships from attack, and that was your job. I feel you made the right decision," Doyle reassures him. Coming from the skipper, this comforts him, to a degree, though by now Stimpson strongly suspects none of the three missing pilots will be recovered.

In spite of his gloom, Stimpson had achieved one of the war's great individual successes in turning back the thirty enemy planes with seven fighters. He was officially credited with five confirmed kills and two probables in the action. And though cruiser *Houston* took a torpedo hit that day from a Japanese torpedo plane (the second cruiser to be torpedoed by Japanese airmen in two days), *Hornet,* Carrier Group 1, and Task Force 38, withdrew from the massive Formosa strike without losing a single ship to enemy bombs or torpedoes.

Lieutenant Stimpson's interception on the afternoon of October 14 prevented the dive bombers of the enemy formation from hitting any American warship. The seven American fighters were credited with destroying thirteen enemy planes, plus four probables. Blair, Dayhoff and Goldberg died in the action. Ensign Lepianka, with wounds in the arm and head, recovered.

The impressive score was achieved not with the outdated Zero, but with the fastest and latest enemy fighters—Hamps, Tonys and Zekes. The Navy thought so much of Stimpson's conduct in the action that shortly afterward Admiral Jocko Clark, in a special ceremony aboard *Hornet,* presented him the Navy Cross for his conduct in the battle.

The five confirmed victories, added to his six victories achieved at Guadalcanal, gave him a total of eleven. But he had not finished. While still aboard *Hornet,* on this same tour of duty, which soon involved support for the American landing on Leyte and the resulting aerial battles

A Japanese suicide plane misses and crashes alongside U.S.S. Sangamon. (Official U.S. Navy Photo)

in the Philippines area, Stimpson added six additional kills. This gave him a final total of seventeen confirmed victories (a number of his probables were almost certainly kills) and made him one of the Navy's top World War II aces.

In early 1945 he returned to the United States, and to his wife, the former Mary Bills of Santa Barbara, whom he had married in July of 1942, after winning his wings in June of that year, in Miami. He was soon discharged from the Navy.

For some years after the war Stimpson operated a ranch in Arizona, and more recently he and his family (which now includes four boys and a girl) moved to Walnut Creek, near San Francisco.

Throughout the years he has maintained an interest in naval aviation, as is demonstrated by a letter he wrote Admiral Arleigh Burke, then Chief of Naval Operations, in Washington, D.C. In the letter he apologized for his boldness in writing the Chief of Naval Operations, but confessed to a yearning to fly, once more, in a Navy fighter—a jet.

Burke proved that the Navy had not forgotten its greatest wartime aces. Stimpson was invited aboard a carrier, off the California coast, and given his ride in one of the latest jet fighters.

The United States Navy looks after its own; it has not forgotten the hero of that bitter fighter battle off Formosa, on Saturday afternoon, October 14, 1944.

The Navy Cross citation Stimpson received in recognition of his mission of October 14 reads in part:

For extraordinary heroism as Pilot of a Fighter Plane in Fighting Squadron Eleven, attached to the U.S.S. HORNET, in action against enemy Japanese forces in the Philippine Islands Area, October 14, 1944.

Instantly taking over the lead of an eight-plane combat air patrol when his flight leader's radio became inoperable, Lieutenant Stimpson boldly intercepted and attacked a large formation of enemy aircraft headed for our surface forces.

Courageously and skillfully pressing home his attacks, he shot down five and possibly seven of the fourteen enemy planes destroyed in the engagement and aided in dispersing the remainder. His skillful airmanship, initiative and exceptional courage reflect the highest credit upon Lieutenant Stimpson and the United States Naval Service.

10 The Ace of Aces' Flight of Nine

OCTOBER 24, 1944:

Commander DAVID McCAMPBELL, U.S.N.

OF the greatest Navy and Marine Corps fighter aces of World War II, Commander David McCampbell was unquestionably the nonpareil. This ace of aces led Air Group 15 of Task Force 38, in the U.S. Third Fleet.

McCampbell ended the war with 34 confirmed aerial victories (tops in the Navy) and estimated destruction of 21 enemy planes on the ground. He was thus responsible for the destruction of 55 enemy planes. His actual total was probably higher. Yet McCampbell and his record are still largely unknown to the American public.

He commanded U.S. fighters in many of the greatest aerial battles in the Pacific. He shot down more enemy planes on one mission than any other American fighter pilot. His service included duty in the Mediterranean, Guadalcanal, and in the South China Sea. It spanned most of the war.

He won just about all of the country's most coveted medals, including the Congressional Medal of Honor. He saw his carrier (*Wasp*) sunk beneath his feet in 1942. He was almost shot down by the guns of the Third Fleet while returning from his most successful mission—on the first day of the greatest naval battle of World War II.

McCampbell's record is little known because World War II fighter battles, apart from naval and land battles, have received little documentary, detailed attention—being difficult to reconstruct, covering such wide areas in so brief a time. And—in McCampbell's case—news of the great naval battle off the Philippines naturally overshadowed his most extraordinary mission.

But if McCampbell's exploits are unknown in American households, they are nonetheless incredible.

His naval career began with dismissal. Graduated from Annapolis in 1933, the depth of the depression, with the Navy lacking funds, he was "rewarded" with an honorable discharge. In June, 1934, however, he was recalled and commissioned. Two years later he received his first assignment involving aircraft: he was made gunnery observer in Scouting Squadron 11, aboard U.S.S. *Portland*.

The next year, 1937, he reported for flying instruction at the Naval Air Station, Pensacola, Florida, and in 1938 won his wings. He began the war aboard *Wasp*, served on that famous carrier from 1940 until she went to the bottom in September, 1942.

Wasp was a fighting ship with a proud record. Among her achievements were two runs into the hotly contested Mediterranean in the spring of 1942, delivering desperately needed Spitfires to beleaguered Malta and saving that British fortress from strangulation by the Luftwaffe. Then she played a vital role in supporting Americans on Guadalcanal, in that grim campaign which began in August, 1942.

Steaming with *Hornet*, new battleship *North Carolina* and destroyers, five weeks after the opening of that battle, *Wasp* was hit and sunk by three torpedoes on September 15. (*North Carolina* also was hit, as was destroyer *O'Brien*—a devastating attack by two colluding enemy submarines, I-19 and I-15.)

McCampbell survived that sinking and, returning to the United States, commissioned and fitted out a new fighter squadron (with *Wasp*'s spirit) within the year. In February, 1949, he was given command of Air Group 15, aboard *Essex*. With this group, beginning early in 1944, McCampbell was to make aerial history—and compile a record unique in the annals of air warfare.

In seven months Air Group 15 participated in attacks on Iwo Jima, Formosa, the Marianas, Palau, Philippines, and Nansei Shotos, as well as in the first Battle of the Philippine Sea, climaxing this operational period by participating in the Battle for Leyte Gulf. During this period McCampbell became the highest-scoring ace in the Navy. His group earned the admiration of fliers everywhere, and the nickname "The Fabled Fifteen."

McCampbell's cool, calculating ability as a fighter pilot was strikingly exhibited on June 19, 1944, in the Battle of the Philippine Sea (the "Marianas Turkey Shoot"), when he led his fighters against eighty enemy aircraft, personally destroying seven. His group virtually annihilated the sizable enemy force. This was one of the great individual and group fighter victories of the war and occurred in the same day that Lieutenant (j.g.) Alexander Vraciu shot down six enemy aircraft—as related in an earlier chapter.

By the time October, 1944, rolled around (the month with which we are concerned) the men and ships of Third Fleet Task Force 38 carrier groups had been in continuous action for two months. In the two preceding weeks, while softening up Japanese defenses to the north with strikes on Luzon, Formosa and Okinawa, they had been subjected to the heaviest enemy air attacks of the war. Many of the fleet's ships had been on operations for nine to ten months without rest or rehabilitation.

Admiral Marc A. Mitscher, commanding Task Force 38, wrote at this time that "No other force in the world has been subjected to such a period of constant operation without rest or rehabilitation." The reactions of crews were slowing down as a result of the long strain. Medical officers were recording increasingly frequent signs of fatigue among the men of the ships' companies. In this condition, carriers of Task Force 38 entered the war's greatest naval battle—the Battle for Leyte Gulf.

The Japanese considered the U.S. landing in the Philippines (October 20) the showdown crisis of the war. They viewed the resulting naval collision as its decisive battle. Vice Admiral Takeo Kurita, rallying his command at the start of the attack, put it simply: "We are about to fight a battle which will decide the fate of the Empire."

The American advance westward had reached Japan's lifeline. If U.S.

forces retook the Philippines, Japanese supply lines to the south would be severed, the fleet's source of oil cut off. In Tokyo the high command conceded that if this happened the outcome of the war would be settled. The enemy, therefore, gathered every available warship in an effort to deliver a crippling blow against the two U.S. fleets supporting the invasion of Leyte—the Third and Seventh.

The job of Third Fleet, and of carrier pilots of Third Fleet's Task Force 38 (to the north), was to protect the vast armada of ships and men (Seventh Fleet) to the south, which was rapidly disgorging men and equipment on Leyte.

McCampbell was flying an F6F Grumman Hellcat off *Essex*—one of sixteen carriers in Third Fleet's Task Force 38. Task Force 38, as we have seen, contained the preponderance of striking power of U.S. naval forces—eight large aircraft carriers (CV's), eight light carriers (CVL's), six big, new battleships with sixteen-inch guns (BB's), six heavy cruisers (CA's), nine light cruisers (CL's), and fifty-eight destroyers (DD's), and was divided into four groups, each in itself a powerful force. The task group to which *Essex* was assigned was Task Group 38.3, comprised of four carriers, two battleships, four light cruisers and thirteen destroyers. It flew the flag of Rear Admiral Frederick C. Sherman.

On the morning of October 24 three of the four groups were strung out 125 miles apart, in assigned positions off the east Philippine coast. The northernmost group (Sherman's) was located due east of central Luzon. The central group was fifty miles off San Bernardino Strait. The southern group was sixty miles off the tip of Samar Island. The fourth was reprovisioning and rearming.

For two days electrifying evidence mounted—indicating a major naval battle was impending. Not all of the enemy's designs were yet known that morning, but two different fleets had been sighted—both apparently heading for Leyte Gulf, to the south.

There, vulnerable to enemy warships, lay the largest aggregation of thinly armed U.S. amphibious craft ever seen in the Pacific. More than 150 LST's dotted the coastline and more than 300 other ships (transports, LCT's and LCI's) were clustered in Leyte Gulf. Four days earlier troops of General Walter Krueger's Sixth United States Army had planted the U.S. flag on the Philippines. Over 100,000 men had gone ashore.

In the early morning hours of the 22nd the first evidence of the enemy's reaction had reached Third Fleet headquarters. Submarine *Darter,* patrolling the Palawan Passage west of the Philippines, reported sighting three enemy cruisers. But *Darter* lost them before dawn. All day the vigil was kept. Then, at sixteen minutes past midnight, October 23, *Darter* and sister submarine *Dace* made another contact. This time the game was bigger—the two subs raced to stay ahead of 32 warships, among them five battleships, steaming northeastward, up the Palawan Passage.

This was one of three major enemy forces converging on Leyte Gulf. The enemy's carrier forces (not yet sighted and being positioned to decoy Third Fleet) were moving south from Japan toward Luzon. Sherman's group formed the northern shoulder of U.S. forces in this area. A third Japanese fleet, consisting of battleships, cruisers and destroyers, was closing the western approach of the Mindanao Sea—headed for Leyte Gulf via Surigao Strait, far to the south.

Darter and *Dace* opened the attack on the enemy as Kurita's central fleet negotiated Palawan Passage. After staying ahead of the oncoming force until just before dawn on the 23rd, *Darter* fired ten torpedoes and sank one heavy cruiser, damaged another. *Dace* sank a heavy cruiser with four hits. The battle was on.

The sighting of Kurita's force, moving toward San Bernardino Strait, had caused Third Fleet Commander Admiral William Halsey to alert his three carrier groups. Each was to launch a patrol at dawn on the 24th—in an effort to locate and attack the approaching enemy central force—the most powerful of the three Japanese fleets.

From the three groups patrols took off shortly after six next morning (the 24th). Search planes from the middle U.S. carrier group spotted Kurita's fleet at 7:46. It was still on course for Leyte. About an hour later, planes from the *Enterprise* (of the southernmost carrier group) sighted Vice Admiral Shoji Nishimura's southern attacking force, consisting of two battleships, a heavy cruiser and four destroyers, southwest of Negros Island in the Sulu Sea, also on course for Leyte.

McCampbell had gone to bed the evening of the 23rd aware of dramatic developments. In the middle of the night an orderly woke him with news that a large enemy fleet was being tracked and that there would probably be a dawn launch from *Essex.* He was not to participate in this first strike. He would lead the second strike, several hours later.

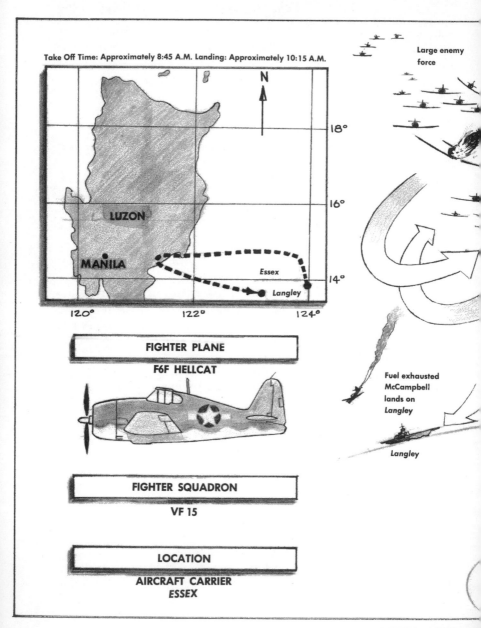

Take Off Time: Approximately 8:45 A.M. Landing: Approximately 10:15 A.M.

Large enemy force

18°

16°

LUZON

MANILA

Essex

Langley

14°

120°   122°   124°

Fuel exhausted McCampbell lands on Langley

Langley

FIGHTER PLANE
F6F HELLCAT

FIGHTER SQUADRON
VF 15

LOCATION
**AIRCRAFT CARRIER
*ESSEX***

MISSION FLOWN BY

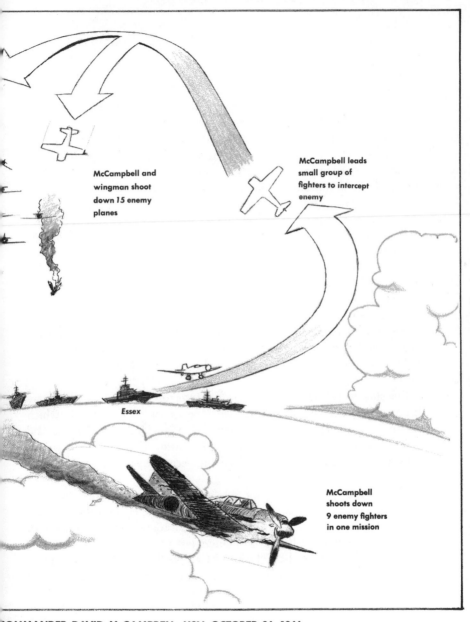

McCampbell and wingman shoot down 15 enemy planes

McCampbell leads small group of fighters to intercept enemy

Essex

McCampbell shoots down 9 enemy fighters in one mission

COMMANDER DAVID McCAMPBELL, USN, OCTOBER 24, 1944

The alarm jangles at 5:30 on the morning of the 24th in McCampbell's room. He pulls on old green coveralls, an escape kit in one pocket, and in others maps, money, vitamin pills, medicine and a flag. After lacing up his high, old-fashioned composition brown shoes, he grabs a .38 revolver and a knife and bounds through the door. He turns right and descends a ladder, crosses the hangar deck, port to starboard, and sits down for breakfast in Wardroom 1.

Three cups of coffee and orange juice later, before 6:30, he is in his office four decks up (02 level) checking weather and developments. This is the office-ready room of *Essex*'s fighter squadron.

The latest information shows the central enemy fleet approaching San Bernardino Strait, to the southwest. McCampbell looks outside at the weather—it is good. There are high clouds and a few thunderheads, but patches of blue show through, and there is only a gentle breeze. *Essex* plows ahead through a gentle sea. As he looks out over the water and scans the sky, the roar of planes taking off from *Essex* begins to die. The last of the dawn strike is taking off.

McCampbell's second strike is due to be launched at 9:00 A.M. Now he settles down to paper work, so much of which was required of group commanders. During the next hour no sighting of the enemy fleet or action report comes from the airborne strike, which consists of fighters, torpedo bombers and dive bombers, and McCampbell continues to "fly" his desk.

But shortly before 7:30 his ordeal is interrupted. Sudden orders are issued for a surprise launch—it will consist only of fighters, which will make a sweep of airfields around Manila. This is not the second launch against Kurita's central fleet. Therefore, McCampbell is not to lead it—he is still scheduled to lead the second strike against Kurita's fleet.

He continues with desk work, while more of *Essex*'s fighters are preparing to take off. Shortly, he watches them launched into the morning sky. As the last one takes off, McCampbell tabulates his fighter strength remaining aboard. He has seven fighters left (out of 36).

It is now almost eight o'clock. McCampbell settles down again to paper work, and after only a few minutes is interrupted for the second time within the hour. The central enemy fleet has been sighted—by a plane from *Intrepid*, a carrier of the middle carrier group. All hands at once begin preparations for the second strike at the enemy fleet—which is now nearing San Bernardino Strait. McCampbell drops the paper work and hurriedly begins preparing for take-off.

But he is due for another quick surprise. At this very moment *Essex's* radar picks up an air contact. As men scurry here and there, readying planes for the second strike on the enemy fleet, and getting them on deck, radar screens show a large number of suspicious specks to the west. The ominous diagnosis . . . an enemy air strike headed for the group's carriers! Like *Essex,* all four carriers in the group are short of Hellcats. Only twelve fighters circle above the group on routine defensive station.

Officers aboard each carrier move hurriedly to assemble everything available to intercept the newly located enemy planes. Now they are surprised again. Radar reports another enemy air group behind the first! The first is estimated at forty planes. Orders flash from flagship *Lexington* to carriers *Langley, Princeton* and *Essex*—launch all defensive fighters. *Langley* would launch twelve, *Princeton* twelve, and *Essex* whatever she could. *Lexington* would hold the group's only fighter reserve.

Aboard *Essex* the horn blurts: "All fighter pilots, man your planes." McCampbell has only seven fighters. He has standing orders not to participate in defensive scrambles. But he takes the announcement to mean he is included in the "all fighter pilots," since this is an emergency.

With him in the squadron room at this moment are his plane captain, E. E. Carroll, his intelligence and administrative officers, and a yeoman. Explaining his intention, he dashes into the passageway, yelling to Carroll to get his plane ready as soon as possible—lugging his back pack, helmet and oxygen mask.

Meanwhile, more alarming news comes from the radar room. A third enemy force has been picked up to the northwest—the largest of the three, estimated to contain sixty aircraft! It is only forty-two miles away! Promptly, from Admiral Sherman, come order for the remaining carrier with fighters not committed, *Lexington,* to launch her last planes. It is 8:31.

The mystery, which few have time to analyze, is where the three groups of bandits have come from. No enemy carriers were sighted with Kurita's central fleet. Therefore, the enemy air strikes must be coming from Luzon, or from undiscovered enemy carriers to the north.

McCampbell is now fully dressed and ready to start for the hangar deck. Just as he is about to dash through the door, an officer hands him orders from Pri-Fly (the control tower of the carrier).

The Chief of Staff has forbidden him to take off! He cannot disobey direct orders, so, disappointed, he slumps into a chair and begins to strip off his flying gear. Minutes, and every available pilot, are precious— with the enemy so close—and now he has to sit back and watch while *Essex*'s few fighters are scrambled to defend their floating base.

The group's carriers change course, heading for nearby rain squalls, in an effort to hide from the approaching Japanese planes. McCampbell tugs lifelessly at his flying gear, but, instinctively, doesn't make much progress. He is reluctant to give up all hope. Then over the horn come new orders for "all available fighter pilots" to man planes immediately. This is all the encouragement McCampbell needs. He is certainly available.

McCampbell bolts through the door—toward MINSI III—his F6F. He reaches MINSI while she is still on the hangar deck, before she is carried to the flight deck by the elevator. On the flight deck, McCampbell in the cockpit, MINSI is quickly pushed into position on the No. 1 catapult. Maintenance crewmen still hold gasoline hose nozzles in tank openings on both wings. There has not been time to get MINSI fully fueled. Activity on the flight deck reaches a frantic pitch. The air officer in Pri-Fly is yelling, "Let's go!" with fearsome urgency. Impatiently, he screams over the bull horn: "If the Air Group Commander's plane is not ready to go, send it below!" Obviously, there is no more time for fueling. Those ready will have to go—now. The enemy planes are only minutes away.

McCampbell hesitates only briefly and glances at his fuel gauges. His belly tank is full. His two main tanks are half full. That gives him 275 gallons. He will go with that. He checks out on the radio with CIC (Combat Information Center), and waves to crewmen to stop fueling MINSI and get clear. He jabs a finger in the air as he revs up the engine, pushing the throttle forward.

The Hellcat thunders and the launching officer, in front, left, looks him in the eye. McCampbell gives him thumbs up, signifying engine okay. The two-finger turn-up follows immediately from the launching officer, the wind rippling his T shirt. The carrier heads into the wind at better than twenty knots. McCampbell rests the back of his head solidly against the head rest, pushes the throttle all the way forward, and gives the left-hand salute. The launch officer's right hand comes down sharply to his knee. With a roar, the hydraulic catapult throws

MINSI out over the sea. The first of *Essex's* last seven fighters is airborne.

With less than a full fuel supply, MINSI hardly dips off the end of the carrier. McCampbell flips on gun switches and fires a few rounds from his six guns. No jams. He banks slowly to the left, climbing steadily, and orders the other six fighters, following at five-second intervals, to join up on the inside of the turn. The first of the six is Ensign Roy Rushing, McCampbell's wingman, whose F6F has been deck-launched, not catapulted. Soon McCampbell can see Rushing's spinning prop and wing silhouette off his left, behind, closing the gap.

Japanese aircraft attacking Essex *in low run over water amid anti-aircraft bursts.* (Navy Department Photo)

McCampbell points MINSI north on a zero-degree heading. Radar places the bandits due north at about 18,000 feet. They are, according to the contacts, only 22 miles away. McCampbell puts MINSI's 2,250-horsepower engine on maximum climb. Rushing, though fully loaded with fuel, is close.

The other five fighters are farther behind. The two lead F6F's pull relentlessly upward, reaching 8,000 feet, 9,000, 10,000 feet. The enemy should soon be in sight. McCampbell calls CIC aboard *Essex.* He is given a new vector and passes the 12,000-foot mark, now on oxygen, superchargers engaged. McCampbell and Rushing reach 13,000, then 14,000 feet. The other five American fighters are strung out some distance back, lower.

Climbing at 150 knots, McCampbell scans the sky ahead. He looks up. Some 4,000 feet above him . . . a large formation! They're neatly stacked—unlike the Japanese. McCampbell thinks they must be American planes.

"Are there any friendlies in the area?" he queries *Essex*. "Negative, negative," comes the reply. "Well, in that case, I have the enemy in sight!"

By now MINSI is at 15,000 feet, still straining to reach enemy altitude. McCampbell had hoped to get to 22,000 feet, which is standard operational procedure, before intercepting the enemy. But he won't have time for that. Up ahead the dots in the enemy formation grow larger and larger. It looks like about sixty bandits altogether—bombers below, fighters flying top cover. Some of the bombers are twin-engine Bettys and some single-engine Val dive bombers.

The fighters number approximately forty, Zekes, Oscars, Tonys. McCampbell estimates the bombers at 18,000 feet, the fighters at about 21,000 feet. By this time he and Rushing are at 16,000, beginning to bank slightly to the left. Since his other five fighters are lower, McCampbell orders the trailing Americans to hit the enemy bombers.

"I'll take the fighters," he transmits. The lower five Hellcats go after the bombers. McCampbell and Rushing are left to intercept forty Japanese fighters. He suddenly realizes how lonely these odds are, picks up the mike: "This is Nine-Nine Rebel. I have only seven planes. Please send help." (Nine-Nine is the code name of the Air Group Commander, Rebel the code designation of *Essex*.) "Sorry. Nobody available," comes the reply from *Essex*.

By now the enemy planes are ominously close. The gaggle begins to turn right, while McCampbell and Rushing continue their climbing left turn—by now almost on a level with the top enemy fighters at 21,000 feet. McCampbell and Rushing watch, spellbound, as the big enemy gaggle turns almost all the way around, in a right turn. Obviously the enemy hasn't spotted the carriers or the two F6F's. McCampbell and Rushing are now trailing the gaggle, gaining an altitude advantage. Apparently the enemy pilots have reached the end of their search radius, and are turning back, or taking up another heading. Whatever the reason, McCampbell, now looking down on the enemy fighters, ahead on his left, knows they haven't seen him. He has the advantage of surprise and altitude for a firing pass.

Now a stroke of good fortune—the enemy spreads into three V formations. McCampbell is 2,000 feet above and in position to attack. He picks out a straggler on the starboard side of the V farthest right, moves stick forward and left. His right wing rises smoothly as he heads down for the first pass at the enemy—two against forty! He reverses his bank, to the right. Rushing follows closely behind.

Eyes on the enemy straggler through the gunsight, McCampbell flashes down with increasing speed on the unsuspecting enemy. (MINSI carries 2,400 rounds of 50-caliber ammunition, divided equally among armor-piercing, incendiary and tracer shells.)

The brownish-green enemy straggler to the right is clearly a Zeke. The enemy pilot flies on unaware of the swooping Hellcat to his rear. McCampbell eases the stick back, shallowing his dive. He is almost on his victim; the wingspan of the enemy aircraft is growing wider second by second. Now McCampbell can see the red meatball painted on the Zeke's wing.

Fire! His finger squeezes the trigger. All six of MINSI's fifties open; a stream of tracers marks the converging path of shells on the enemy fighter. Pieces of the Zeke begin to fly backward almost immediately. McCampbell—with superior speed from his dive—closes rapidly from the rear, his shells pouring into the Jap. The Zeke's fuel tanks ignite at the wing roots! Smoke and fire stream back. He is on top of the enemy fighter, pulls back and right, gently, on the stick, and zooms past the stricken, burning Zeke. Victory! No chute appears. McCampbell points MINSI's nose skyward to regain all-important altitude he surrendered in the dive. Rushing is behind. But he has not been idle. He also knocked down an enemy fighter. They climb back to 2,000 feet above the enemy gaggle. Surprisingly, no reaction comes from the Japanese fighters. It is as if nothing had happened. The enemy flies on. McCampbell wonders why they haven't spotted the two Hellcats.

For a few seconds he watches his victim spiral down, smoking. Then he picks out another Zeke to the right of the gaggle, lagging behind, and pushes over into another gunnery pass. (McCampbell had taught classic fighter passes to trainees for many years, first on *Wasp*, and in recent days to younger pilots aboard *Essex*.) Down below, the five U.S. fighters have dived into the enemy bombers. A wild melee is developing.

It is time for McCampbell and Rushing to score again. Wind screams as MINSI, nose down, picks up speed. McCampbell maneuvers to fix his gunsight on the second Zeke victim. Rushing is immediately behind, also preparing to fire. The distance closes faster and faster. McCampbell is rushing down on the doomed enemy. He squeezes the trigger! Tracers again show a straight and converging path of shells into the Zeke. McCampbell holds the button down. The Zeke appears to stagger from the impact. He is taking perhaps seventy-five hits per second!

Smoke begins to stream back, a flash of yellow flame! Victim No. 2 falls out of formation—out of control. But this time the enemy gaggle wakes up to the situation—enemy fighters turn sharply and string out into a long formation. McCampbell and Rushing, again pulling up, are once again above the enemy. They can clearly distinguish Tonys, Hamps, and Zekes. Most of the enemy fighters carry a belly tank, or bomb. The line is now forming into a Lufberry! McCampbell and Rushing watch, surprised, as the Japs begin assembling in the tight counterclockwise circle.

An attacking fighter, to gain a firing position behind an aircraft in a Lufberry, must inevitably pull into a position ahead of another enemy fighter. It is a tactical problem. McCampbell hesitates to attack. It would be suicide to pull in behind any of the enemy fighters. But, possibly, he could make a successful head-on attack. He will try.

He noses over and starts down. MINSI is diving faster than before; this will be a split-second attack. Making almost 300 knots, McCampbell pulls out of his steep dive, points his nose toward the Lufberry. He picks out an enemy fighter and closes him. At maximum distance that he can fire effectively, at 1,500 feet, he opens with all guns. The two planes literally flash together, at a combined speed of over 400 knots, on a converging course. The enemy pilot is not surprised, and tracers streak past MINSI's wings. McCampbell fires away with all six guns.

Time is short—only seconds. McCampbell sees his hits registering—then he shoots past the enemy so fast he can hardly take his finger off the trigger button in time. Looking back, as he pulls up, he sees no falling enemy plane. He regains his altitude. Rushing is still with him. Maybe he can do better. He will attack the Lufberry again. He wings over into another dive and picks out another enemy fighter. He attains good diving speed. This time, again, he opens fire at maximum distance. Again he sees hits registering on his enemy, but tracers streak toward him again. It's over in seconds—he is pulling back up.

On his wings he notices small holes. He has taken hits from the enemy. In the excitement and noise from the dive and his guns he hadn't heard or felt the enemy shells scoring. His engine is still running smoothly. Probably no serious damage, but once again he's failed in a head-on pass, and wasted precious ammunition.

His speed carries him back up above the enemy Lufberry. McCampbell tries to think of a new approach. He doesn't like the chances in head-on attacks. The enemy gaggle continues to fly counterclockwise. At a loss, McCampbell decides to relax and think things over before making his next move. He leans back and stretches. The two F6F's circle slowly—looking down on the big Jap fighter force continuing its circle. It is a strange and unrealistic interlude.

Knowing he doesn't have the strength to go down and mix it with the greatly superior enemy force, McCampbell calls *Essex*. He explains the problem and asks for fighter support. "No help available" is the answer from *Essex*. He asks instructions. "Use your own discretion," Rebel Base answers.

So the problem is placed squarely back in his lap. The last two head-on passes were unproductive, and dangerous. He and Rushing continue to circle above the enemy and the strange scene is unchanged. McCampbell calls the other five F6F's—who had taken on the bombers. Only one replies. He will be on the scene in minutes. McCampbell wonders why the enemy doesn't come up after the two Hellcats. Whatever the reason, they continue their circle, and soon McCampbell spots the lone American reinforcement climbing to join them. He has already destroyed two Japanese bombers, but has enough ammunition to join in the fighter battle. As he approaches the two Hellcats, the Japanese fighters make the next move. They begin to pull out of the circle, and set a course of 325 degrees.

They are stringing out into a long line, heading for Luzon. They must have come from land bases, are perhaps worried about their fuel supply—which might explain their strange behavior. They have barely missed the carriers. If the Jap fighters are low on fuel, McCampbell has them at a grave disadvantage.

McCampbell and his two supporting Hellcats set a course following the enemy fighters—to the rear and above. The enemy seems to be forming into a wide V, with the point forward. Some are inside the V, flying in line astern of the leader, but most are edging out to the sides. Because the enemy formation is strung out, McCampbell soon spots one lagging behind the others. The straggler is banking out to a position on the starboard end of the inverted V. He is trailing far behind. MINSI immediately responds to McCampbell's push of the stick, and starts down after him. Rushing picks out another straggler. Soon all three Hellcats are diving to the attack.

The dirty-green enemy fighter McCampbell closes is caught napping. He grows larger and larger in McCampbell's sights. Death is a matter of seconds. Within 900 feet of his adversary, McCampbell squeezes the trigger. At that distance 92 per cent of MINSI's shells are concentrated in a three-foot pattern. McCampbell aims at the wing roots. The concentration of shells begins to smash the light Japanese fighter to pieces. The enemy plane explodes in a flash, falls drunkenly out of position. Again the pilot fails to get out. Victim No. 3!

McCampbell couldn't watch Rushing on this pass, but he also ignited an enemy fighter—his second victim. The three Hellcats pull back up to regain their altitude advantage. The Japs fly on! Obviously, they are too low on fuel to engage in a dogfight. They have probably searched too long for the U.S. fleet. (Though they missed the group's carriers, one of the other enemy gaggles fared better. They found and attacked *Princeton*. And, as McCampbell continues his running fight, *Princeton* is sinking.)

Now McCampbell decides to start down again, seeking a fourth victim. He picks out an Oscar or a Hamp—he isn't sure—and closes rapidly in a diving pass from behind. It is a perfect firing pass. The red rising sun on the wings of the enemy come into distinct view. McCampbell opens with a short burst. At the same moment he sees tracers flying past his wing—from behind! Where had the enemy come from? Caught by surprise, McCampbell jerks the stick back. MINSI skyrockets upward. The tracers disappear. He levels out.

Another Hellcat, flashing past below, is the culprit! He was firing at the same enemy McCampbell was attacking. Saying a few appropriate words over the radio, McCampbell, still above and behind the enemy formation, prepares for another attack. He selects another plane, chooses a fighter trailing the V. This time no one is behind him, except Rushing, and he closes the enemy deliberately.

It's now obvious the enemy is not going to turn and mix it up. McCampbell becomes more relaxed, even begins thinking about the types of fighters he is attacking. He can see he is now closing an Oscar. The enemy plane carries a belly tank beneath the fuselage.

McCampbell is on him. He presses the trigger button. Once again six fifties roar and the pattern is concentrated. Hits streak into the wing roots, a trail of smoke immediately stretches out behind the stricken Oscar. Soon it tumbles into a dive and out of formation. Again the pilot burns in the cockpit. McCampbell pulls back on the stick and cuts up into the blue. Victim No. 4!

The third Hellcat pilot is now out of ammunition and going home. McCampbell and Rushing stay on for the finish. By this time McCampbell has scratched four enemy fighters and Rushing three; the score, so far, is 7–0 in their favor. But McCampbell and Rushing are not through. MINSI roars smoothly. McCampbell selects another victim.

The deadly toll being exacted by the two Hellcats continues at a dizzy pace. McCampbell dives again, misses, but after pulling back up, dives again, and this time a burning Tony spins out of the wide V. Victim No. 5. Again they dive. McCampbell's deadly, short bursts rip open the gas tanks of a Zeke. It is kill No. 6! And on and on the Japs fly, now getting close to the shores of Luzon.

McCampbell glances to the left corner of his instrument panel. His fuel is low—he had taken off with only half-filled tanks. He begins to wonder how much longer he can chase the enemy. Rushing's supply is adequate—but his ammunition is getting low. McCampbell is in no mood to call off the attack, even with fuel getting low. Above the enemy again, they head down. Rushing scores kill No. 4. McCampbell breaks off his pass when his victim, pouring smoke, dives off and down. He can't follow. There are too many enemy planes in position to dive in pursuit.

As long as he maintains his speed (which is also his altitude advantage) he will be relatively safe. The smoking, diving enemy fighter McCampbell can't count as a kill—though he will probably never make it home.

Two more passes later, however, McCampbell boasts seven kills, Rushing five! Between them they now have a score of 12–0. The enemy formation, as a result, is down to something over twenty planes! Still, the two Hellcats continue to press their attack. On the next pass, McCampbell again hits victim. Smoke trails backward, but the Jap banks away and down, flying upright. McCampbell can't claim him.

Looking back as he pulls up, Rushing is nowhere in view. McCampbell begins to rubberneck, to be sure no one slipped into position on his tail unseen. Without a wingman behind, to guard the rear, death can come suddenly from behind. He is worried about Rushing—have the Japs gotten him?

His thoughts are interrupted by a distant silhouette in the sky behind him, climbing slowly into firing position. At last the Japs had decided to come up after him! Had they shot down Rushing this same way? The bogey in the rear moves in—with a speed advantage. This shocks McCampbell. He rams the throttle to the wire stop—and MINSI picks up speed. Still the bogey closes.

Desperate, McCampbell slams his left hand forward, and the throttle through the wire check. The engine bursts into a loud roar. It is his last trump card—water injection into the cylinders. For a short time, in an emergency, it gives the engine a tremendous power boost.

McCampbell continues to gain speed. But it takes time to reach the maximum, and the gap behind continues to close. Tension building fast, McCampbell calls Rushing. "This is Rebel Leader, Roy," he yells. "Waggle your wings." Eyes straining, engine going all-out, McCampbell watches the silhouette behind him. The wings go up and down!

Rushing had stayed down too long on his last pass, but had scored another kill. Thus, when he pulled up, McCampbell had been taken by surprise, had mistaken him for an enemy fighter. Rushing now has six victories, but the sixth was his last. He is out of ammunition. Moreover, he has caused McCampbell to use a considerable amount of precious fuel. Now he calls over the radio: "Dave, I'm out of ammunition." McCampbell replies: "Roy, this is Dave. I've got a little left. Do you want to stay up here and watch, or go down on each pass with me?" "I'll go down with you," Rushing answers.

And, one Hellcat out of ammunition and the other low on gas, the two pilots resume the fantastic battle. McCampbell sees an island ahead. He knows he is getting close to Luzon, that other enemy fighters might soon be encountered. But he picks out one of the enemy trailing the V and noses over into a firing pass. Rushing wings over behind.

The Japs are now descending—another sign they are nearing home. So it is a long pass. McCampbell catches the Zeke just off the coast of the island and, waiting until within about 900 feet, opens fire on the wing roots. Two short bursts, a flash of flame, confirm victory No. 8! MINSI rushes over and by the side of the stricken enemy fighter points her nose skyward again. The enemy pilot didn't get out. It is 14–0 now!

Ahead the coast of Luzon now is in view. McCampbell glances again at his gas gauges. It will be a close thing—getting home. But his guns are still firing. He must be almost out of ammo, but maybe there's enough for one last pass. As the coast of Luzon becomes clearer and clearer, he pushes MINSI over into the last dive. The engine roars as he builds up speed. By now the enemy has descended to 12,000 feet. It is another long dive. MINSI is closing the rear of victim No. 9. McCampbell coolly eyes his gunsight, finger on the trigger button. The wingspan fills the yellow sight ring. The red rising suns are visible. He opens fire.

Hits are striking the enemy plane. But he can hear his guns giving out. Some continue to fire, others stop. But they have scored again! The enemy fighter jerks convulsively, rolls over on its back, and takes the plunge. A vertical trail of black smoke marks the descent. It had been the gas tanks again. No chute.

The record is now at least 15–0, an amazing score! But it is time to go home. There is not a second to lose. McCampbell banks into a sharp right turn, Rushing behind, and sets course 145 degrees. Now he begins to sweat his fuel supply. Can he find *Essex* in time? Had she been hit? Had the five fighters which attacked the enemy bombers succeeded—in driving them off?

McCampbell's gauges show 45 gallons of fuel left. "Roy, I've only got forty-five gallons left. I'm slowing to thirteen fifty revolutions," he calls over the mike. Rushing acknowledges, says he has plenty of fuel, will stay with him. Down to 1,350 revolutions, the two Hellcats barely fly at 130 knots. McCampbell calls *Essex*. But his YE (antenna) will reach only eighty or ninety miles. There is no reply. Every few minutes McCampbell picks up the mike. "Rebel Base, Rebel Base, this is Nine-Nine Rebel. How do you read me?" Silence.

On fly the two Hellcats, three-blade props spinning slowly in front of the big Pratt and Whitney engines. McCampbell continues trying to reach *Essex*. At last comes the familiar voice: "Nine Nine Rebel, you're coming in loud and clear." McCampbell fires back: "Rebel Base, am low on gas . . . request landing as soon as possible . . . I think I'm about fifty miles away." (Actually, McCampbell was sixty miles away.) *Essex* gave him a steer—to bring him in on the carrier. By now MINSI is down to 6,000 feet, still on a southeasterly course.

McCampbell's gauges show something less than twenty-five gallons. Over the mike comes disturbing news from *Essex*. "Continue on in . . . Will be able to land you in about fifteen minutes." *Essex*, the radio operator tells McCampbell, is preparing to launch a strike. The planes are already on deck and armed. They would have to get off before *Essex* could receive MINSI! McCampbell knows it will be close. Suddenly it seems like days since he had been planning tactics to lead that same strike on the enemy fleet. He looks at his watch; it's not yet ten in the morning!

The two lone Hellcats descend lower, still barely flying at 130 knots, and a big ship comes into view ahead. Could it be *Essex*? Soon McCampbell and Rushing recognize *Hornet*—a sister carrier. They will pass quite close. Black puffs appear in the sky nearby. McCampbell and Rushing jerk sticks and begin to jinx violently. *Hornet* has opened fire on them! McCampbell screams into the mike for *Hornet* to withhold fire. But the five-inch guns continue to fire. And over the earphones McCampbell hears *Hornet's* fighter director vectoring *Hornet's* fighter patrol toward the two lone Hellcats.

Hornet continues to throw shells at the Hellcats—by now some fifteen rounds! And then McCampbell sees the friendly Hellcats from *Hornet* closing in from above, for an attack! He calls C.I.C. aboard *Hornet*—constantly identifying himself. Still *Hornet's* patrol closes to attack.

The five-inchers cease firing. The patrol leader peels off and starts down on the two Hellcats in a firing pass. By this time McCampbell and Rushing are down on top of the waves. They have dived all the way to avoid *Hornet's* guns, and there is nowhere to go. They watch the closing Hellcat. And then, at the last minute, *Hornet's* Combat Air Patrol leader recognizes the two Hellcats, breaks off the attack.

McCampbell realizes, ironically, he has just missed death at the hands of his fellow pilots. His desperate maneuvering used up much of his remaining fuel. Once *Hornet's* air patrol called off its attack, he hardly looked back. His eyes strained forward. He had to land soon or he would be forced to ditch in the ocean.

Up ahead, after what seems hours but is only minutes, destroyers appear. *Essex's* outer screen! MINSI, with Rushing behind, aims for the center of the ring of ships. And there lies *Essex*, straight ahead. Agonizing minutes pass, and then McCampbell is over the carrier. He is dismayed when he sees the deck still fully loaded with armed aircraft. The strike has not yet begun to take off. His gauges show about ten gallons left. *Essex* says it will be fifteen minutes before he can be landed.

McCampbell replies: "I've only got ten minutes' flying time left." Rushing's gas supply is adequate; he can circle and wait. But McCampbell has to act. He picks out another carrier, *Lexington*, several thousand yards away, and finds her decks also full. He points MINSI's nose toward the other carrier in the formation, *Langley*. In a couple of minutes he is above her—and, to his dismay, she also is loaded with planes ready to launch a strike!

McCampbell considers ditching. But now *Essex* comes in over the horn: "We're launching *Langley's* deck load in order to take you aboard." With relief, McCampbell sticks by *Langley*, on *Essex's* port side, about a mile or two ahead. Luckily, the carriers are in close formation.

The last planes are being launched. He has only minutes left; he can just make it. It will have to be fast. He gets the signal to land.

He approaches *Langley's* stern before the deck is fully ready and has to be waved off by the landing signal officer. The absolute crisis is at hand. McCampbell's gauge has long ago passed the ten-gallon mark. The red line on the gauge shows 10, 6 and 0, and the gauge is accurate! He pulls the stick tightly into his belly, banks MINSI into a daringly sharp left turn, never climbing above 200 feet, and approaches the end of the carrier again. The yellow and red diagonal flags wave. He is thirty feet above the rear of the carrier as he comes in over the end. The landing signal officer holds the flags straight out. At last the sign— the landing officer crosses his throat with his right hand. McCampbell "cuts the gun" (closes the throttle all the way), MINSI dips, thumps the deck, and is caught by the No. 2 wire of some eight or nine on the 300-foot landing area. MINSI jerks to a stop in ninety feet.

The taxi director of the deck came up, began to signal where MINSI should be parked. McCampbell eased the throttle forward and MINSI began to cough—fuel giving out. Now the warm air began to stream into the canopy, which McCampbell had cranked open on the approach. He began to relax. He was safely down, could get out and walk again. As soon as he was parked, McCampbell unbuckled. No one aboard *Langley* knew this had been a memorable mission, that he had shot down nine enemy fighters and probably two more in less than two hours.

Slowly he climbed out. On both wings were damage and gashes. A close inspection, however, revealed the gashes weren't bullet holes. They were caused by pieces of enemy planes which had exploded in front of his guns, coming back and striking his wings. The ordnance man who rearmed MINSI's guns reported that of 2,400 rounds of ammunition, McCampbell had fired all but six rounds. This remained in one gun because of a feed stoppage.

Wearily, though it was still early in the morning, McCampbell climbed the steps to report to Captain Wallace M. ("Gotch") Dillon, skipper of the *Langley*. Traditional courtesy required he pay a call on the carrier's captain, and thank him for taking him aboard. McCampbell did that. Dillon told him *Princeton* had sunk. The captain was busy—his first strike was just about to come in and he was readying a second strike on the Jap fleet approaching Leyte. McCampbell stayed only a minute and headed for the ready room. There he at last sat down and relaxed, with sandwiches and coffee. *Langley*'s air group commander entered, elated. He had shot down five Japanese planes that morning! When McCampbell was asked if he had made any kills, he replied that he had made nine or ten. Eyes popped in disbelief.

McCampbell was not through for the day, however. He was called on to fly a combat air patrol mission from *Langley* before the day's action was over. At last, he landed back on *Essex* later in the day. He immediately started out to pay his respects to the captain, after which he always called on Admiral Sherman. On the way to the captain's bridge, he was intercepted by Admiral Charles R. ("Cat") Brown, Chief of Staff to Admiral Sherman.

"The Admiral wants to see you," Brown said. McCampbell headed for Sherman's bridge. As soon as he entered, Admiral Sherman roared: "Dammit, I told you I didn't want you flying in these scrambles."

"Sir, I asked if 'scramble all fighter pilots' meant me too, and the answer was first 'yes,' then 'no,' and then 'yes.' I figured the captain had come to you for a decision," McCampbell replied.

"Dammit, don't ever let it happen again," Sherman barked. (Such a mission never occurred again and had never occurred before.)

Japanese suicide plane dives on U.S.S. Suwanee *as F6F prepares to land. Action took place off Leyte two days after Commander Mc-Campbell's Flight of Nine.* (Official U.S. Navy Photo)

As for the three enemy fleets, American planes from carriers of Task Force 38 wrought heavy destruction on the main (central) Japanese fleet. More than 250 sorties were directed at that fleet, and one of Japan's two greatest battleships, *Musashi,* with eighteen-inch guns, was hit by no less than nineteen torpedoes and seventeen bombs!

When McCampbell landed on *Essex* during the afternoon of the 24th, *Musashi* had dropped behind the Jap fleet and was still afloat, but at 7:35 P.M. she rolled over and sank. Some of the hits on *Musashi* were scored by *Essex* planes. In addition to sinking *Musashi,* Task Force 38 carrier planes scored two hits each on two other Japanese battleships, five near misses on another battleship, and damaged a cruiser so badly it had to retire from the battle.

Admiral Halsey, at the end of the day, assumed (mistakenly) that the enemy's central force had been so devastated by his carrier attacks that it was no longer a danger to the ships of Seventh Fleet unloading supplies on the beaches to the south. And—after his scouting planes had sighted the enemy's decoy fleet of four carriers and other ships, to the north—Halsey turned his attention toward the northern fleet, leaving the eastern end of San Bernardino Strait relatively unguarded.

With sixty-five ships he steamed northward at 25 knots. A number of subordinate officers (including Commodore Arleigh Burke) questioned this strategy, especially because of aerial reports which showed the enemy fleet very much afloat and still steaming eastward. But they were overruled. Task Force 38 proceeded north.

Japanese battleship Ise *photographed from one of* Essex's *planes just after being hit by bomb in Battle of Leyte Gulf.* (Navy Department Photo)

Because of this, Admiral Kurita's central fleet reached the landing beaches the next morning (the 25th) and for a short time caused havoc and confusion. Kurita retired prematurely, however, after suffering more losses at the hands of weak American forces than he caused.

The southern enemy fleet was more roughly handled in what is known as the Battle of Surigao Strait. On the night of the 24th-25th, that fleet ran into the American battle group led by Rear Admiral Jesse B. Oldendorf, under Vice Admiral T. C. Kincaid's command. Oldendorf sank two Japanese battleships and a number of cruisers and destroyers in one of the most one-sided victories of the war. United States forces didn't lose a single ship.

On the 25th, then, Admiral Kurita, with the big central fleet, had inflicted the only major damage on American ships. With four battleships, six heavy cruisers, other cruisers and destroyers, he had surprised American ships off the beaches, having passed through San Bernardino Strait undetected on the morning of the 25th. He sank several ships, including a baby carrier and destroyers.

Halsey engaged the northern decoy fleet on the 25th-26th, sinking several carriers, cruisers and destroyers.

The last day of the battle, the 26th, was largely concerned with the chase of the retiring enemy carriers by Halsey's forces, and with rescue operations.

It was, in summary, the greatest naval battle ever fought, a resounding victory for American forces. And not the least exciting and memorable single action of the battle was Commander David McCampbell's unforgettable "flight of nine" on the morning of the opening day.

Commander McCampbell understandably received the Congressional Medal of Honor for this and another mission—in which he destroyed seven carrier-based enemy aircraft. The citation of the Medal of Honor award, in part, read:

During a major fleet engagement with the enemy on October 24, Commander McCampbell, assisted by but one plane, intercepted and daringly attacked a formation of sixty hostile land-based craft approaching our forces . . . shot down nine Japanese planes and, completely disorganizing the enemy group, forced the remainder to abandon the attack before a single aircraft could reach the Fleet. . . .

And, in addition to the nine victories, and the seven, for which he won the Medal of Honor, he shot down another eighteen enemy planes to end the war with thirty-four kills—the highest scoring ace of the Navy and Marines in World War II.

Thus, when the native of Bessemer, Alabama, was appointed to the U.S. Naval Academy by a Florida senator, after having attended Staunton Military Academy and Georgia Tech, in 1929, it was an appointment to be felt around the world, to the great good of the Navy and the United States.

Today McCampbell, still in the Navy, is on the staff of the Joint Chiefs of Staff in Washington, at the Pentagon.

11 The Flying Circus at Okinawa

APRIL 17, 1945:

Lieutenant EUGENE A. VALENCIA, U.S.N.R.

CONTRARY to the popular belief, the heaviest losses in U.S. warships in World War II, as a result of aerial attacks, occurred in the last year of the war.

These losses were largely caused by Japanese Kamikaze attacks. The first major Kamikaze offensive against U.S. warships was launched during the invasion of the Philippines, in October, 1944.

The Flying Circus: left to right, Valencia; Lieutenant (j.g.) Harris Mitchell, U.S.N.R.; Lieutenant Clinton L. Smith, U.S.N.R.; Lieutenant (j.g.) James B. French, U.S.N.R.

On the morning of October 25, Kamikaze Zeroes, led by Lieutenant Yukio Seki, began what proved to be the war's most successful assault on American warships.

On that day an explosive-laden Zero plunged into the small carrier *Santee,* exploding just forward of the deck elevator. Two others missed *Sangamon* and *Petrof Bay.* A fourth crashed into small carrier *Suwanee,* exploding in the ship's hangar. Other Kamikaze Zeroes plunged into the small carriers *St. Lo, Kitkun Bay,* and *Kalinin Bay.* (Two exploded on the flight deck of *Kalinin Bay.*)

It was an auspicious beginning for the Japanese Navy's surprise weapon. Understandably, Vice Admiral Takijiro Onishi, commander of the First Japanese Air Fleet, at Manila, was well pleased with the first day of Kamikaze operations.

Onishi was a Navy pilot himself and had served under the famed Admiral Isoroku Yamamoto earlier in the war. He had played a leading role in the build-up of the Japanese Navy's air arm in the prewar years and had helped draw plans for the Pearl Harbor attack.

Now, comparing Japan's air strength in the Philippines with the massive American force approaching, he had come to the conclusion that only through Kamikaze attacks could the victorious American tide be stemmed. Onishi, however, didn't begin the Kamikaze offensive by ordering his pilots to crash their planes into American ships.

On the evening of October 19, just after arriving at Clark Field, on Luzon, he called a meeting of his executive officers. At this meeting, held at the main Japanese fighter base in the Philippines, Onishi made a request for Kamikaze volunteers.

The pilots at that meeting unanimously agreed to the Admiral's request, and Onishi designated the groups which would inaugurate suicide operations as the *Kamikaze Tokubetsu Kogekitai* (Kamikaze Special Attack Squad).

Onishi was, naturally enough, encouraged by the destruction achieved by Kamikazes on October 25 off Leyte. He hastily began recruiting new suicide forces for the Japanese Navy's air arm. In addition to Zeroes, Val and Judy dive bombers and Frances twin-engined bombers were modified for suicide attacks. In the days to follow, Army aircraft also were modified for such attacks.

The Japanese estimated that in the next three months, between October 25, 1944, and January 25, 1945, their suicide pilots inflicted damage on some fifty American ships of all kinds. This was only the beginning.

Kamikazes were used in considerable numbers against American ships off Iwo Jima, in February, 1945, and after March, 1945, according to Masatake Okumiya, in *Zero,* more than half of all attacking planes were Kamikazes. In the Okinawa campaign Kamikazes were credited with more than 275 hits or near misses on U.S. ships. One Japanese source reports that more than 2,300 Japanese Navy planes took off on Kamikaze flights. The suicide attacks took the lives of more than 2,500 Japanese Navy pilots and air crew members, and probably at least an equal number of Army pilots and crew members.

The suicide attacks were carried on until the very last, and on the day that Japan surrendered the Japanese Vice Admiral who had commanded the suicide bombings from Kyushu, Matome Ugaki, flew

Japanese Navy's Frances bomber, used extensively in suicide attacks off Okinawa. (Navy Department Photo)

the last Kamikaze mission of the war, diving at a United States warship off Okinawa. Vice Admiral Takijiro Onishi, the originator of the Kamikaze operations, committed hara-kiri rather than surrender.

The American public is still largely unaware of the crisis caused by Kamikazes during the Okinawa campaign. On April 16, during that operation, the Japanese launched more than a hundred Kamikazes at U.S. ships off Okinawa. That day destroyer *Pringle* was sunk and eleven other ships, including carrier *Intrepid*, were hit.

Up to that date in the Okinawa campaign (the first landings on Okinawa had occurred on March 26) Kamikazes had sunk fourteen warships and damaged several times that many. The Navy high command was so concerned that Admiral Chester Nimitz, Commander of the Pacific Fleet, tried to borrow destroyers from General Douglas MacArthur's command. (He was turned down.)

The U.S. Army's Twentieth Air Force, under the command of General Curtis LeMay (now Air Force Chief of Staff) was ordered to bomb Kamikaze nests on Kyushu, in an effort to ease the Navy crisis.

U.S.S. Bunker Hill *burning after being hit by two Kamikazes during bitter battle off Okinawa described in this chapter.* (Navy Department Photo)

Off Okinawa the greatest naval force ever assembled, Task Force 58, was conducting the largest amphibious landing operation in history, in the face of the heaviest Kamikaze opposition of the war. When *Intrepid* was hit, April 16, she was the fifth carrier of eleven in the operation to be struck by Kamikazes.

Among Task Force 58 carriers participating in the Okinawa operation was famed carrier *Yorktown,* known the world over as the Fighting Lady. *Yorktown* had departed Ulithi with Task Force 58 on March 14, and as of April 17, the day with which we are concerned in this chapter, personnel aboard were weary of the sound of general quarters —the signal to prepare for air attack.

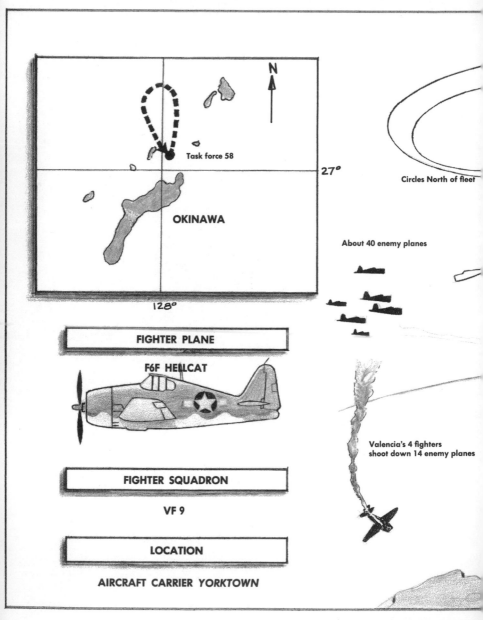

N

27°

Task force 58

OKINAWA

128°

Circles North of fleet

About 40 enemy planes

Valencia's 4 fighters
shoot down 14 enemy planes

FIGHTER PLANE

F6F HELLCAT

FIGHTER SQUADRON

VF 9

LOCATION

AIRCRAFT CARRIER *YORKTOWN*

MISSION FLOWN BY:

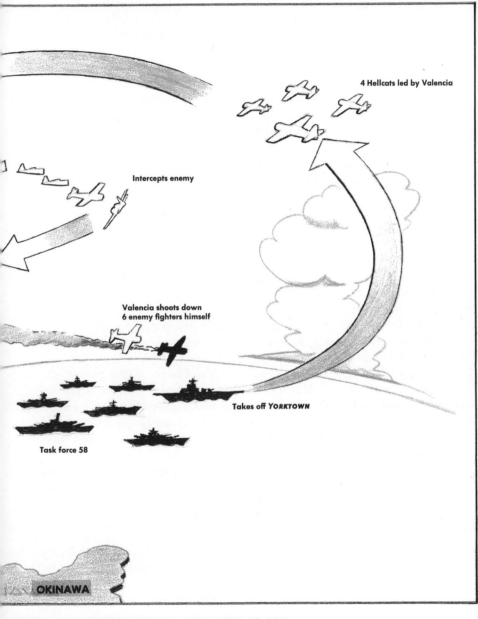

4 Hellcats led by Valencia

Intercepts enemy

Valencia shoots down
6 enemy fighters himself

Takes off *YORKTOWN*

Task force 58

OKINAWA

LIEUTENANT EUGENE VALENCIA, USNR, APRIL 17, 1945

Many aboard had seen *Intrepid* struck by Kamikazes the day before. They had ripped a 12-by-14-foot hole in her flight deck, destroying forty planes, killing nine and wounding forty. Aboard nearby *Yorktown* was the most successful Navy fighter division (four planes) of World War II. That division was to become known as "Valencia's Flying Circus" and it was a part of VF 9. The leader of the division was Lieutenant Eugene Valencia, of San Francisco, California. Both Valencia and the division had had an interesting history.

Eugene Anthony Valencia was born in San Francisco, California, April 13, 1921. He attended Alameda High School and San Francisco Junior College, where he played football and boxed.

After World War II began, but before the United States became involved, Valencia received an appointment as an aviation cadet. During his flight training, between August, 1941, and April, 1942, Japan attacked Pearl Harbor.

Thus, when he won his wings as an ensign, early in 1942, his country was at war. His first wartime duty as a pilot, which failed to thrill him to the quick, was as a flight instructor.

By the end of 1942, however, Valencia had begun his carrier training, and on February 3, 1943, he reported to Fighting Squadron 9 aboard U.S.S. *Essex.*

In 1943 he saw his first combat, in the Pacific, taking part in the actions at Wake and Marcus islands. Later in the year, on a mission to Rabaul, with which the reader has now become familiar, Valencia shot down his first three enemy planes. At Tarawa he got another, and at Truk—the enemy's major Central Pacific naval base—he scored three more victories.

During the fighting over Truk, Valencia conceived the four-plane fighter tactic which was to make his "Flying Circus" famous the world over. There Valencia was jumped by thirty enemy aircraft, and in a series of up-and-down firing passes he thought he detected a weakness in the enemy's fighter tactics.

Returned to the States, and training for a new combat tour, Valencia carefully selected three eager and capable pilot trainees, whom he thoroughly indoctrinated in the offensive tactic later called the "mowing machine."

The three were young pilots who loved flying and were willing to fly overtime to perfect the new tactic. They were James B. French, of Oakland, California (who ended the war with eleven victories), Harris E. Mitchell, of Richmond, Texas (ten victories), and Clinton L. Smith, of Jackson, Mississippi (six victories).

These four pilots flew night and day, so many extra hours, in fact, that other pilot trainees ridiculed them as fanatics.

They logged three times the necessary number of hours required during the training period.

When this division and others of VF 9 were ready, the squadron went aboard carrier *Yorktown*. *Yorktown* was one of the carriers of Task Force 58, which in the spring of 1945 was to become embroiled in the battle with the Kamikazes.

On the afternoon of Sunday, April 15, 1945, *Yorktown* fueled, and next day she and other ships of Task Force 58 withstood the attacks of more than a hundred Kamikazes. On that day the Japanese registered their first hit with an Oka glide bomb, a piloted suicide bomb far heavier than the normal weight of explosives in the Kamikazes. It was another desperation weapon introduced by the enemy.

On the 16th crewmen aboard *Yorktown* saw *Intrepid* struck by one Kamikaze and narrowly missed by another.

The next day, Tuesday, April 17, Valencia was roused from his bunk two hours before dawn. He began his morning push-ups. Without fail, each morning Valencia did forty push-ups. He pulled on his green flight suit, picked up his 45 caliber pistol and escape kit, and walked forward about a hundred yards to Wardroom 1. There he enjoyed a good breakfast.

Valencia was flying Combat Air Patrol (C.A.P.) and so he hustled up one deck to VF 9's radio room. Sixteen planes were to comprise the patrol that morning; Valencia would lead four—the four different divisions orbiting in four different areas.

At the radio room Valencia learned he was to orbit north of *Yorktown*, at 25,000 feet. Lieutenant Ralph Murphy, the A.I.O. (Aircraft Intelligence Officer), warned the pilots they could expect a renewal of the heavy Japanese attacks which had continued throughout Monday. The weather was excellent outside, a few low cumulus clouds scattered about in the predawn gray, but generally fair. Pilots pulled on their flying gear, and shortly, from Pri-Fly, came the announcement: "Pilots, man your planes."

In minutes Valencia and the other three F6F Hellcat pilots of his division were in their cockpits, propellers spinning, ready to be launched. It was close to dawn; the sky was lighting up in the east. Valencia roared down the deck and the black fighter lifted off *Yorktown's* bow. After him came Mitchell, French and Smith—pulling off the carrier into the wind, climbing behind the division leader.

F6F Hellcat about to take off from deck of U.S.S. Yorktown. *Note moisture halo.* (Official U.S. Navy Photo)

Valencia checked in "airborne" and the other three members of the division closed into proper formation, Mitchell in close, as wingman, French and Smith, together, a little off to the side. He set his prop on a setting to reach 25,000 feet in thirty minutes. The four black fighters knifed up into the blue, and through white cumulus clouds, on a zero-degree heading.

They switched on gunsights and pulled the "charge" handles to load their guns. As the division reached 10,000 feet, each checked his oxygen, and on they climbed, higher and higher into the sky.

Valencia knew his division's chances for action were unusually good. He was patrolling to the north of the fleet, the direction from which the enemy's Kamikazes came. American troops farther south were encountering a stubborn and resisting enemy on both northern and southern Okinawa, in the seventeenth day of the largest amphibious operation of the Pacific war, an operation which Task Force 58 was shielding.

And though the expected air reaction from the enemy had been slow to materialize, beginning April 6 the Japanese had struck with a fury never before encountered in the Pacific.

The relatively short distance from Japanese air bases on Kyushu, and on Formosa, enabled the enemy to throw almost every type of aircraft into the battle.

Task Force 58 had already been hurt, but few suspected that twenty-eight more warships would be sunk by air attack (twenty-six by Kamikazes), and another 225 damaged, before the campaign was over.

The capture of Okinawa, then, was to take a considerable time and require the support of Task Force 58 for more than two months. All through April and May the fleet, constantly battered by Kamikazes, doggedly maintained its position in support of the Okinawa operation. It was not until June 21 that all organized resistance on Okinawa ceased, and the last escort carrier departed after a stay of eighty-eight days in this area.

Valencia's Hellcat division reached 20,000 feet—now well north of *Yorktown*. Valencia contacted C.I.C. aboard *Yorktown*. Nothing was up yet. The four black fighters continued to climb northward—the sun now above the horizon in the east. It was a brilliant morning. A clear blue sky arched upward in every direction. Below, at about 5,000 feet, small white cumulus drifted over the shimmering Pacific.

The glare of the sun in the east was almost blinding, and revealed every line in the glass on the right side of the canopy. Except for the roar of the engine, loud and constant, the only sound in the cockpit was the strange wheezing of the oxygen mask, as Valencia breathed. The small, yellow, half-moon blips on the flow indicator moved open and shut silently, indicating oxygen was flowing into the mask.

The division reached 25,000 feet. Valencia signaled his comrades they would begin to circle, now being on station. The four Hellcats began to weave back and forth, circling. Each pilot scanned the sky to the north, and elsewhere, in an effort to detect the approach of any unidentified aircraft. But no bogeys were sighted.

Time passed pleasantly, minute by minute, and soon the division had been on station half an hour. The planes continued to circle; over the radio no action was reported. The fighters continued to weave and circle. Now an hour had passed.

There was little indication that this was to be the division's greatest day of the war, as the morning continued to pass. The division had been in action two months, having received its baptism of fire in the carrier strike on Tokyo, on February 16, and having gotten off to an impressive start. Though few Jap planes opposed them, the Flying Circus claimed six on that day.

Since that time, however, the division had encountered few enemy planes. Valencia had thought opposition would be almost certain on this patrol, in view of the attacks on the fleet in recent days, but the patrol was now half completed and nothing had happened. Disappointment began to set in.

But aboard *Yorktown* radar reports now caused a stir . . . enemy aircraft were picked up on the radar screen—to the north. At least three large groups of enemy planes were detected, all closing fast. Combat Information flashed the warning. In the cockpit, Valencia heard it. He alerted the division and each pilot searched the sky harder than before. All four kept their eyes fixed on the blue to the north.

Valencia glances back over his shoulder—the spinning props of the other three Hellcats denote perfect formation. Mitchell is slightly back, left, French and Smith are farther back, right. All four fighters are banking, left wings down, into the west.

Smith, last man in formation, sees them. "Tally-ho! Bogeys! Three o'clock!" he yells.

French, section leader, kicks right rudder and moves stick right, and takes the lead, heading toward them. He is in the best position to reach them first, and the division had been trained so that any one of the four could take over. With French leading, and pointing the way, all four pilots now see a number of dots in the blue to the north. *Yorktown* is informed.

The bogeys are closing fast; Valencia estimates them to be ten miles away. The number of planes grows even larger. At first it looks as if the gaggle might include ten or fifteen. Now it seems twice that number are in the formation.

"You've got it, Jim; go to work," Valencia radios French. French acknowledges the call. The Hellcats, at full throttle, streak north to intercept the bogeys. Now Valencia positively and finally identifies the bogeys as bandits . . . definitely enemy aircraft. He identifies Franks, Zekes and Oscars. He estimates their strength at thirty-five to forty aircraft.

The bandits approach in a number of small V's, which make up a large, loose V. Over the radio comes French's exclamation: "Jeez, there must be fifty of 'em!"

The enemy is only slightly below the four-fighter division now at full throttle, heading north, to intercept them. Valencia estimates the distance from *Yorktown* at sixty miles. He reports to C.I.C. that the division is about to go into action.

The enemy planes are so close Valencia notices their silver color—unusual for enemy aircraft, which are usually brown or green.

Valencia again checks his gunsight and the four F6F's begin a shallow dive toward the big enemy V, growing larger and larger, directly out front.

Aboard *Yorktown*, general quarters is sounded. It is 8:17 A.M.; this is the fourth general quarters which has sounded aboard her since yesterday afternoon.

French maneuvers rudder and dives for one of the leading enemy planes—a Frank. At full throttle, and descending, the four Hellcats ring up considerable speed, are closing the enemy V at a speed of approximately 500 knots. French will make the first attack from the port quarter, forward, with Smith diving in to the attack at the same time. Valencia and Mitchell will wait until these two firing passes are completed, before starting down, and French and Smith (after climbing back up above the enemy) will act as top cover for Valencia and Mitchell, as they execute passes three and four.

Now French is approaching the enemy Frank ahead, whose silhouette grows larger and larger in the sight ring. The enemy makes no move. Valencia and Mitchell remain above, watching the initial pass. The enemy planes come on, as if they've seen nothing, holding formation and proceeding toward the fleet. Obviously, the enemy knows the location of Task Force 58, and if unmolested, the gaggle will reach the ships in twenty minutes.

The silver Frank is in range of French's guns and the leading Hellcat opens fire; thin streams of white smoke trail backward from his wings. Smith, off to the side, picks out another silver Frank. His six guns open on the enemy aircraft. Valencia watches the action below. The two American fighters below are converging as they pile into the big enemy V, all guns still blazing. Both are aiming for the enemy's wing roots. Now, in quick succession, one of the enemy Franks and then another disintegrate in a blinding flash. The Franks are carrying high explosives!

As Valencia watches the disintegration of the Franks and realizes how important it is to prevent these enemy planes from reaching the fleet, French and Smith have crossed and are pulling back up above the enemy gaggle. It's Valencia's turn. He and Mitchell now bank into a descending pass, French and Smith providing top cover.

Valencia picks out a Frank, as does Mitchell, and they rapidly close in widely separated passes. The enemy gaggle continues toward the fleet, none breaking formation. The silhouette of the silver enemy victim grows wider and wider in Valencia's sights. He grips the stick trigger. The rate of closure is so fast that Valencia must move quickly; the wingspan grows wider and wider. It fills the yellow ring on the sighting glass. Valencia pulls the trigger. The six 50-caliber guns shake the F6F and the noise drowns out the roar of the engine. Tracers mark a straight path into the onrushing Frank. Valencia holds the trigger down. He is almost on his victim. A flash! The third Frank has exploded! Valencia pulls back on the stick and crosses the enemy formation, Mitchell now approaching from his pass. With their greater speed, they climb above the enemy gaggle. Valencia notices smoke and debris below—the fourth enemy victim—Mitchell's kill. Four enemy aircraft in four firing passes!

The four Hellcats now reverse direction, as the enemy continues to fly southward toward the fleet. The enemy commander is gambling he can reach the fleet before the Hellcats decimate his force. It takes a little time for the Hellcats, after reversing course, to catch up with the enemy. Valencia is in a hurry because no other American fighters are in sight. It is four against more than thirty. The Japanese gaggle is now fifty miles north of *Yorktown*. Aboard the carrier preparations to deal with the enemy are under way, and all gun crews have been alerted.

Now Valencia's four black Hellcats are in position, behind and above, for another firing pass, headed south, with the enemy. Valencia is ready to go down, begins his pass. Mitchell, off to the side, also starts down. Valencia continues to work on the Franks. He selects another, its red rising suns clearly visible on the wings, and points his nose at the victim. Valencia is impatient. A lot of planes must be knocked down if all are to be prevented from reaching the fleet.

Finally the wingspan of his victim widens. Valencia and Mitchell close the ragged enemy V from the sides, behind, on something of a converging course, as they ease into position to fire. Valencia presses the trigger, and aims for the wing roots, as he did on the first pass. Tracers show his shells striking the enemy up and down the fuselage, especially in the right wing root. Pieces fly back and smoke begins to trail from the Frank. Valencia closes to less than a hundred yards, less than seventy-five. He continues to fire. The concentration of shells is too much. A burst of light, directly in front of his eyes, marks the explosion of Valencia's second victim!

Valencia jerks his stick left and kicks left rudder, lines up another enemy fighter in a split second. He opens immediately with all guns, sees tracers streaming into the enemy victim. However, he must pull up to avoid a collision, hauls back on the stick, and the F6F cuts up into the blue. He crosses Mitchell, who has flamed his second. The division has already knocked down six enemy fighters. As Valencia and Mitchell regain altitude, French and Smith start down on their second pass. Both pick out two of the remaining Franks, scream down on their intended victims.

The division is operating just as Valencia intended. Long days of training and practice are paying off. As each section makes its pass from above, the enemy fighters cannot pull up and behind them. If they could, they would expose themselves to the fire of the two cover fighters—above.

Valencia watches the other two Hellcats again closing the big enemy V, both American fighters now firing away with all six guns. French's victim explodes in another brilliant flash—the seventh victim! Smith's victim, another Frank, pours black smoke. The two American fighters cross and knife back up into the blue.

The enemy V is getting close to the fleet. The passes laboriously worked out by the Flying Circus are working to perfection, but the question is now whether the four fighters can destroy the large enemy gaggle before it reaches Task Force 58. As Valencia is pondering the dilemma and preparing for another pass, the enemy V begins to break up into smaller V's—of three planes each. Groups of enemy fighters are turning to each side. The enemy leader is dispersing his forces, forcing the Hellcats to concentrate on one or two separate small groups, rather than the entire gaggle. This will make the job tougher.

Now, over the horn, Valencia picks up a comrade calling C.I.C. He recognizes the voice—one of his *Yorktown* comrades, leading another four-plane division on the same C.A.P. mission. Valencia hears him message *Yorktown* he can't spot the enemy aircraft, though he has seen antiaircraft fire to the north. (The antiaircraft fire was exploding Franks knocked down by the Circus, and visible for miles and miles.)

Aboard *Yorktown* it is reported the enemy planes are only thirty miles away. Over the tubes comes the warning: "Raid still closing . . ."

Valencia grabs the mike: "Break tactics—select targets of opportunity." The four Hellcats will go after victims separately, in an effort to knock down as many as possible before the enemy planes reach the fleet. Valencia is reluctant to terminate his mowing machine, but the enemy is rapidly scattering and results will be better if the division breaks up.

The four Hellcats now spread into two pairs, as the Franks, Zekes and Oscars scatter widely, all still heading generally south toward the fleet. Valencia sees a flight of three Franks ahead, below, and starts down on them. Mitchell sticks close, flying now as section wingman. Valencia will approach from six o'clock. At full throttle, he gains only slowly on the silver Frank ahead.

Just as he is beginning to realize his division cannot possibly wipe out the enemy, off to the side comes a reassuring sight—other Hellcats. The Japanese are getting uncomfortably close to *Yorktown* and other ships, and Valencia is relieved to see other American fighters joining in the interception.

Meanwhile, French and Smith are after another enemy trio. Smith, roaring down from the left, behind, firing on another Japanese plane. Now Valencia looks to his right, ahead, sees the enemy.

He kicks left rudder again and slides back into his firing pass on the three-plane enemy division ahead. He will continue his pass. Shocked momentarily by the tracers, which might have been from an enemy fighter, Valencia recovers his composure. Once again he begins to close the enemy trio ahead. He's confident Mitchell will not hit him. Valencia is on his fourth victim. He walks up on him from behind. Fire! The enemy planes turn, but too late. Valencia stays on his victim, pouring shells toward the enemy fighter at a rate of a hundred a second. It's too much for the silver fighter. At this moment Valencia sees that Mitchell has crossed under him, is off to his right, slightly behind, in position again. He is joining in the attack on the three Franks ahead.

Valencia's victim is pouring smoke. Mitchell opens fire on another one of the three, as all rack around into a tight turn. The two Hellcats stick with the Franks, in the turn. Mitchell's fire begins to tell on the Frank just to the right of Valencia's victim, and he begins to trail smoke. Now Valencia's victim streaks a long tail of yellow flame. Victim No. 4! Mitchell's victim bursts into flame. Eleven kills, two probables, for the division! Valencia watches his victim, for a second, start its fatal plunge.

Now he maneuvers stick and rudder, points his nose at the remaining plane in formation. He gains quickly and is soon in range. He opens fire. Valencia hangs on the remaining fighter, as the enemy pilot turns to move out of the line of fire. Valencia stays with him in the turn, pouring shells into the trapped Frank. In seconds he, too, streams smoke and flame, suddenly disintegrates! It is victim No. 5! Valencia has knocked down two of the three, and glances around him, but sees no enemy aircraft nearby.

Mitchell is in position off to his right, having flamed one of the three enemy fighters and observed Valencia's two kills. Valencia hauls back on the stick and begins to level off. He scans the sky in all directions. American fighters are appearing in increasing numbers. Dogfights are raging all over the sky; the Japanese attack at this moment is being turned back. Few of the enemy planes are able to continue south. Some which have not been shot down are turning back.

As the victory is being gained, just in time, Valencia spots an enemy fighter closing the rear of two Hellcats to his right. The two F6F's are,

flying French's wing, has already seen four parachutes—the Jap
bailing out today. Radio chatter begins to come in over the earphor
other Hellcats join the fray. This, along with the sight of fa
Japanese planes, and parachutes, adds to the excitement of the dev
ing battle. And only minutes are now left to stop the er
planes.

Valencia is closing the Frank ahead, has him in his sights.
enemy pilot obviously hasn't seen the diving F6F behind him. Val
waits the last, dragging seconds. He is looking down, through a y
light circle, on his victim from behind and above, range less than
hundred yards. One hundred yards. Valencia opens fire. Shells s
straight into the helpless silver fighter ahead, rip holes in the fuse
Valencia knows it's only a matter of time. Smoke streams back.
Frank's wing goes up, as if the enemy pilot is attempting to turn o
the line of fire. At this instant the Frank explodes in a violent f
Victim No. 3 for Valencia!

He is so close, he applies right rudder and aileron, pushes stick
ward, and streaks by the debris and smoke, diving downward, r
Meanwhile, French has claimed his third victim, as another of
enemy planes explodes into a ball of fire in front of the section le
twinkling guns. Valencia already has three victories, French t
Mitchell two, Smith one and a probable. Valencia also has a pro
. . . a total for his division, so far, of nine kills and two prob

Valencia has little time to think this over as he hauls back o
stick to level out after his third victory. He leans into a slight ba
the right, and looks around him. Streaking by, from left to right,
turns, is a flight of three Franks! He slams throttle all the way for
steepens his bank to the right, rolls out behind the three-plane e
formation.

A glance behind reveals Mitchell still in position. Valencia
again squints through the gunsight glass. The Pratt and W
engine, wide open, roars and the distance behind the enemy trio
to lessen. The Japs are getting closer and closer to the ships of th
and beginning to descend. Time is short, but he will soon be in

Tracers . . . streaking by, left to right, in front! Valencia st
looks back, sees nothing. More tracers streak by out front, h
downward, off to his right. He kicks right rudder and glances l
again. Up above, behind, to the left, a Hellcat! Mitchell! Mitc

in turn, closing a lone Jap fighter, unaware of the Frank on their rear. The Hellcats are in trouble, and Valencia once again rams his throttle all the way forward and banks into the chase. He must get the enemy fighter off the tail of the two unsuspecting F6F's ahead.

Meanwhile, French is blasting another enemy fighter out of the sky, and this and Mitchell's third victim a moment earlier gives the division a score of thirteen confirmed kills and two probables.

Valencia's thoughts, however, are on the enemy fighter ahead. Can he close him before he opens fire on the two Hellcats? Valencia and Mitchell are closing, but the Jap is close behind the two F6F's which, in turn, are almost within range of their intended victim.

Valencia dumps his stick a little more, picks up speed as he turns inside on the enemy fighter ahead. All the fighters appear to come within range of each other almost simultaneously. Valencia pulls the trigger. All six of his guns are still firing. The enemy ahead is caught by surprise as tracers streak into him and past him. Once again, Valencia's gunnery is deadly. His shells tear into the fuselage of the enemy fighter. The F6F continues to pour out fire as it moves closer and closer. A blinding ball of flame! The victim explodes in front of Valencia's eyes. The debris forces him to turn suddenly; Mitchell stays with him in the turn. Six kills for Valencia! Fourteen for the division! And it's still early in the morning. Valencia eases back on the throttle. The oil-streaked engine is still running smoothly, but gas is low. Ammunition must be all but exhausted. Valencia looks around. The enemy has been turned back. Hellcats are dealing handily with the few scattered enemy planes, now on the run.

Out front a smoking enemy cripple crosses in view. He is probably doomed, but Valencia will make sure. He stands the Hellcat on its right wing and banks in behind. In a few moments he is on the hapless victim. A short burst from Valencia's guns completes the job. The enemy fighter wings over and heads for the water, out of control, streaming black smoke. Valencia won't claim him.

Valencia levels off; he can no longer ignore fuel tank gauges. And since his guns must be about empty, he must return to *Yorktown.* A glance around the sky finally convinces him the crisis has passed. However, he can't spot French and Smith anywhere. Mitchell is on his wing, right. To the south, ships of the fleet are in view, though *Yorktown* is not in sight.

Valencia points his nose south, toward the position over which the division had planned to orbit after the battle. *Yorktown* should not be far from that area. Valencia has enough fuel to reassemble the division, and lead it to *Yorktown,* but none to spare. The sky is rapidly clearing. One or two planes are visible in the distance, but no enemy plane is headed south, for the fleet.

He proceeds to the rendezvous point. He lowers his tail hook, the join-up signal. The rendezvous area is just ahead. He and Mitchell begin to circle, slowly, scanning the sky in all directions. They orbit for several minutes. But there's no sign of French or Smith. Valencia can't orbit much longer or he won't have enough gas to get aboard *Yorktown.*

About to break out of orbit, he spots an aircraft approaching. French or Smith? Valencia hopes it's not; if it is, one might have been shot down. The oncoming silhouette grows larger. Valencia eyes it suspiciously. It's not an American! Enemy fighter! The enemy pilot hasn't seen the two F6F's, for he flies quite close to the Hellcats.

In a flash, Valencia is standing on a wing, and, once more at full throttle, though low on gas, roaring after the unsuspecting enemy fighter. The gap closes quickly, and Valencia is on him. This will be victim No. 7. The sudden maneuver has left Mitchell behind, but Valencia will be able to handle the enemy fighter without help. Now the enemy's wingspan stretches across the sight circle. Valencia presses the trigger. Nothing! Not a sound! With a start, Valencia presses the trigger again. He's in perfect firing position and, desperate, almost wrenches off the top of his stick. But nothing happens. His guns are empty!

Disgusted, Valencia tries the button several more times, but nothing happens. He banks away, uncomfortably close to the enemy, unarmed. The enemy fighter, now suddenly aware of the danger to his rear, banks and streaks away. Valencia turns back toward the orbiting area, and in the turn, Mitchell kills the distance between them.

They must head for *Yorktown;* Valencia cannot wait longer for French and Smith. Accordingly, he calls *Yorktown* for a vector and points his nose toward the carrier.

Yorktown is not far, has picked up the two Hellcats on its radar screen. Pri-Fly messages Valencia *Yorktown* can take them aboard immediately. The morning is still sparkling clear and Valencia soon spots the big carrier ahead, surrounded by lesser warships. *Yorktown* is making approximately thirty knots, headed into the wind.

As Valencia's two Hellcats come into view, crewmen aboard *Yorktown* observe a red ball of fire in the sky to the north. It is an enemy aircraft exploding. Other ships of Task Force 58, to the north, open fire with their antiaircraft guns.

Now, as Valencia and Mitchell approach, *Yorktown* is warned, once again. Bogey closing from fifty degrees! Valencia and Mitchell are already turning on their final approach to put down on the carrier deck. The carrier will take them aboard. Now Valencia can see the landing signal officer. The deck of *Yorktown* looms ahead, larger and larger. He awaits the signal from the landing deck officer, maneuvers rudder to come in on a straight line with the carrier deck. The landing signal officer gives him the sign; he chops his throttle, all the way back, and the big black, oil-spattered Hellcat settles toward the hydraulic cables, stretching from side to side.

Valencia must make it on this pass, being low on gas, and because *Yorktown* has already been warned of a bogey closing. With a thump, the Hellcat hits the deck. The tail hook engages. The cable yanks him to a stop. He breathes a sigh of relief as he taxies off the landing area and Mitchell is safely taken aboard.

Yorktown waves off another Hellcat. The bogey is now reported only twenty-five miles out, bearing fifty degrees. Valencia climbs out of his now-still Hellcat, and crewmen surround him. They've heard about the running fight. They want to know the details. Valencia smiles as he tells them he downed six enemy planes. The word spreads quickly through the ship. Everyone is exhilarated over the achievement. Captain Walter F. Boone, soon to take over as skipper of *Yorktown,* remarks: "How about that boy who just shot down six Japs? It wasn't so long ago that stuff like that was getting the Congressional Medal!"

In a short while, French and Smith land. When scores are totaled among the four the division has fourteen confirmed kills and three probables. It is the best day of the war for the Flying Circus. VF 9 scored seventeen confirmed kills and four probables in the battle.

Yorktown was well protected. She was destined to survive two desperate months off Okinawa, when the Japs threw more than a thousand Kamikazes at Task Force 58.

The Flying Circus was to continue its deadly work on the enemy. Seventeen days later Valencia, Mitchell, French and Smith were to knock down eleven more enemy planes, in a hot fight off Okinawa, protecting the fleet. On May 11, just seven days afterward, they knocked down another ten enemy aircraft, likewise protecting the fleet.

An enemy torpedo plane takes the plunge after missing U.S.S. York-town. (Navy Department Photo)

By the end of the war all four had becomes aces. They had bagged fifty planes, and Valencia had become the third-ranking Navy ace of World War II. Moreover, he had personally proved his "mowing machine" was an effective offensive and defensive fighter tactic.

Valencia's performance on the morning of April 17 did not go unnoticed. A short time afterward the Navy took official notice of it by awarding the San Francisco pilot the Navy Cross. The citation, in part, read:

For extraordinary heroism as Pilot of a Fighter Plane in Fighting Squadron Nine, attached to the U.S.S. *Yorktown,* in action against Japanese forces at Okinawa, April 17, 1945.

Leading his Combat Air Patrol in an aggressive attack against an overwhelming force of enemy fighters attacking our Fleet units, Lieutenant Commander (then Lieutenant) Valencia engaged the enemy and, although outnumbered ten-to-one, personally shot down six hostile planes, probably destroyed another, and damaged one. By his expert airmanship, gallant fighting spirit and devotion to duty, he contributed materially to the ultimate destruction and dispersal of the enemy formation. . . .

Valencia remained in the Navy after the war. Today he is active in a newly organized association of U.S. fighter aces. In 1961 he traveled to Germany to meet with fighter aces of the Luftwaffe, to help establish the international organization of fighter aces of the various nations which participated in World War II.

In addition to the Navy Cross, Valencia was awarded the Distinguished Flying Cross and five Gold Stars in lieu of a second, third, fourth, fifth and sixth Distinguished Flying Cross. In addition, he received the Air Medal, and five Gold Stars in lieu of additional Air Medals. After the war, he transferred to the regular Navy, and, as *Greatest Fighter Missions* goes to press, is stationed in Los Angeles, California.

INDEX

245